The Helmsleys

Other Books by Richard Hammer

Dance Down the Mountain
(NOVEL)

Hoffa's Man (with Joseph Franco)

The CBS Murders

The Vatican Connection

Mr. Jacobson's War
(NOVEL)

An End to Summer
(NOVEL)

Hoodlum Empire

Gangland, U.S.A.

The Illustrated History of Organized Crime

The Last Testament of Lucky Luciano
(with Martin A. Gosch)

The Court-Martial of Lt. Calley

One Morning in the War

Between Life and Death

The Helmsleys

The Rise and Fall of Harry and Leona

by

Richard Hammer

NAL BOOKS

NAL BOOKS
Published by the Penguin Group
Penguin Books USA Inc., 375 Hudson Street, New York, New York, 10014 U.S.A.
Penguin Books Ltd, 27 Wrights Lane, London W8 5TZ, England
Penguin Books Australia Ltd, Ringwood, Victoria, Australia
Penguin Books Canada, Ltd, 2801 John Street, Markham, Ontario, Canada L3R 1B4
Penguin Books (N.Z.) Ltd., 182-190 Wairau Road, Auckland 10, New Zealand

Penguin Books Ltd, Registered Offices:
Harmondsworth, Middlesex, England

First published by New American Library, an imprint of Penguin Books USA Inc.
Published simultaneously in Canada.

REGISTERED TRADEMARK—MARCA REGISTRADA

First Printing, April, 1990
10 9 8 7 6 5 4 3 2 1

Copyright © Richard Hammer, 1990
All rights reserved

LIBRARY OF CONGRESS CATALOGING IN PUBLICATION DATA

Hammer, Richard, 1928–
    The Helmsleys : the rise and fall of Harry and Leona / by Richard Hammer.
        p. cm.
    ISBN 0-453-00682-5 : $18.95
    1. Helmsley, Harry. 2. Helmsley, Leona. 3. Businessmen—United States—
Biography. 4. Women in business—United States—Biography. 5. Real estate
developers—United States—Biography. 6. Hotels, taverns, etc.—United States—
History. 7. Helmsley, Leona—Trials, litigation, etc. 8. Trials (Tax evasion)—
New York (N.Y.)
    I. Title.
HC102.5.H45H36 1990
333.33′092′27471—dc20
[B]   90-30810
                                                                                  CIP

Printed in the United States of America
Set in Times Roman
Designed by Nissa Knuth

To Mel Berger

*He remembered poor Julian and his awe of them
and how he had started a story once that began,
"The rich are very different from you and me."
And how someone had said to Julian, "Yes, they
have more money."*

—Ernest Hemingway
The Snows of Kilimanjaro

The Helmsleys

Author's Note

THIS IS A story of money, power, and fear—too much money, too much power, and too much fear. It is the story of two people, Harry and Leona Helmsley, and the creation of an empire ruled with all the arrogance and imperiousness of latter-day absolute monarchs.

It is, perhaps, a cautionary tale of America in the last half of the twentieth century, when old values eroded, culminating in a decade when greed and disregard for others were elevated to virtues, when acquisitiveness became an end in itself, and when few gave much thought to the moral implications of the means used to amass inordinate power and wealth. The power of Harry and Leona Helmsley to control individual destinies and exact retribution often seems to the outsider to defy logic. But so great is the fear that they have spread in their wake that during the course of research for this book, the majority of the more than 150 people contacted refused to talk about them at all.

The Helmsleys themselves, of course, did not respond to repeated requests for interviews, even if they were permitted to set the ground rules. Through spokesmen they replied, "Mr. and Mrs. Helmsley have no desire for a meeting nor any intention of cooperating." Though I saw them on occasion in the lobbies of the Park Lane Hotel, where they lived in a nine-room duplex aerie, and the Helmsley Palace, it was always at a distance and there was never an opportunity to exchange a word.

Then, for eight weeks in the summer of 1989, the chance

3

came to observe Leona Helmsley from a distance of perhaps a dozen feet in a federal courtroom on New York's Foley Square. It was, in many ways, illuminating. Still there was no communication between us. But as her trial was nearing its end, I happened to take my ten-year-old daughter to court with me. Leona Helmsley approached her, had conversations with her then and in the days that followed, and because of that chance encounter, Mrs. Helmsley and I had our first and only conversation, an exchange that, perhaps, provided me with some insight I would not otherwise have had. I will not describe here what passed between us. That belongs in the context of the moment and I will leave it to then.

There were many others who had known the Helmsleys or worked for them over the years who would not return repeated phone calls. Others said simply that they had no desire to discuss the Helmsleys, and when pressed would give no reason for that decision. A number went so far as to say they would not talk because they were afraid. Even the promise of anonymity could not dissuade them. As one former Helmsley executive said, "Even if I talk off the record or just for background, if you use anything, they'll know where it came from. They're very vindictive and they've got more power than you can imagine. I'm in this business and I want to stay in it." Of those who did talk, most did so only on the promise that they not be identified.

Many people did agree to meet with me, though, and without their recollections and their insights, this book could not have been written. It would be impossible to name them all, and, indeed, many would not want to be named. But to all of them I offer my gratitude.

The Helmsleys are very rich. But the differences between them and the rest of us lie in far more than mere wealth. In this book we will discover where the use and misuse of money and power and fear ultimately lead.

Prelude

1

THE QUEEN WORE red. Even at the uncivilized hour of seven-thirty on a spring morning, she was all smiles, all confidence, regal. The height of fashion in her expensive custom-tailored red coat-dress, open-necked white blouse, and off-white pumps, she looked, as she invariably did, a decade younger than her sixty-eight years. Her makeup was expertly applied and her crown of tousled short brown hair was painstakingly coiffured to look natural. She traded idle pleasantries with the crowd of reporters and the curious by-standers who had gathered outside the office of New York Attorney General Robert Abrams in lower Manhattan in anticipation of her arrival. At her side, her consort, who had once owned this very building, stood tall and straight, his thinning gray-white hair slicked straight back, not a strand out of place, white mustache nearly invisible as it blended into the pale skin beneath his prominent nose. His face was stoic, expressionless.

It was veneer. And hardly had they passed through the doors and ridden the elevator to Abrams' office than the first cracks began to show. Members of the attorney general's staff had congregated to watch with fascination the couple's arrival. Under the disconcerting scrutiny of these secretaries, clerks, and attorneys ("I never realized she was that tall," says one, "or that underneath all that makeup her complexion was terrible; you could see the acne scars"), tears seemed to well in the lady's eyes. She headed for the

7

rest room to do some minor repairs. When she emerged, the watchers noticed only a slight redness around the eyes.

Within the next hours, though, the confident smile disappeared, the arrogant manner vanished, the glib banter was silenced. Her eyes grew increasingly hollow, ringed by black smudges as tears streaked the mascara. The face took on such a raddled look that, for one of the few times in anyone's memory, she looked her years.

And always at her side, he looked stricken, uncertain, bent, older than his nearly eighty years. His normally self-assured and imperious manner was no longer in evidence. His frailty gave credence to the rumors that he had suffered not one but several small strokes and had not fully recovered. In time, these ravages of old age would be asserted by his attorneys in his defense.

There was reason enough for the despair.

Leona Mindy Rosenthal Roberts Panzirer Lubin Helmsley, the "Queen of the Palace," and Harry Brakmann Helmsley, ruler of a real estate empire that spread from coast to coast with holdings in seventeen states, including more than a score of hotels and hundreds of office buildings, apartment complexes, and other properties valued between $5 billion and $10 billion, had just been put through the traumatic experience usually reserved for common criminals.

The offices of the New York State attorney general had been just the first stop on this day of tribulations. They stopped next at police headquarters, to be booked, photographed, and fingerprinted. Though spared the ignominy of handcuffs, it was on then to state supreme court, to the courtroom of Acting Justice Carol Berkman. She knew they were coming, but she played by the rules and gave them no special treatment. For more than a half hour they sat in her small paneled courtroom and waited while she heard the pleas of a group of alleged narcotics pushers. Then it was their turn. They stood before the bench, surrounded, as though by a protective shield, by their lawyers. The tears were now evident in Leona Helmsley's eyes, and Harry Helmsley seemed to visibly shrink as they pleaded not guilty to a 188-count indictment returned against them and two key executives of the Helmsley organization, Frank Turco, who had been her right-hand man, and Joseph Licari, who had been his, by a New York grand jury.

It was only the beginning. Within the week, they would be forced to repeat the degrading experience, this time in federal court, to plead once again not guilty, this time to a 47-count indictment returned against them and the same two co-defendants by a federal grand jury.

The charges: evasion of more than $4 million in federal and state income taxes, fraud, conspiracy and extortion. The crimes, the government said, had taken place over a three-year period, from 1983 to 1985.

It boggled the mind. Harry and Leona Helmsley were one of America's richest and most prominent couples. Their personal fortune was estimated to be in excess of $1.5 billion, and they claimed to have paid more than $240 million in taxes over the previous five years, including the three cited in the indictments. And yet if the charges by New York and federal authorities were true, they had tried to get away without paying what was, for them, a picayune sum. A few weeks of the interest on their personal fortune alone could have paid it off. But, the charges read, they didn't. And what was worse, they went to extreme and intricate lengths to avoid paying.

The Helmsley scheme to evade those few million dollars in taxes began, the government said, on June 20, 1983, when Harry bought Leona a palace.

Three years earlier, he had built her the gaudy fifty-one-story Helmsley Palace on Manhattan's Madison Avenue. It was the gem in his chain of twenty-six hotels, and he gave it to her to run. She became the "Queen of the Palace," so dubbed by the press and her advertising and publicity people. And she became, as well, president of all the Helmsley Hotels. Now, perhaps to reward her for all her successes in

that venture, and as another grandiose display of his uncon-
cealed, almost idolatrous exhibitions of love, he decided to
indulge her even more and give her a palace of her own.
Never mind the penthouse duplex on top of their Park Lane
Hotel on Central Park South, with its private swimming pool
and breathtaking panoramic view of the city, or the condominium in Palm Beach, or other homes around the country.
This would be something special. Indeed, it was.

It had been built in 1918, at what was then considered the
staggering cost of $1 million, by steel and banking tycoon
Daniel Grey Reid as a wedding present for his daughter,
Rhea, when she married Henry Topping. She named it Dunnellen Hall in honor of her mother, Ella Dunn, and though
it continued through the years to bear that name, old residents with long memories invariably refer to it as the Topping House. A twenty-eight-room Jacobean mansion on
twenty-six rolling acres, the manor stood on a hilltop in the
exclusive back country estate section of Greenwich, Connecticut, and from that hilltop were vistas sweeping all the
way to the blue waters of Long Island Sound. If those in
the house could see in all directions, those on the outside
could see little. The house and most of the grounds were
invisible and inaccessible to the curious, ringed by hedges
and stone walls topped by wire-mesh fences.

Those walls, fences, and hedges might keep the interlop-
ers out, but they could not keep ill fortune from overtaking
those within, and over time the estate gained the reputation
as a place of ill omen. The Toppings had two sons, Dan
(who at one time owned the New York Yankees) and Bob.
Both squandered fortunes in extravagant living and frequent
marriages and sometimes messy divorces. The estate passed
out of the Topping family's hands in 1950 when it was sold
to Loring Washburn, president of a steel-fabricating company. He went bust, and in 1963 Dunnellen Hall became
the property of a finance and factoring concern. For three
years it remained empty, until it was bought by a partnership that subdivided some of the land and sold the bulk,

including the mansion, to Gregg Sherwood Dodge Moran, a one-time showgirl and former wife of an heir to the Dodge automobile fortune. She was then married to a New York City cop named Daniel Moran, who later committed suicide. Mrs. Moran owned the house only two years and then sold it to a financier named Jack R. Dick for $1 million, then a record price for Greenwich real estate. In 1971 Dick was indicted by a New York grand jury on charges that he had stolen $840,000 by using phony documents to obtain a loan. He died in 1974 before the case went to trial. Dunnellen Hall next passed to an Indian-born owner of oil supertankers named Ravi Tikkoo. The cost: $3 million, including $1 million for the furnishings. But Tikkoo's wife hated the place, and when the oil tanker market slumped badly in 1983, he sold it to Harry Helmsley.

If Helmsley was aware of the ghosts that hung over the estate, they bothered him not at all. He didn't haggle over the Tikkoo asking price of $11 million for the land and the house and its contents, the highest price ever asked for a property in the community. Leona wanted it and so Leona would have it, regardless of price.

But as it stood on that June day in 1983, it wasn't quite good enough for Harry and Leona Helmsley. It needed, they were sure, a lot of work to make it the palace of their dreams.

The Helmsleys loved to swim, in the morning before breakfast and in the late afternoon or evening after a hard day of work. Pools, then, were essential, one outdoors for warm weather and one indoors for the rest of the year. The Helmsleys had a passion for dancing, imagining themselves latter-day incarnations of Vernon and Irene Castle, masters of the fox trot, the waltz, the rumba, even of disco dancing. Whenever the music started, out they would move to the floor, crooning to each other as they glided expertly. And so their house would need a dance floor, and where better to have it than above the indoor swimming pool? Inside and out, they were certain, their new mansion needed major renovations, new furniture and furnishings and knick-knacks, new landscaping. And with the Helmsley billions, they had the funds to indulge every whim.

So they spared no costs. They hired workmen of all kinds, and they went on shopping sprees to transform Dunnellen Hall. The work commenced and the bills mounted. The construction of an elaborate brick, limestone, and marble structure to house the indoor swimming pool, an adjacent breakfast room, and a second floor dance hall ran to $2 million, more than Daniel Reid's original cost in building the entire house. The Helmsleys had a passion for jade, and so they thought objets d'art of jade might be a nice touch scattered about Dunnellen Hall, and as long as they were buying jade for the Connecticut mansion, they decided to add to the collection in the penthouse at the Park Lane. They went to a San Francisco dealer in Oriental art who found them a number of exceptional pieces, at a cost of only $500,000. They loved music, so what could be more natural than a system that would bring music to them wherever they were. An indoor-outdoor stereo system was installed and cost just $130,000. Another million went for furniture, antiques, works of art, and the like, including $210,000 for a mahogany card table, $150,000 for a cherrywood highboy and some carved walnut chairs, $80,000 for side chairs, $60,000 for a side table, more thousands for a tall musical clock in an ornate case, at least that's what invoices called them. The list went on. And on.

And then there were little personal items, gifts from Harry to Leona, and from Leona to Harry. There were toiletries and perfumes and clothes, and a $45,000 silver clock in the shape of Harry's Helmsley Building in New York that Leona had specially designed and made as a birthday present. And more.

There was just one small problem with all this extravagance. Harry and Leona, the authorities charged, didn't reach into their own pockets to pay for them. The millions they spent on Dunnellen Hall and the Park Lane duplex, and on themselves, were charged instead to nineteen different companies that were part of Helmsley Enterprises, and then the books were phonied up to make the costs look like business expenses of those companies, which would be, of course, tax deductible.

For instance:

- The swimming pool and the marble dance hall and all the accouterments were charged as construction and repair expenses incurred by a number of Helmsley properties, including the Graybar Building, Helmsley Building, Helmsley Hotel, Park Lane Hotel, Windsor Hotel, and Garden Bay Manor.
- The jade wound up on the books of the St. Mortiz, Park Lane, Windsor, and Carlton House hotels as antique furniture bought for redecorating.
- The indoor-outdoor stereo system became the cost of an electronic security system supposedly installed in the Helmsley hotels and the Helmsley Building and charged to them.
- Furniture, antiques, and art were marked as costs incurred by Deco Purchasing and Distributing Company, a Helmsley subsidiary based in Florida, which acted as the central purchasing agent for the entire Helmsley network and which had been run by Leona's son, Jay Panzirer, until his death.
- The more than $370,000 in gardening and landscaping were entered as costs incurred by the Harley Hotels in Cleveland and the Harley Hotel in Enfield, Connecticut.
- That $45,000 clock in the shape of the Helmsley Building was charged to the Park Lane Hotel, and stacks of Leona's clothes, toiletries, and other gifts ended up on the books of the Park Lane and the

Helmsley real estate company, Brown, Harris, Stevens.

- A white-lace-and-pink-satin dress that Leona bought for herself, along with a jacket and white chiffon skirt, was paid for by the Park Lane, whose books said they were hotel staff "uniforms."
- They went so far as to make out a fake invoice to cover the moving expenses of the Dunnellen Hall housekeeper and had those few thousand dollars charged to the Park Lane.

It's one thing, perhaps, to cheat a little on the income taxes by diverting personal expenses to businesses; a lot of people take the risk and do it, and some even get away with it. But, according to the government, Harry and Leona Helmsley did more than just a little creative tax accounting, aided and abetted by a couple of top executives of their organization.

They were allegedly engaged in a scheme to defraud the minority stockholders in Realesco Equities Corporation, of which the Helmsleys owned seventy-eight percent of the stock. In one of those complicated business arrangements linking a multitude of subsidiary companies, under Realesco's corporate umbrella fell the Park Lane, Carlton House, and Helmsley Windsor, whose operations were the responsibility of the Helmsley Hotels, whose president was Leona Helmsley. According to the government charges, she rewarded herself by having Realesco pay more than $1 million of her personal expenses, and the Park Lane reward her with an $83,333.34 monthly "consulting fee." This, the government said, amounted to defrauding the minority stockholders of Realesco, since no stockholder approval was sought or granted for either the payment for expenses or the "consulting fees," though under law that was a requirement.

And then there was the little matter of extortion. That was something that didn't involve Harry. It was, the government charged, Leona's sole province, and that of her chief aide, Frank Turco. They demanded, and got, monthly cash payments from liquor salesmen in exchange for throwing the Helmsley hotel business their way, demanded and got free television sets from RCA as a condition to giving the electronics giant entree into the hotel chain, demanded and got from other suppliers free kimonos for use around the Dunnellen Hall swimming pool, free mattresses for use in the Dunnellen Hall bedrooms, and a lot more.

These little forays into extortion, which is what they were, if true, didn't extend just to outsiders. Those in the Helmsley organization itself found themselves targets as well. Some employees were ordered to prepare fake travel vouchers and endorse blank reimbursement checks so that Leona could cash them in whatever amounts she wanted. Behind the demand was the threat that if they didn't do precisely what was dictated, they'd better look for jobs somewhere else.

New York State Attorney General Robert Abrams and United States Attorney for the Southern District of New York Rudolph Giuliani and their investigators and grand juries had taken more than a year of digging and questioning a hundred and more witnesses, including two dozen former and current employees of the Helmsley companies who were granted immunity from prosecution in exchange for their testimony, to put together their cases. They had been prodded initially by a series of articles in the *New York Post,* which reported that LaStrada Contracting Company, the major contractor at Dunnellen Hall, had been ordered by two major Helmsley executives, Turco, the chief of financial services for the Helmsley Hotels, and Joseph Licari, the chief financial officer of Helmsley Enterprises, and by Leona Helmsley herself, to send the bills to the Helmsley-owned building at 420 Park Avenue and "concoct detailed descriptions of work that was never actually performed in the office buildings."

It was the start. And the end was not over even with the

announcement of the indictments. Less than two months later, in June 1988, Assistant United States Attorney James DeVita, who was handling the case against the Helmsleys for the government, revealed that he was preparing to move against them with new charges. Apparently they had been using their private jet—first an eight-passenger Sabre Liner and then a newer one for which they had traded in the Sabre. (According to Leona Helmsley, they needed a "larger plane because of Harry's size"—at six feet three, he "had to stoop to get on it.") The new one was a $5 million hundred-passenger BAC-1-11, about the size of a DC-9, and the interior was redecorated in inimitable Leona Helmsley style at a cost of three hundred thousand dollars. The jets were used not merely for business purposes, for which they were writing off its costs, but for their personal pleasure as well. "There's a lot of money involved, several hundreds of thousands of dollars," DeVita said.

If successfully prosecuted, the accumulated charges would, at the very least, hit the Helmsleys with heavy fines. A maximum sentence of between three and five years in prison could be levied on every one of the tax evasion and conspiracy charges, and in the case of Leona, reserve a jail cell for her for up to twenty years on the extortion counts.

But the state and federal governments weren't the only ones who had set out after them. A lot of others, people who had been doing the work turning Dunnellen Hall into Leona and Harry's dream palace, had been taking aim at them, too.

Not only had the Helmsleys attempted to use their various companies to pay their private bills, but when it came to paying the contractors for their work at Dunnellen Hall, they acted like deadbeats. Almost everyone they hired eventually ran to the prosecutors with stories of the Helmsley peculations and ended up being forced to bring suit against them in civil court in Connecticut when the Helmsleys simply refused to pay their bills.

• Mike DiSisto, a Scarsdale, New York, building contractor, was hired in November 1983 to do the excavation and concrete work on the enclosure for the new indoor pool. By late spring 1984, DiSisto had finished the job and handed in a bill for $102,496.15, the price agreed on at the beginning. But the Helmsleys hedged and delayed, and doled out payments in dribs and drabs. They came up with $39,090 over the next several months. That left a balance of $63,406.15. DiSisto sent bills regularly. The Helmsleys just as regularly ignored them.

By October 1986, two and a half years after he had completed the work, DiSisto's patience ran out. He felt he had no alternative but to sue. When he did, however, he discovered there was a distinct possibility that even that action might result in nothing. For it seemed that the Helmsleys no longer owned Dunnellen Hall. In February 1986 they conveniently sold the estate to a newly formed Delaware corporation known as Five Twenty-One Corporation. The purchase price: $1.00. Of course, Five Twenty-One's address just happened to be that of Dunnellen Hall on Round Hill Road, and the sole owners of the new Delaware corporation were Harry and Leona Helmsley. But legally they no longer owned the estate, the corporation did, and the corporation was in Delaware, not in Connecticut, and so it was outside the jurisdiction of the court.

Still, DiSisto and his attorney persisted. They summoned Leona to appear for a pretrial deposition to find out just what was going on. Leona refused to appear.

For the next eighteen months the case remained in

never-never land. The Helmsleys resorted to legal maneuvers to delay, and DiSisto became ever more frustrated, stuck not only with an unpaid bill for work long finished, but also with mounting legal bills.

Suddenly, just after Christmas in 1987, something persuaded the billionaire couple to call off the charade. They paid the bill (without three and a half years' interest, naturally), and DiSisto withdrew the suit.

DiSisto's misadventures with Harry and Leona were hardly unique. They were repeated time and again with practically everyone who had been hired to work on the house or the grounds.

• J. O'Brien and Sons were hired by the Helmsleys in November 1984 to do extensive pruning and grooming of the trees and shrubs about the grounds in anticipation of the approaching winter. The work was finished by the end of January. It had been a big job and the Helmsleys had run up a bill of $48,818.65. O'Brien asked to be paid. The Helmsleys apparently didn't think the request merited their attention. O'Brien sent bill after bill. All were ignored. He phoned. His calls were not returned. Finally, in March 1986, fourteen months after he had completed his work, he felt he had no choice but to go to court and file suit for payment and seek a $50,000 attachment on the property. If O'Brien thought he would have little trouble winning and then collecting, since he had the papers and the evidence to prove his case, he soon discovered, as had DiSisto and would others, that when dunning Harry and Leona Helmsley, nothing is quite as simple as it seems. The case dragged on as the Helmsley attorneys filed motion after motion. In the fall, O'Brien's lawyer filed papers demanding Leona's appearance for pretrial depositions. But Leona played by her own rules, and she simply ignored the summons.

And then, in a repeat of the DiSisto episode, the dispute came to a sudden end. In early February 1987, two years after the completion of the job, the Helmsleys decided the time had come to pay. Check in hand at last, O'Brien withdrew the suit.

• John Fahey Landscaping did $6,600 of work on the Dunnellen property in July 1983, a month after the Helmsleys had bought the estate. Two years later, his bill still not paid, he went to court. Another year of motions and delays would ensue before the Helmsleys came across. Embittered, Fahey summed up his experience by declaring, "I'd work for bag ladies before I'd work for someone like that again."

• From the beginning of April 1984 to the end of December, Vasileff Nurseries planted new gardens and did extensive landscaping around Dunnellen Hall. The bill came to $9,448.37. The Helmsleys disregarded it. Nevertheless, knowing he was working for billionaires and unaware at that moment of the plight of other contractors, Vasileff had no reason to think that the omission was anything more than an oversight. And so, in January 1985, when the Helmsleys asked for additional pruning work on the trees and general cleanup of the grounds, Vasileff did as they asked. Then he submitted another bill, this one for $5,519.25.

Like everyone else, Vasileff, too, wended his way into the legal underbrush after a year of fruitless attempts to collect the outstanding $14,967.62. Two more years went by. Vasileff's legal fees climbed. His motions were ignored. And then, as if on sudden impulse, the check was in the mail and the suit was withdrawn.

• Post Road Iron Works did $8,631.99 worth of construction and renovation at Dunnellen Hall from the end of 1985 into early 1986. Not until May 1988, a year after their suit for payment had been filed, was the payment at last made.

• And that luxurious indoor swimming pool of which Harry and Leona boasted during a television interview with Mike Wallace on *60 Minutes*? What the couple neglected to tell the nationwide audience was that they hadn't bothered to pay E. L. Wagner, Co., for building it. Wagner billed and billed and finally brought suit at the beginning of 1987. When the attorneys summoned Leona to a pretrial hearing to answer questions and give a deposition, as usual she didn't bother to show up at the scheduled time and just refused to be examined. Not until February 1988 did the Helmsleys finally decide the time had come to satisfy the Wagner claim.

• The pool, of course, was housed in a baronial structure that contained on its second floor the marble dance floor. The work on the private ballroom had begun in 1984 and was completed early the following year. According to the bills submitted by Bergen County Cut Stone, the builders had provided:

1. Labor and materials for a limestone and bluestone pool installation, at a cost of $97,000
2. Labor and materials for limestone bay windows, at a cost of $130,000

3. Labor and materials for limestone coping for the stairs, at a cost of $4,975
4. Limestone trim for a new bathroom window in the cabana, at a cost of $4,884
5. Cutting and resetting the bluestone near the pool enclosure and repairing bluestone steps to the courtyard, at a cost of $1,200
6. Materials and installation of a retaining wall in front of the pool's mechanical room and an enclosure for an air conditioning condensing unit, at a cost of $7,190
7. Work on the limestone coping on the pool house roof, at a cost of $8,647.83
8. Stonework around the pool, at a cost of $8,289.40
9. Repairs on the limestone balustrades on top of existing fieldstone walls, at a cost of $15,500.

The grand total of the bills submitted by Bergen County Cut Stone came to nearly $300,000. Their only problem, naturally, was how to collect. The only way was the same way everyone else had taken, go to court, which the company finally did in January 1987.

A year later, as other claims were gradually being settled, this one remained unresolved. The Helmsley attorneys pleaded for more time, especially when it came to the demand to produce various documents. "This action," they said, "was one of eight cases involving construction work performed on the Helmsley residence in Greenwich, Connecticut. Three of the eight Connecticut actions have now been resolved. At about the time of the commencement of this action a joint investigation was undertaken by the office of the attorney general of New York and the United States attorney for the Southern District of New York into income tax matters including the returns of all the defendants.

". . . over two million documents have been produced for the government and the subject matter of the investigation is directly related to the payments made for services encompassed by this and the other pending actions."

In short, the Helmsleys claimed their other legal problems would take precedence and the builder would just have to wait before they could get to him.

A sleazy story. Here were the billionaire Helmsleys, cheating on their income taxes for what was for them a pittance, extorting money, gifts, and services they hardly needed, trying to stiff the people they hired to create their dream palace.

It was incredible, if true.

But it did not emerge of an instant, full-blown. The precedents had been established in all the years that had gone before. And so few shed any tears for them in their plight. "It couldn't have happened to people who deserved it more," said one former Helmsley employee, now a successful real estate broker on his own. "Not that anything's really going to happen to them," he added, "not with their money and their clout. Hell, they'll buy their way out. Do you think a little fine's going to make a dent? No matter how much, it'll be small change. But it was worth the price of admission just to see them like that in the courtroom, even if nothing else happens."

These sentiments were widely echoed, and not just by former employees or business associates or rivals, many of whom voiced them discreetly, fearing retribution should the Helmsleys, and especially Leona, discover what they had said. The tenants of Parkchester and Tudor City and other apartment complexes gobbled up over the years by Harry Helmsley had come to think of him as one of New York's worst landlords. Others had fought to save priceless landmarks and parks from his determination to raze them and erect faceless skyscrapers in their stead. Still others had been objects of Leona's sudden fury when they had somehow displeased her. All those and many more had little reason to feel compassion for Harry and Leona Helmsley in a time of trouble, the trouble of their own making.

There were, to be sure, some who were certain that behind it all loomed the dominating presence of Leona, a Lady Macbeth insidiously leading a docile if arrogant king along a road to destruction. She was the one responsible, these were all her ideas. Harry had either been unaware of what she was doing or, because he loved her so uncritically, and love is blind, had gone along with anything she wanted. Given Leona's history, there is ample cause to credit this view.

Still, there were many who disagreed. Perhaps the Macbeth analogy holds, but Macbeth and his lady were truly joined, and if she led him, it was in directions he was prepared to go. "If you think Leona did it on her own," says a man who has known Harry Helmsley for years, "you couldn't be more wrong and you don't know Harry Helmsley. She would never have dared do a thing without Harry knowing about it and giving his okay. If he didn't know, then he's stupid or a fool, and nobody ever accused him of being either. Just look at his whole career. He always knew everything that was going on. If you crossed him, forget it."

The Helmsleys are richer than most people ever dream of being. With their riches, the Helmsleys are more powerful than many can imagine. With their riches and their power, the Helmsleys inspire inordinate fear among many who know them, depend on them, deal with them, even compete with them.

Still, certain questions remain. How did they become what they are? What drove them to believe that the law does not apply to them, that rules are for other people, that morals and morality are outmoded conceptions to which they need give no heed, that if you are rich enough and powerful enough and spread enough fear about you, there is nothing you cannot do with impunity?

"I need the money," Harry Helmsley, the billionaire, has said on more than one occasion when questioned about why he has come down hard on someone.

"Nobody really likes anyone," Leona Helmsley has said. "Nobody really likes me. What they like is my money."

Who, then, are these two people, Harry and Leona Helmsley? Are they, indeed, the MacHelmsleys?

Part One
The Broker

HARRY HELMSLEY, WHO would become a billionaire, who would become the preeminent figure in American real estate in his time, was born March 4, 1909, in the Bronx, into a family just on the edge of the middle class. He was the first child of Henry and Minnie Brakmann Helmsley. (A second son, Walter, was born a few years later.) Minnie's father was a small landlord. Henry was, Harry later said, owner of a moderately successful dry goods wholesale company he had founded, though there are others who say he was only a notions buyer for a wholesale firm owned by others. As with so many other stories about the Helmsley past, the truth is buried somewhere in the mists of time.

In the first decades of the twentieth century, the Bronx was a quiet, middle-class borough of small homes and graceful apartment houses, especially along its main thoroughfare, the Grand Concourse. In this neighborhood, by then becoming a magnet for upwardly mobile Jewish businessmen and professionals escaping the poverty of the Lower East Side, Harry Helmsley grew up in a family of practicing Lutherans. Bright and quick, he earned high marks in school, particularly in subjects related to economics and mathematics, things he would put to good use in the years to come. By the time he graduated from Evander Childs High School in 1925, he had had enough of formal education. It was time to make his own mark. He debated only briefly a choice of directions—either into the garment world of his father or the real estate world of his Brakmann grandfather. Even in the boom time of the mid-1920s, the garment industry was volatile, more bust than boom. Real estate, on the other hand, was the rock on which the nation was founded; real estate would always prosper. People needed places to live and places to work, and they would always need them. And so he made the rounds looking for a job and accepted the first one he was offered, as a twelve-dollar-a-week office boy in the mail room of Dwight, Voorhis and Perry.

Though venerable and respected, dating back to its founding in 1866 by S. B. Goodale, Dwight, Voorhis was hardly a major force in New York real estate. It concentrated on Manhattan's West Side in the Forties, what was then Hell's Kitchen, and in the loft district stretching north of Fourteenth Street. It bought, sold, and managed properties, mainly small and undistinguished.

Still, sixteen-year-old Harry Helmsley saw it as an opportunity to make something of himself. Within a few months he was out of the mailroom and on the streets. The tall, slim young man began climbing tenement stairs and beating on tenement doors; he had become the dreaded rent collector. And in the years that followed, he became ever more feared as rent collecting became ever more difficult, especially in those poor neighborhoods that were his beat. At first, the stock market crash of October 1929, though devastating the paper fortunes of the rich, seemed of little moment to the Hell's Kitchen poor who had nothing and so, it seemed, nothing to lose. But the tidal wave engulfed them as the Great Depression quickly followed and there was no work, and so no income, for anyone. The rent collector became the man who threatened to strip the roof from a family, the man to hide from when his knock resounded on the door. Even a youth could not escape that stigma. But, perhaps, given a stern and often unbending Lutheran heritage, Harry Helmsley had no desire to escape it. Perhaps it bothered him not at all. Certainly, in the years to come, he would exhibit an imperviousness to the plight of the less fortunate who lived in the buildings he controlled; that indifference may have been an ingrained trait.

Rent collecting, though, was not what Harry Helmsley envisioned as his life work. He saw in the economic collapse an opportunity for a bright young man who knew where to look and find openings and seize them. And how could he do this? The rule of the day was foreclosure, all around the city. Landlords of buildings large and small were unable to keep up their mortgage payments, and the holders of those mortgages, the banks and insurance companies, were calling them in and taking over the properties. Financial institutions, though, were not only unprepared to be landlords, they didn't want to be landlords; they wanted only to make good investments that paid off with good returns. So they were desperate to rid themselves of that new responsibility. Every week they posted notices of the buildings they had foreclosed and asked for bids from people willing to take over the mortgages. Helmsley began reading the notices, trying to spot those buildings that might be good investments.

He spotted prime properties waiting for the right taker, but to do the taking he needed money, and he had little to spare on what in those perilous days had to be considered a risk, and neither did Dwight, Voorhis. So Helmsley came up with an idea to circumvent that shortage of funds and those risks. He cultivated good contacts at the banks and insurance companies, growing a mustache along the way, some said, to make himself look older, and persuaded them that the way out of their dilemma was to give him and Dwight, Voorhis contracts not to assume the mortgages on the foreclosed properties but to manage the buildings. This, of course, required no outlay of money, only the application of the expertise he had been learning.

A wise alternative, and as it turned out, a lucrative one. Dwight, Voorhis was propelled from a minor factor in the real estate market into an increasingly important force in the city. More crucial, it made Harry Helmsley a force to be reckoned with.

So Dwight, Voorhis began to move upward, and as it did, Harry Helmsley, no longer a rent collector but a property manager and a broker now, began to emerge as its spokesman. The older executives, enjoying the success and prominence that grew from Helmsley's enterprising ways, stepped back and let him take the lead in public. Young, aggressive, and articulate, he did not hesitate to volunteer his views on his industry's role in the city whenever those views were solicited. By 1933, he was appearing in the public press, and to some, especially in the real estate community, what he had to say made sense. He spoke out against high real estate taxes, of course. Under the tax system as it then existed, he declared, "a man is forced to tear down his building because of inability to secure sufficient income to meet the taxes, whereas in three years time he would find the building again profitable. The demolition of this building would be a sheer economic waste. If the tax laws of our city were changed to allow owners of vacant buildings to lock their buildings and to secure the same benefits that the owner of unimproved property enjoys, it would eliminate the destruction of valuable property. In addition, it would help the owner of buildings which are still occupied" by, naturally, bringing him more tenants. It was not the first time real estate operators would make this argument, nor was it the last. And if some saw good sense in it, others in the years to come, as laws changed and new factors came into play, would see it as a ploy by owners and operators to "warehouse" apartment buildings and then convert them into high-priced cooperatives and condominiums.

And Helmsley was extensively quoted when he advocated a sliding rather than fixed scale for apartment and commercial rentals, thereby allowing the owners to reap what he called a fair return as times changed for the better. He complained often and loudly about the hardships landlords faced because of the city's multiple-dwelling laws, which, he said,

prevented them from earning a fair return on their investments and inevitably led to the deterioration of property
since owners would necessarily be reluctant to make capital
improvements when they could not pass along the costs. His
wisdom, then, was sought on just about every real estate
issue.

By 1938 he was doing well enough so that he was able to
buy a partnership in the company, whose name was changed
to Dwight, Voorhis and Helmsley. Within a few years, its
name would be changed again, to Dwight-Helmsley, Inc.
Indeed, the company had grown mainly through his efforts
from a small handful of employees to a staff of twenty,
among whom was his brother, Walter, who would continue
to work at his side until he retired in 1966. (Walter Helmsley
died in Florida in 1974.)

This was a seminal year for him. He not only became
ruler of this small realm, but took two other crucial steps.
The first was business related. The mortgage on a ten-story
commercial building on East Twenty-third Street between
Fifth and Madison avenues was about to be foreclosed.
Helmsley decided to make his first move into the personal
ownership of a property. He didn't need any great outlay,
only $1,000 down to assume the $100,000 mortgage. Rapidly he set about making that investment pay off. He cut
costs everywhere he could, and he put members of his family to work in the building, running the elevators and collecting the rents. The building superintendent's job he gave
to his father, whose company had vanished in the economic
chaos of the Depression. "I was supporting him anyway,"
Harry Helmsley would later say, "and one of the reasons I
wanted to buy the property was so he could get a job." The
building soon turned into a winner. Eight years later, at the
end of World War II, he sold it and reaped a profit of
$65,000.

In 1938, too, Harry Helmsley got married. The bride was
a young widow, born Eve Ella Sherpick, whose husband,
Arthur Greene, had been killed in an auto accident a few

years before and whose only child had died soon after birth. They had met through Eve's brother, Eugene Sherpick, a lawyer who had done legal work for Helmsley on some of the early real estate ventures. It was her money that enabled Helmsley to buy his partnership in Dwight, Voorhis. On February 28, they were married at the Church of the Transfiguration. It was a small wedding, attended only by the immediate families, with no bridesmaids and Walter Helmsley the best man. From the church the couple went to the S.S. *Europa* at its pier on the Hudson River and in their stateroom gave a small reception for family and friends before setting sail for a European honeymoon. It was the first vacation Helmsley had taken in years, and they spent a month sightseeing in France, Austria, Italy, and Switzerland. Back in New York, they settled into married life in an apartment at 31 Park Avenue, in what was then a comfortable middle-class residential neighborhood just north of Thirty-fourth Street.

Eve Helmsley was a quiet, reserved, unpretentious Quaker. Within a year, she brought Harry into the fold, and the two regularly attended services at the meeting house on Twentieth Street. As time passed, Harry became more active, eventually becoming an auditor at the annual meetings. The Quaker credo seemed suited to the lifestyle the newly married couple adopted. They lived quietly and modestly, entertained seldom, and then only small groups of friends, and went out infrequently. From the recollections of those who knew them, their relationship was a comfortable one, if not particularly warm or loving.

Harry Helmsley's passion was work and where it could lead him. "Real estate," he would say later, "is the best game around—and when you're ahead in the game, you like to keep playing." He played the game and he played it hard and he played it well and he played to win. As he would say, "If you're a good player, you're rich." He was almost always the first one in the office in the morning and the last one to leave at night, and when he left, he carried a briefcase crammed with papers. His evenings, for the most part, were spent absorbed in calculating potential deals and potential profits. "The only deals that interest him," said one lawyer who came to know him well, "are those where there's an enormous profit. He's not interested in a deal that someone else in real estate would consider damn good."

His goal was to build Dwight-Helmsley into a major force in New York real estate and in the process turn himself into a mover and a shaker. "Harry," remembers a one-time friend who was involved in a number of deals with him, "wanted to be number one. He thought he was smarter than anyone else, he was sure he knew the business better than anybody, and he was sure he belonged at the top. I suppose you could call that arrogance, but he was just so confident about his own ability that people around him believed it."

In those years, though, he was by no measure a rapacious proponent of greed, an attribute that would appear and deepen in later years as his fortune multiplied in exponential proportions. Among his peers, he was building the reputation of a man of sterling character. In a business where a deal is not a deal until the papers are signed and the check clears, with Helmsley a handshake was enough. There are tales that he would shake hands on an agreement one day and be approached a couple of days later by someone offering to pay half again as much, and Helmsley would shrug and say, a deal is a deal whether it's on paper or not. "He was a real gentleman," remembers one rival, "and in this business, you don't find many."

In addition, he was a good man to work for, quick with praise, understanding with those who made mistakes, willing to give a second chance, and generous with rewards for those who did a good job, rewards that sometimes included taking his people in with him as partners in a deal, especially if they happened to have been the one to turn up that deal, and so making them rich in the process.

He had an eye, too, for comers and go-getters, and when they proved themselves, he moved them ahead, which did much to win loyalty. Robert Drewes, now senior partner in London and Leeds Development Corporation, began in the Helmsley organization as a seventeen-year-old delivery boy in the mailroom and worked his way to a top position before his departure. He told a reporter for the business weekly *Crain's* how one afternoon in those early days he had to deliver two briefcases to Helmsley at the St. Moritz Hotel, where the broker maintained an apartment. It was pouring that day and Drewes had to wend his way on foot through the downpour because the rules at Helmsley-Spear (as Dwight-Helmsley would later become) were: no cabs for delivery boys. He was drenched when he reached the Helmsley apartment and rang the bell. Helmsley's maid refused to let him through the door, but Helmsley himself spotted Drewes, sodden, water dripping off him. "Get in here and get out of those clothes," the boss ordered, then led Drewes, wrapped in a towel, into the dining room for milk and cookies while the maid dried his clothes. Helmsley sat with him, chatted in a casual, friendly manner, led him over to a window overlooking Central Park, waved his hand over the view, and said, "Isn't all of this the most wonderful thing?"

That experience and more won Drewes' devotion. Soon afterward he was drafted, and when he returned from the service, he didn't even wait to get home. He called Helmsley as soon as he got off the bus at the Port Authority Bus Terminal. Helmsley took the call and offered Drewes a job learning building management. And from there it was onward and upward until, finally, Drewes went out on his own. But his memories of the old Harry Helmsley are still fresh and his feelings still warm.

In these years, however, the top rung eluded Harry Helmsley. Real estate in New York required capital, and a lot of it, to acquire the choicest properties. Control of them meant power, and that control rested in the hands of the banks, insurance companies, financial institutions, and a few of the wealthiest families. Harry Helmsley might be smart, talented, and ambitious, but he didn't have the money.

He was a broker, the middle man between the seller of property and the buyer, earning a five percent commission on the sales he arranged. He needed more leverage, and he found it. Throughout the final years of World War II and into the early postwar years, he made a number of what proved farsighted gambits. Since there had been a major building shortage during the war, demand was mounting for what little was available. With the coming of peace and the return of millions of servicemen to civilian life, the demand for offices and homes would rocket almost beyond the nation's ability to provide it. Returning veterans would be desperate for homes, and since living space in the city was at a premium, that meant there would have to be a home-building boom in the outlying suburbs within easy commute to the city.

Helmsley had little interest in providing living space for those who needed it. (He had been rejected for wartime service in the army himself because of poor eyesight.) He was concerned about working space. And so he set out to find business properties close to the commuter railroad depots, Grand Central and Penn stations. If the giant sky-scrapers that were headquarters to major corporations were out of his reach, plenty of other smaller buildings were there for the taking. He couldn't afford to buy them himself, of course, but what he could do was find buyers and then use his five percent commission to cut himself in for a piece of the action. And that action meant not only a part-ownership but a management contract as well, paying him additional fees to run the buildings.

In this way he began to put together a growing portfolio of moderate-sized office buildings in good locations, and he began to acquire a reputation in the business as a man who knew how to run those buildings well and turn a good profit. There were the complainers, naturally, the tenants who said that when Harry Helmsley took over a building, his first step was to pare expenses to a minimum, which invariably meant that services tenants had come to take for granted suddenly disappeared. Light bulbs were replaced by others with lower wattage, and some of the lights in lobbies and halls were removed, all to knock pennies off the utility bills. Repairs weren't always made with the alacrity of before; and cleaning and maintenance staffs were reduced. Some of the elevators were shut down during slow hours, and when they became available self-service elevators were installed. "He would cut the payroll and run the elevators less," was the way one critic put it. These were complaints that would resound through the years and would grow louder, and they would earn Helmsley the reputation among tenants as a landlord who demanded top dollar and squeezed it, and gave as little as possible in return. Still he managed to produce a return of about twelve percent on the buildings he took over. So even the carpers agreed that Harry Helmsley ran a tight ship, even if those inside might find it a little too tight.

All the same, he was only a broker. He was not a Fred Trump, building apartments in Queens, or a William Levitt, carving inexpensive homes out of potato fields on Long Island, not a Tishman or a Zeckendorf or one of those beginning to erect the skyscrapers that would change the face of Manhattan. He was simply a broker, a man in the middle of the deals, and thereby a man in the middle ranks of his chosen profession.

And then one day in the spring of 1949, soon after his fortieth birthday, he met a man named Lawrence Wien. New vistas opened up, and with them the chance to realize all his ambitions.

3

To THE CASUAL observer, Lawrence Wien and Harry Helmsley would have seemed an odd pair to become not merely business partners but abiding personal friends as well, so different were their backgrounds, outlooks, and interests.

Helmsley had grown up in a lower-middle-class family in the Bronx, his father a notions peddler. Wien, six years older, was a child of affluence. "My father," he said, "was a prosperous silk-cloth manufacturer, and I'm not the Horatio Alger type." Helmsley was a Lutheran turned Quaker; Wien was Jewish. Helmsley's formal education stopped with high school. Wien graduated high in the class of 1925 at Columbia University, and then went on to Columbia University Law School. Helmsley set out as a twelve-dollar-a-week office boy. Wien, law degree in hand, founded his own law firm, which eventually became Wien, Malkin and Bettex, of which he was, even into his eighties, still senior partner and still active. Helmsley was single-minded in his devotion to real estate. Wien was a cultivated man with wide interests in the arts and the city's social life. Wien's manner and soft-spoken speech exuded a sense of culture and breeding. Helmsley's inflections remained redolent with the "dese," "dems," and "dose" of the Bronx.

What brought them together and forged their close personal relationship was a fascination with the possibilities in the world of real estate and a mutual respect and admiration for each other's ideas, insights, abilities, and ambitions.

Soon after Lawrence Wien embarked on his legal career,

he found himself representing a number of small business-men and professionals. In the process he became ever more deeply involved in real estate law. He was drawn as well into the management and operation of Manhattan and Brooklyn apartment houses of his clients.

By the late 1930s an idea was germinating in his mind, one that would both help his clients and make him very rich. The stark fact of life in real estate at that moment was this: Lots of first-rate buildings were available around the city, but only a very limited group of buyers could afford to purchase them—financial institutions and the wealthiest families, all with nearly unlimited funds available. Because of the paucity of potential buyers, prices were often lower than they might otherwise be, and the return on investments was extraordinarily high, between fifteen and twenty percent a year. So Wien began to ponder whether a small man might somehow get his foot in that door and realize some of those profits. This led to the brilliant stroke of putting together groups of small investors, people with limited funds individually but collectively a force with considerable capital. Still, a second problem remained. Even if he could put together such syndicates, how could he do it so that the investors avoided high corporate income taxes?

The main reason he was drawn to this problem, he says, was that a great many of his clients were growing older and facing retirement. In many cases they had no family members to keep their businesses going. They and their families, then, had a need for a second income to support them in their declining years.

Wien began to do research in the law, and that investigation led him to a solution. A large group, he discovered, had banded together in the Midwest and invested in what was called the Cleveland Trust Company. It was strictly an investment, and those who had put their money in the trust had nothing to do with the operation of the company. As a result, the trustees maintained that they were "passive" investors, neither a corporation nor operators of a business, and therefore they were not liable for the heavy corporate income tax on top of their own personal income taxes. The government, naturally, held otherwise and took the trust to court. In a landmark decision, an appeals court in the Middle West held for the trust and ruled that as long as the investment was passive, any income from these holdings was not subject to corporate taxes. The government did not appeal, and so the rule stood.

When Wien read this decision, he said he immediately understood how it might apply to real estate and so redound to the benefit of both his clients and himself. He could set up real estate-investment syndicates, with large numbers of limited partners and himself and one or two others as the general partners responsible for operations and legal matters. The investment syndicate would then purchase the property and the new owners would create a net lease, which Wien would assume personally; then, for a fee, of course, he would proceed to operate the business. Thus, he, and not the limited partners in the syndicate, was responsible for the building and earned income from that direct involvement, while the limited partners would be receiving only the income he managed to generate, at a remove from anything else relating to their investment.

He began to put the idea into practice just before World War II. Still worried that he might be treading on treacherous legal and tax grounds, since no one had done anything like this before in real estate, he prepared a lengthy brief outlining the legal reasoning that buttressed his plan, using the Cleveland Trust Company decision as one precedent, and supported it by other interpretations of tax laws. He then took that brief to Roswell Magill, senior partner in the prestigious law firm of Cravath, Swaine and Moore, and to Randolph E. Paul, senior partner in the equally prestigious firm of Paul, Weiss, Rifkind, Wharton and Garrison. Both were experts on tax matters. If he could win their backing for his reasoning, he was sure he would be on smooth ground. "I convinced both of them," he said, and with their written opinions in hand, he put together a syndicate of two hundred investors to buy a building at 25 Broad Street in Manhattan's financial district for $7 million. Then he filed a registration statement with the Securities and Exchange Commission outlining the deal and in addition sought approval from the Internal Revenue Service. Once that was done, all he could do was sit back and wait. After reading his brief and the opinions of Magill and Paul, the IRS agreed that members of a passive real estate trust were exempt from corporate income taxes.

Wien was off and running. And the world of buying and selling real estate would never be the same again. No longer would the major deals be the sole province of the huge institutions and the very rich. Small investors anteing up $5,000 or $10,000 each could compete on nearly equal footing when formed into syndicates. Wien did just that and went looking for prime properties. In the process he became a major force in the postwar real estate market. He would always claim modestly, "I'm a lawyer, not a real estate man." Perhaps. But he was also widely heralded as the father of real estate syndication, and such syndicates were soon springing up everywhere as the Wien idea won wide acceptance. "A lot of other people started doing it," says Peter Malkin, Wien's son-in-law and partner both in the law firm and in many of the syndicates, "but then many converted syndication into publicly traded stock corporations, taking out and selling stock, and then they got right back into the double tax situation, which didn't make sense. We never did that."

What Wien did was to continue following the course he had charted. The small investors who put up the money received in return about fifty percent of the profits, on which they paid no corporate taxes. The general partners—himself and a few others—who found and then ran the property, received for their efforts the other fifty percent of the profits in addition to legal, operating, and other fees, and paid the corporate taxes.

He had conceived this plan, he always maintained, essentially as a way to give his clients a secure income free of onerous taxes. But there were critics who regarded Wien's altruistic declarations with skepticism. "Larry Wien got rich off the backs of these little people," says one. "He came up with the idea, yes, but it was their money that made it work, not his, because he didn't have to kick in a dime. Without them there would have been nothing. And he charged them plenty for finding the investment in the first place and for his legal services and then for operating the buildings. And then he took half the profits. If you really look at it, altruism had nothing to with it. Larry Wien and the people who were close to him got rich, that's what it was, and they got rich using other people's money."

Few of his little investors complained, though. Wien gave them what he promised, if not quite as much as they might have hoped. He gave them relatively safe investments, for most people were convinced that nothing was quite as safe as real estate; he gave them a steady return on those investments; and he gave them a return free of corporate taxes. "Sure, Wien got rich," says one investor in several Wien syndicates, "but he had every right to. It was his idea in the first place. And we didn't do so badly."

In the spring of 1949, Harry Helmsley was acting as broker for a building in the Columbus Circle area. He, like everyone in the business, was well aware of the Wien syndicates and of Wien's constant search for worthwhile properties. And so he made an appointment to see the lawyer and arrived with a proposal for a Wien syndicate to take on that building.

Wien not only took to Helmsley's proposal and formed a syndicate, but he took to Harry Helmsley himself. "Mr. Wien," says Peter Malkin, "was very impressed by Mr. Helmsley. He thought he was one of the brightest people he'd ever met. He said, 'Any time you have other properties available, bring them to me.' "

And Wien himself said, "He found investments and, when necessary, entered into negotiations for purchase. He's the best negotiator I've ever known. My job was to provide the money." Wien, though, was being overly modest. His own abilities as a negotiator were unquestioned, and those who dealt with him say he was, at the very least, Harry Helmsley's equal.

The door swung open and Helmsley strode through it onto a higher plane. Over the next decade and a half, he brought a steady parade of good properties to the attention of Lawrence Wien, and Wien formed syndicate after syndicate to buy them. This time, however, Helmsley was not only earning his broker's commission on the sales but was taken in frequently as one of the Wien general partners. He thereby gained a stake in the ownership of a growing portfolio of prime properties, and shared in the profits without risk of his own money. And since Wien was less than enamored with the day-to-day running of the properties, and Helmsley had considerable experience and expertise in just that, the responsibilities for operating the buildings were turned over to Helmsley and his company. With those responsibilities came a growing fortune. He had to pay rent on the sublease, naturally, but it was always a fraction of the rents he was reaping from the building's tenants. Even when his operating costs and other expenses were added in to his rent, his total bill was still usually less than a third of his total income. The Helmsley coffers, then, were filling with substantial profits steered his way by Lawrence Wien. Further, Helmsley was building a reputation now as one of the major movers on the New York real estate scene. In 1958 his peers named him Realty Man of the Year, and in the years that followed, those peers and business groups of all kinds would heap honor after honor upon him. "You couldn't turn around," a fellow realtor says, "without going to a dinner where Harry was getting some award or other, or without reading in the papers about Harry getting another plaque." He had come a long way.

Through these years, dozens of prime office buildings up and down Seventh Avenue in midtown Manhattan and in the downtown financial district were turned up by Helmsley and brought to Wien's door. As Helmsley's reputation grew, an increasing number of owners began to seek him out when they wanted to sell, or were receptive when Helmsley, scanning New York real estate, set his eyes on a building he thought he and Wien might do well with. In the Grand Central area, for instance, they picked up the Lincoln Building on Forty-second Street, where both maintained their offices (Helmsley had moved from smaller offices in the Flatiron Building twenty blocks south), and the Graybar Building on Lexington Avenue.

In many respects, then, Helmsley seemed locked in tandem with Wien. But not completely. His own company, Dwight-Helmsley, was expanding, its growing staff of bright young men scouring the city for bigger and better properties, making bigger and better deals.

Perhaps the brightest in the early years was Alvin Schwartz, a man with a keen eye for the right property at a bargain price. He had joined Dwight-Helmsley shortly before the war, and before long he was the boss's most valued and trusted employee. Along with Irving Schneider, who would later become a partner with him in many building purchases and so become a millionaire in his own right, Schwartz's future at Helmsley's side seemed unlimited.

But in 1949, just as Helmsley was forging his union with Wien, Schwartz decided the moment had come for him to move elsewhere. His uncles owned Spear and Company, a real estate concern which specialized in managing office buildings around New York, and he went to work for them. The desertion distressed Helmsley greatly. "He looked on Alvin Schwartz as a son or a younger brother," says a former Helmsley executive. "Schwartz was somebody he could trust. It often seemed that they communicated without words, that both of them knew what the other was thinking. When Alvin Schwartz talked, Harry Helmsley paid attention, which wasn't always true with other people. He could understand why Schwartz left to go with his uncles, but it hurt.'' It hurt enough so that Helmsley wanted Schwartz back. Over the next few years he made repeated overtures, but Schwartz was not receptive.

Helmsley did not give up, though. The clout provided by Wien gave him the opportunity to win back Schwartz by another tack. One morning in 1955, he walked into the offices of Spear and Company, and by noon he had bought out the uncles. Once more he had Alvin Schwartz at his side, in a venture that would henceforth be called Helmsley-Spear and would become the cornerstone of this growing empire.

And grow it did. Over the next ten years he added Charles F. Noyes, Co., one of the city's most prominent real estate firms, and used to it to handle his expanding portfolio of lower Manhattan properties. A little later, as he began to expand into the housing market, he swallowed Brown, Harris, Stevens, a hundred-year-old real estate firm that specialized in both rental and cooperative apartments.

With these subsidiaries, which all one day would be grouped under the banner of Helmsley Enterprises, and with all he learned about syndications and financing from Lawrence Wien, he was able in later years to reach out on his own and take control of properties that once would have been beyond his capabilities, if not his dreams.

He was on a roll, both alone and together with Lawrence Wien. The buildings were falling his way, and with them increasing riches, no little the result of Wien's beneficence. So generous was Wien to Helmsley, in fact, that some of the investors in his syndicates began to complain that they were getting the small leavings while Wien and Helmsley, who put up little or no money of their own, were reaping bountiful harvests. (At that time, there were only complaints; decades later, though, some of those investors took other steps and carried their disenchantment into the courts, challenging the arbitrary way the syndicates were being run.)

"For Mr. Helmsley and Mr. Wien," says Julien Studley, a major real estate broker and a sometime investor in the syndicates, "the properties were just a stream of money. The buildings are the investors' property, but they thought of them as theirs."

Such complaints bothered Harry Helmsley not at all. He considered them mere carping by those who should have been grateful for all that he was giving them, never mind all that was coming his way.

But all these early deals, with all their great personal rewards, were merely prelude to what Helmsley would later call the crowning achievement of his life, and what the press and the public would come to think of as his, and his alone.

4

ON THE BOOKSHELVES behind his desk in his office on the fifty-third floor of the Lincoln Building, Harry Helmsley kept two replicas of the Empire State Building. From his windows he could look eight blocks south and see the real thing. It is something he did nearly every morning, he once said. It towers there, dominating the skyline. He has called it the apex of all he has accomplished, the jewel in the Helmsley crown.

The Empire State Building. More than just a building. It conjures up visions, real and fanciful, that make the imagination soar to equal its height. There did King Kong, arm wrapped around its tower, clutching Fay Wray in one enormous paw, swat at swooping, machine-gunning biplanes and then tumble to the earth far below. Cary Grant waited forlornly for Deborah Kerr, William Holden came on to Maggie McNamara, Charles Boyer was abandoned by Irene Dunne, Victor Mature was trapped in an elevator, Tarzan let loose his jungle howls as he leaped here and there to the admiring gaze of Jane, and dozens more heroes and heroines of the movie dream world wandered through its vast high-ceilinged, ornate marble lobby on some errand of romance or adventure in the 150 films that used it as a backdrop. In real life, a World War II B-25 bomber, lost in the clouds, crashed into the seventy-ninth floor, creating havoc and leaving thirteen dead, twenty-six seriously injured (including two women who somehow survived a seventy-five-story plunge in an elevator whose cables snapped), and more

46

than half a million dollars in destruction. Grimmer still, because more personal and individual, a score and more of the despondent, to the horrified shrieks of sightseers, have suddenly climbed a parapet and leaped from the observation deck.

The Empire State Building. Nearly anywhere in the world, mention "skyscraper" and it is the first name that comes to mind. It is *the* skyscraper, Promethean in conception and execution, rising 1,472 feet above Fifth Avenue between Thirty-fourth and Thirty-third streets, with setbacks and embellishments on a scale to fit the building itself, a lance piercing the sky, called by critics and laymen alike the most beautiful, graceful, the most majestic edifice of such enormity on earth.

It was the dream of a group of private citizens, led by New York's one-time governor and Democratic presidential candidate, Alfred E. Smith, and General Motors executive, financier, and Democratic political power, John Jacob Raskob. It was a time when men dreamed outsized dreams, when the Roaring Twenties roared ever louder, when the direction was up, always up, when the boom was forever. It was 1928 when Smith and Raskob and Mayor Jimmy Walker and other worthies, shovels in hand, turned the first earth. It was three years, $40,948,000, and the lives of seventeen construction workers later, most dreams in shambles, the city filled with bread lines and soup kitchens and apple sellers and the unemployed, when the last rivets were driven.

At that moment there were those who looked at the skyline it dominated and called it a monstrous monument to fatally flawed visions and grandiose ambitions. It would stand forever as an empty shell, a reminder of an ever-overreaching age. They dubbed it derisively "The Empty State Building."

For a time the scoffers seemed prophetic. In the first years of the Great Depression the building was less than a quarter full, and the corridors echoed with the footsteps of the few

who inhabited it. But by the beginning of World War II the
Empire State Building became not a reminder of a lost past
but of hopes reborn. New tenants appeared, not the hoped
for corporate giants making it their headquarters, but rather
about 650 small professionals and businessmen, one third
from the garment trades, who carved out offices sometimes
little larger than cubicles throughout the building's two million square feet of space. And the sightseers flocked to the
observation deck, paying $1 million a year for the privilege
of standing on the highest man-made point on earth. Looking out in every direction, they could see for miles, the
cities and farms of New Jersey to the west and south, the
fields and towns of Long Island to the east, even the suburban bedrooms of Connecticut to the north. The Empire
State Building had become by the end of the 1930s the most
profitable building in New York, testimony to the Smith-
Raskob vision.

By 1950 the dreamers were dead and the heirs, with interests in other directions, began to look for a buyer. They
found one not in New York but in Chicago, in Colonel Henry
Crown. A year later, the Crown interests took over, paying
$54 million for the building alone. The land on which it
stood was sold separately, for $17 million, to the Prudential
Insurance Company, which charged Crown $1,020,000 a
year in rent.

Under Crown the building continued to prosper. In 1958,
though, aging and thinking about retirement, he quietly let
out word that he might be willing to sell if he got the right
offer. The word got to Lawrence Wien. He could not resist.
This was, after all, the Empire State Building. And so, in
semi-secret, negotiations got under way. Not until mid-
August 1961 did most of the public and those in real estate
hear the news. Crown called a meeting of his board of directors and simultaneously sent out a notice to tenants and
the press, announcing that he was considering a sale of his
building.

The suspense over the identity of the buyer lasted three

days, until August 22, and then it was revealed that Lawrence Wien was the man who would be buying. As the details emerged, they were staggering. This would be the most
spectacular and complex real estate transaction ever. The
cost of the Empire State Building had risen more than twenty
percent in a decade, to $65 million, the highest price ever
paid to that time for a single piece of property.

It had taken all of Wien's ingenuity and negotiating expertise to put the deal together. What he had done was this:
During the two-and-a-half-year course of the negotiations
with Crown, Wien was well aware that the Prudential Insurance Company, which owned the land upon which the
building rested, had a vital interest in the future of the
building itself. Prudential would have bought it if it could.
But it could not. At that time, the law prevented an insurance company from investing more than $50 million in a
single piece of property. Since Prudential already had $17
million sunk into the land and Crown was not about to let
the building go for a mere $33 million, Prudential was sty-
mied. But for Wien to come up with Crown's asking price
would be no easy task, not even with his books replete with
lists of potential investors.

So Wien, with his usual resourcefulness, took a different
tack. When he was certain of the price he would have to
pay, he approached Prudential and entered into lengthy dis-
cussions to reach a resolution agreeable to both. The result
was that the moment Wien signed his contract with Crown
to buy the Empire State Building for $65 million (to which
would later be added about $5 million in closing costs, var-
ious expenses, and legal fees, $1.1 million of which was
earmarked for lawyer Wien), he turned around and sold the
building to Prudential at a price it could legally afford—a
bargain price of $29 million.

But this was a bargain not just for Prudential but for Wien
as well. In exchange for his generosity, Prudential handed
over a 114-year lease on the building to a Wien-created Empire State Building Associates, a partnership of Wien and

his law partners, Peter Malkin and the late Alvin Lane. The master lease gave Wien, Malkin, and Lane the entire income from the building, then running to $10 million a year, out of which they were to pay Prudential an annual rent of $3,220,000 for the next thirty years, after which the rent would gradually decline until, after ninety-three years, it would be $1,610,000 a year.

So both Prudential and Wien got what they wanted. Prudential owned both the land and the building, and its investment remained within the legal strictures. Wien had a century-long lease, which amounted essentially to ownership, and would collect income that would far exceed the rent he was paying Prudential.

The next problem was to raise the money to pay Crown and the other costs. That was no problem at all. The first $29 million, of course, was put up by Prudential. Another $13 million was raised through mortgages on the lease. Then he turned to the tried-and-true formula of the syndicate, creating one whose limited partners would buy another $33 million in shares of $10,000 each, with a promised return of nine percent, or $900, a year. More than 3,300 investors quickly grabbed the shares.

The cost to Wien and his partners was practically nothing: a $4 million deposit to seal the deal with Crown, and $3 million of that they borrowed from shipping magnate Daniel Ludwig. And that was a short-term outlay. The instant all the papers were signed and some of the other money was in hand, the loan from Ludwig was repaid, and so was the $1 million Wien and his partners had advanced.

And where was Harry Helmsley all this time? As the negotiations were reaching a climax, Wien brought him in as the broker on the sale. That earned Helmsley a $500,000 fee. Then Wien decided that somebody would have to run the building under the new ownership. Who better than Harry Helmsley? An operating sublease was thus created, given the name of Empire State Building Company, and then handed over to a partnership to do the actual operating. And who were the partners? Lawrence Wien and Harry Helmsley, with the day-to-day operations falling to Helmsley. For his labors Helmsley was guaranteed a fee of $90,000 a year, while Wien was on the books for $190,000 a year for handling all the legal affairs of the enterprise. Further, the partners in that operating sublease, Wien and Helmsley, were also entitled to a tad more than half the profits after the investors got their $900. The cost to Helmsley for acquiring all this? Not a penny.

The building became increasingly profitable as Helmsley put his managerial talents to work. He slashed operating costs sharply, computerized the bookkeeping system, thereby cutting the staff from twenty-eight people to four, fired the outside cleaning company and assigned that job to one he controlled, and then proceeded to stagger the hours of his maintenance staff, which did away with overtime. He dispensed with the alterations department, which was costing, he said, ten times more than it was bringing in. He installed air conditioning and self-service elevators and then raised the rents of the tenants. (They now pay upward of $50 a square foot, still a bargain compared to the rents in the newer glass edifices farther uptown, but sharply higher than what they had been.) After six months, profits of the building were $1.5 million greater than they had been when he assumed command.

Wien and Helmsley gloried in the control of the world's tallest building, but the glory did not last long. Within three years they learned that the Empire State Building was not to hold its exalted title much longer. Taller structures, not one but two, were going to be built right in Manhattan, along the Hudson River, and not by some private developers but by a public agency, the Port of New York Authority, a joint operation of New York State and New Jersey. It was prepared to spend more than $350 million to build what it intended to call the World Trade Center. The twin towers would be a hundred feet and eight stories taller, and contain nearly ten million square feet of office space, about five times as much as the Empire State Building. Though its sheer glass-and-steel walls could not hope to match the architectural elegance of the older skyscraper, sightseers would be able to stand on the observation decks, look uptown, and stare down on the Empire State Building.

Wien and Helmsley mobilized other leading builders and real estate powers to fight the plan. They claimed the new World Trade Center would make office space a glut on the market, for, they said, ten million square feet of office space was already lying vacant. Further, private owners and developers would suffer greatly, some might even be driven out of business, while the World Trade Center and the Port Authority would flourish at their expense, since as public agencies they were relieved of the heavy tax burden carried by private interests.

Port Authority spokesmen scoffed at the opposition. The basic motivation behind it, they said, was an attempt to preserve the status of the Empire State Building. And the Port Authority, with the backing of the political powers of the two states, carried the day. Construction soon was under way, and as later events would prove, the expressed alarm at excess office space was spurious.

If the Empire State Building was to be dethroned, still Helmsley was determined to maintain its preeminent status, at least in the public imagination. Within days he announced that he was installing floodlights to illuminate the top thirty stories of the Empire State Building, making it, no matter what, the most dominant object in the Manhattan nighttime sky. Mounted in setbacks in the building, on the seventy-first, eight-first, and ninetieth floors, and designed so they would not attract or annoy migrating birds, disturb late office workers or interfere with the image transmissions from the televisions towers then on top of the building, the lights would make the top of the building, and hence the top of the city, appear to be crowned with a sheet of ice, a block of solid white light. The cost, he said, would be minimal, only $250,000 for the purchase and installation of the lights and a mere $25 a day to operate them.

If nothing else, the plan was a master stroke of public relations. It was hailed by just about everybody as an adornment that would grace the city's skyline. And so it was when the lights were turned on for the first time on April 1, 1964.

Through the 1960s and 1970s, Helmsley and Wien, the partners in the operating sublease, and the general partners in the syndicate were making ever more money from the Empire State Building. As for the limited partners, they usually earned only the $900 annual return that they had been promised on each of those $10,000 shares. By the 1980s, though, nearly twenty years after the purchase, things began to look up for them. In 1981, for instance, the Empire State Building turned a profit of $36 million, of which $8 million was distributed to the limited partners, a return of twenty-four percent on their investments. And the picture kept getting rosier. In 1986, according to reports filed with the Securities and Exchange Commission, the amount spread among the limited partners had risen to $13.4 million, with each of those original $10,000 shares earning about $5,000.

Still, this was a pittance compared to what has come Harry Helmsley's way through that operating sublease so generously granted. After his initial cost-cutting spree, Helmsley found new ways to reward himself for his efficiency. His subsidiaries doing the maintenance and other necessary services were being paid handsomely for their work, their fees, according to some experts, as much as twenty-five percent more than their competitors. Even with such costs, the Helmsley efficiency has paid off handsomely in profits for Helmsley. In 1981, for instance, when the 3,300 limited investors were splitting up $8 million in profits, Helmsley alone earned a $5 million profit for managing, cleaning, and providing other services to the building and maintaining the insurance, while Wien and the other general partners split up another $6.5 million. Five years later, the report filed with the SEC would note that though $13.4 million was distributed among the limited partners, the Helmsley operating sublease turned a tidy profit of $30 million, more than half of which went into Helmsley's pocket.

Harry Helmsley, then, has made a fortune from the majestic skyscraper on Fifth Avenue. He has managed it efficiently, though there have been continuing complaints about poor maintenance and services, as there have been on almost every building in which he has been involved, and he has made it ever more profitable. And so the stories have spread, fertilized by Helmsley himself and propagated by a less than probing press, to the point where they have become accepted truths, that the Empire State Building is Harry Helmsley's. It is not, of course, and never has been. It and the land on which it stands belong to Prudential Insurance Company. The lease on that land and on the building, for 114 years, is owned by Empire State Building Associates, a partnership of Lawrence Wien, Peter Malkin, and the estate of Alvin Lane. The sublease to operate the building is the province of another partnership, of Wien and Harry Helmsley. Only the actual running of the building, under a contract, is Harry Helmsley's.

Still, the myth flourishes. If Helmsley did not start it, he has done nothing to discourage or correct it. Rather, he has encouraged it and gloried in it. A man of undeniable accomplishments and an immense ego, perhaps he sees in it, and in the skyscraper itself, a fitting symbol of himself and all that he has become, a truth that goes beyond myth.

Lawrence Wien and Peter Malkin watched it happen. "It just doesn't happen to be true," Malkin sighed shortly before Wien's death. But neither he nor Wien were bothered enough to do more than mildly correct those who repeated it to them. After all, Malkin said, "Mr. Wien is not particularly interested in publicity."

5

ON HIS OWN, Lawrence Wien had been a winner, a dominating force in a highly competitive business. On his own, Harry Helmsley, if not a winner and pivotal figure, had been a comer, a man to reckon with. Together, they seemed unbeatable. Anything they wanted, they got, and whatever they got seemed to be prime. And as their reputations spread and flowered, more and more people with deals to make sought them out; now they had choices, bigger and better ones, and could turn down the marginal ones on which they might once have taken a flyer.

Success, and with it riches, became so regular and so expected that neither Wien nor Helmsley was prepared for failure. It was unthinkable. And then they ran up against J. Myer Schine.

Myer Schine was a singular figure, a rough-hewn, self-made, arrogant man with a reputation for getting his own way at any cost. Some called him, charitably, a rugged individualist out of a now-vanished mold, a man who exemplified the American dream, an immigrant who had started with nothing and worked his way to fame and fortune.

He had arrived in the United States from his native Latvia in the early years of the twentieth century, settled in Syracuse in upstate New York, failed in several business ventures, and then moved to the small town of Gloversville near Albany, where he would make his home for the rest of his life. To support himself he tried his hand at anything that came his way, selling garments for a time, peddling candy

on railroad trains, and a lot more, always in search of the
main chance. He found it in 1917, in the American love
affair with the movies. Leasing a vacant building, he converted it into a theater. Audiences flocked to it in even
greater numbers than he had hoped. Before long he was
buying and leasing more vacant buildings and turning them
into theaters until, by the beginning of World War II, he
had established a chain of 250 movie palaces across the
Northeast.

From theaters it was only a short step into real estate and
into other aspects of the entertainment industry, and the
Schine holdings burgeoned, taking in land, hotels, radio
stations, and reaching from the Northeast to Florida and on
to California.

But the Schine hold, particularly when it came to movie
theaters, was inclusive enough to make the government take
a hard look into his empire, and what it saw led to an anti-
trust suit for violation of the Sherman and Clayton anti-trust
acts. By the time the government was through with him,
Schine had been hit with heavy fines and been forced to sell
off seventy-five percent of his theaters. It was a blow more
to his ego than anything else, for it still left him with vast
holdings.

By 1965, Schine's realm took in sixty movie theaters,
twelve hotels, including the six-hundred-room Ambassador
on twenty-one extremely valuable acres on Wilshire Boulevard in Los Angeles, the Boca Raton and other Florida
resort hotels, three thousand acres of prime oceanfront
property in Palm Beach and Boca Raton, a Florida mansion
and estate once owned by the Chicago *Tribune*'s publisher,
Colonel Robert R. McCormick, and a dozen radio stations, among others. The value of that empire was conser-
vatively estimated at $150 million.

Nevertheless Schine was growing old, if not losing his
grip, and his brother, Louis, who had been his partner and
who had shared much of the day-to-day burden, had died.
To follow in his footsteps, Myer Schine had two sons,

C. Richard and G. David.[1] Both worked for Schine Enterprises, Richard in the main office and David as president of the Ambassador Hotel. But Myer Schine didn't think very highly of the abilities of either son to succeed him and take firm control of his empire. So he let out word that he might be open to a reasonable offer for all he owned.

Wien and Helmsley got the word, and so did others. But Wien and Helmsley thought they were the right people to put together a deal Schine could not refuse. They were not alone. Another real estate entrepreneur, Morris Karp, a one-time medical student who had become a developer of homes and apartments in New York City and the suburbs and had parlayed his success in that venture into a $10 million publicly held company called Realty Equities, also got into the act.

But Wien and Helmsley had the kind of power and finances that Karp did not, at least not at that moment, and so after a while Karp dropped out of the bidding. Through May and June of 1965, Wien, with Helmsley in his usual capacity as broker, held a series of meetings with Schine and his representatives. By early June a tentative agreement had been reached. Schine agreed to sell his vast holdings at what could only be considered a bargain price of $64.5 million. "We shook hands on it," Helmsley said.

1. G. David Schine had won a certain notoriety of his own before going to work for his father. His good friend Roy Cohn had been chief counsel to the Senate subcommittee headed by Senator Joseph R. McCarthy, the Wisconsin Republican whose name became synonymous with witch-hunting. During the height of McCarthy's indiscriminate and often specious pursuit of suspected Communists and subversives in the government, Schine had been hired by the senator and Cohn as a subcommittee assistant, and had then proceeded to make headlines when he and Cohn had journeyed to Europe where they attacked American libraries as fronts for the spread of Communist and subversive literature. When Schine was drafted, to become Private Schine of the United States Army, Cohn and McCarthy had sought special favors for him. The Army had resisted, and that resistance led to the Army-McCarthy hearings and ultimately to the censure of McCarthy by his Senate peers and the end of his power and influence.

As far as the two partners, Wien and Helmsley, were concerned, that handshake sealed the agreement. That was the way they always did things. First a handshake and then everything on paper. And so Helmsley announced to the press that he and Wien were buying Schine Enterprises. All that remained was for Wien's office to draw up the contracts.

As far as Myer Schine was concerned, though, a deal was not a deal until it was signed, sealed, and delivered, and the money in his bank account. Until then, he was free to do whatever he wanted.

He began even while the preliminary negotiations were still in progress. His brother's widow and her two children had been left 37.5 percent of the stock in Schine Enterprises. Myer went to them and explained sorrowfully that the company was facing "imminent insolvency and bankruptcy." But he was willing to help them out before that dreaded day arrived. He would buy their 37.5 percent interest for $5 million, would somehow manage to come up with $100,000 within fifteen days and the balance in sixty days if they agreed to accept his offer.

Martha Schine knew her brother-in-law all too well. Before she agreed to his proposition, she wanted proof that he was telling her the truth. She needed concrete evidence, she said, that the company was indeed in dire straits. And so she proposed that three reputable businessmen, two of whom could be named by Myer, be appointed as receivers of Schine Enterprises to make a true assessment of its actual condition. Schine agreed verbally, then refused to sign the papers that would put the agreement into effect. Instead, he mounted increasing intense pressure on Martha Schine and her children, insisting that disaster was just around the corner and if they wanted to salvage anything at all, they had better accept his terms with no more quibbling. Unable to resist, they agreed, and on July 6, 1965, they signed the papers Schine had ready and turned over their stock to him.

Then Schine turned in another direction, back to Morris Karp. "Unknown to us," says Peter Malkin, who was deeply involved along with Wien and Helmsley, "at the same time that we were drawing and finishing the contract, we believe that the same law firm that was representing Schine was taking our draft every day and drawing a similar contract with Morris Karp, who may or may not have known what we were doing. We have no way of knowing and I don't want to indicate in any way that he did anything improper. But . . ."

Meanwhile, the contract was completed, approved by all parties, and ready to be signed. On September 1, Wien and Helmsley had an appointment to meet with Schine and his representatives late in the morning and conclude the deal. "Early that morning," Malkin recalls, "it came over the broad tape that Schine had sold the property to somebody else. We were not even told about it until we read about it. And Karp signed virtually the identical contract that we had been negotiating for many weeks."

About the only difference was the amount of money that would change hands. Karp paid $75 million for the Schine holdings, $10.5 million more than Schine had agreed to accept from Wien and Helmsley.

Myer Schine offered a variety of explanations. He had, he said, been indignant at what he thought was a "premature announcement" by Wien and Helmsley early in the summer that the sale had been arranged. What he didn't say was that the announcement just might have wrecked his deal with his sister-in-law had she been aware of it. In addition, he claimed that he had taken personal offense at what he considered their patronizing attitude toward him, treating him as an old man losing his grip and desperate to dispose of what he owned at any price. And, he said, as far as he was concerned, as long as the papers had not been signed, there was no final agreement and he was free to do whatever he wanted, and if he could strike a better deal with someone else, so much the better.

Wien sighed and wrote it off as just one of those things

that happen. Others did not look on Schine's performance quite so serenely.

Sister-in-law Martha and her son and daughter hired attorney Louis Nizer to sue for $15 million in damages. Schine settled.

Robert Rosan, another attorney, sued Schine for $1.5 million, claiming that he had brought Schine and Morris Karp together and handled their negotiations, yet Schine had not paid him for his services. Schine settled.

And Harry Helmsley, not of a forgiving nature, sued Schine for $1,932,000, the broker's commissions he said were due him and Helmsley-Spear for having negotiated the sale of the Schine properties to Wien and himself, even though Schine had backed out of the sale at the last moment. Schine settled.

The whole Schine affair had been a bitter, perhaps even a traumatic experience for Harry Helmsley, for it meant more than just the money and the properties he stood to gain. "Harry changed after what I suppose you have to call the Schine fiasco," says a former Helmsley executive. "He had always acted like a gentleman. He believed that was the way to behave. If you acted the right way toward other people, they'd act right with you. If you agreed on a deal, then it was a deal even if somebody came along later with a better offer. He'd been around long enough, so maybe he should have known better. But he thought that was the only way to do business. And, remember, he was a winner. I can't remember a time before that when he'd ever lost anything he wanted. He wanted those Schine properties. He had plans for them. He wasn't prepared for somebody like Myer Schine, and he certainly didn't think anyone would do what Schine did. I don't think I ever saw him as furious as he was that day. I don't think he was ever the same after that. He got harder and tougher. He didn't trust people the way he used to. And he got a lot more demanding of the people who worked for him, and a lot less forgiving of mistakes."

Where once he had been generous with his employees, if not his tenants, cutting them in for participation in his deals, handing out Christmas bonuses and raises when things worked out well, now that generosity faded. The bonuses became smaller and so did the raises, and even to get a salary increase often required strenuous bargaining, even pleading. It was demeaning to those who went through it, and the staunch loyalty of the Helmsley organization, which had once been given so unquestioningly, began to fray.

The unexpected collapse of the Schine deal must be seen as a crucial moment in the career of Harry Helmsley. Much would change, both in his career and in his personal life, in the years that followed.

The business partnership with Lawrence Wien that had opened so many doors began to fade, though the two remained close friends. Helmsley was now taking a leading role in finding, purchasing, and syndicating major properties. And some of those properties were very major indeed. There was, for instance, the Furman-Wolfson Trust.

A publicly owned real estate venture controlled by Morris Furman and Herman Wolfson and listed on the American Stock Exchange, the trust's properties encompassed some thirty buildings in seven states, including a twenty-five-story one at Broadway and Forty-first Street in Manhattan, the forty-nine-story One LaSalle Building in Chicago, the tallest building in Newark, New Jersey, rising thirty-seven stories, and others in Los Angeles, Houston, and Des Moines, Iowa, as well as a number of shopping centers. In 1969, Morris Furman and Herman Wolfson decided to sell. Harry Helmsley decided to buy. The price was $165 million, and it was one of the largest real estate deals made to that time. The way Helmsley worked it was to follow the Wien formula and make his own alterations to it. He raised about half the money, $88 million, in mortgages. The rest, about another $80 million needed to purchase the trust's outstanding publicly held shares, he got from his friends at Chase Manhattan Bank on a loan. It was a loan that raised a few eyebrows.

For Helmsley simply went to see his friends, told them he needed the money, then signed some papers and walked out with what he needed. He put up no collateral, put up nothing more than his signature for what was the largest unsecured loan ever given to an individual.

But that was all right. Chase Manhattan had faith that Helmsley was a good risk. He was, indeed, for he had come up with a scheme that would get Chase Manhattan its money back rapidly and would put millions into his own pocket. First he stripped the trust of ten of the best properties, taking them for himself, and put the rest into something he now called Investment Properties Associates. Then, emulating the Wien formula, he set up a syndicate to finance this new group whose general partners were himself and his close aide, Irving Schneider, and whose limited partners would be offered the chance to buy 81,700 shares in Investment Properties Associates at $1,000 a share, for a grand total of nearly $82 million. What he offered the limited partners was a replay of what the limited partners in the Empire State Building had been offered—a nine percent annual return on their investment and half the operating profits above that payout. The shares sold, and Helmsley justified Chase Manhattan's faith by immediately repaying the loan. And so this massive purchase had actually cost Harry Helmsley not a single penny and had gained him free and clear ten major properties, half the profits on twenty others, which, as the years passed were showing net profits of about thirty percent a year, plus his brokerage commissions for handling the whole thing, and on top of that hefty fees for managing all the properties and providing all the services.

Furman-Wolfson had been a coup for Helmsley, one he had done on his own. But there were some who looked at it closely, and though they could appreciate the ingenious way he had manipulated it to his own ends and in his own favor, they noticed something else, they saw sharpness and avarice that went beyond what had once been. He might still stride through the business world with the outward demeanor of the gentleman, but, since the Schine affair, there seemed within a growing element of greed, a sense that no matter how much he had and how much he accomplished, it was never enough, he wanted still more. He now looked on people with distrust, viewed with suspicion the proffered deal, looked for angles, stacked things heavily in his own favor. A handshake was no longer good enough; he wanted to see the papers, too, and he wanted the small print on those papers to read the way he dictated.

He might continue to show the world that old manner of trust and a willingness to compromise, to listen to reason, but, say competitors and even some executives who worked for him, there was always a hatchet man nearby, someone to make the unpleasant moves dictated by Helmsley, and so take the heat. If he wanted someone fired, it wouldn't be Helmsley who would do the firing, he would have someone else do it, and then, not infrequently, he would make apologies and hand over a generous severance check. If tenants brought major complaints to his door, he would listen with what seemed patience and reasonableness, letting someone else turn those complaints away. Always he seemed the model of reason and gentility, and always there was someone else to do the dirty work. In a very real sense, he played the game of good cop–bad cop, with himself in the role of the good, understanding, reasonable cop.

His interests were spreading now, out from office buildings to residences, and in the process he suddenly found himself embroiled in politics and in bitter battles that would do much to change his public image. He would move, too, from the world of brokering into the world of building, and he and his public relations men would carefully cultivate a myth that he was constructing a domain to rival and even outstrip those that he had once envied.

And with all these changes, his personal life would be altered beyond recognition. He would shed the past and show the world an entirely different face.

Part Two
Landlord and Builder

6

HARRY AND EVE Helmsley were married for nearly thirty-
five years, but in all that time, though they shared apartments and a house, they walked apart, a distance always
between them.

"I think it was no better and no worse than a lot of marriages," says someone who knew them. "Harry and Eve
were both pretty private people, and they weren't terribly
demonstrative. They never really let anybody get close to
them. It's hard to tell what goes on behind closed doors,
but I would guess that over the years they just got used to
each other and went their own ways and that was about it.
There was never any obvious friction, but there wasn't much
affection, either. I'd guess the reason they stayed together
so long was simply out of habit. It's a lot easier just to stay
together and let things ride, especially after all those years,
than go to all the trouble that goes along with breaking
up, as long as there wasn't anybody else. I'm sure there
wasn't, until that woman came along."

In those days, of course, married women were supposed
to stay home, tend the children, and take care of their hus-
bands' needs. But Harry and Eve Helmsley had no children,
either because they wanted none or could have none. Nobody is certain which, though those who knew them say that
they were both uncomfortable around small children, kept
their distance, as though they were not quite certain how to
act. And Eve, a tall, handsome woman with a windblown
look, with no career, and few close friends, felt trapped in

the city apartments, their first one on Park Avenue and then a later one on Gramercy Park. She was polite if a little distant with her neighbors; her life, a restricted existence, centered around the Quaker meeting house and her home.

So Harry, in a financial position to buy what he wanted where he wanted began to look at land in the suburbs, and in 1950 found a hilltop acre overlooking the Hudson River in the village of Briarcliff Manor, in Westchester County. It was far enough from Manhattan, almost an hour on the commuter line of the New York Central Railroad, so land prices were cheap. He bought it, built a modest five-room ranch house whose only outstanding features were the view and the large pool. An avid swimmer, Harry was in the pool in good weather for an hour every day, and he considered access to a pool one of life's necessities.

They joined the Sleepy Hollow Country Club in nearby Scarborough, where Harry played a high-handicap duffer's game of golf now and again, usually with someone with whom he had a deal going, and Eve, who was less than enamored of golf, played better-than-average tennis. In the winter, they went skiing, usually to slopes up the Hudson though now and then to tougher hills in Switzerland or to Aspen in Colorado. Harry, in fact, considered himself something of an expert until he got hurt racing down the slopes at Aspen and gave it up. The one thing they seemed to share was a passion for dancing. Both tall, slim, and attractive (though as time passed, Eve put on weight and began to look like a dowager), they made a striking couple as they waltzed around the dance floor at the country club. It was, some people said, the one time when they seemed in harmony. In the main, though, they stayed to themselves and for nearly twenty years played almost no role in the life of their community. Harry surfaced only when there were proposals to change the zoning laws to permit building on smaller lots; he threw his weight behind efforts to keep Briarcliff Manor an exclusive area where homes had to be built on lots of an acre or more. Eve surfaced hardly at all.

She did not join the bridge games, so ubiquitous in suburbia. A practicing Quaker, she devoted much of her time to charities, joining a few committees though she did not play a leading role in them, stayed home, and took care of her ailing mother who moved in with them during her declining years.

Life in suburbia revolves around parties and entertaining, but the Helmsleys remained at a remove from the social whirl. At the parties they did attend, they usually stood to the side, aloof, a distance from each other, had perhaps a single drink, which they often left hardly tasted, and departed early. The only exceptions were the parties given by Mrs. Frank Vanderlip (her husband had owned the land that Helmsley bought). The Vanderlip mansion featured a vast ballroom, and their parties centered around dance contests, so the Helmsleys accepted invitations with enthusiasm. More than once, they waltzed away with the prize as the best dancing couple, and one observer was sure that Harry worked to perfect his dancing technique as hard as he worked at building his business. But that sense of shared pleasure was missing almost everywhere else. Some thought that had Eve not been along Harry might have been more approachable, more outgoing, for the few times when he did appear without her, he seemed far more affable, a man able to mix, to engage in idle conversation, to enjoy himself.

Their own gatherings were perfunctory small affairs of rarely more than half a dozen couples at a time. "Whenever they had people in," says a longtime Briarcliff Manor resident, "it was always like they were doing a duty, paying us back for having had them to our houses. You never felt like they really wanted you in their house or that they enjoyed entertaining. We had them so now they had to have us." And it showed. The hors d'oeuvres were sparse, the drinks limited, usually one to a customer, the conversation stilted, the host and hostess distant, and the affair soon over, to the relief of both the givers and guests. A favorite mem-

ory of those who were there in the old days is of the time
the Helmsleys arranged to repay a number of invitations by
having parties on two successive days. One woman arrived
on the wrong day for the wrong party. Eve Helmsley stood
stiffly in the doorway, blocking her entrance, told her she
wasn't supposed to show up until the following day, and
sent her away.

"In those days we never had any idea that they were rich,
I mean, the way you read about him now. We knew he was
in business, and I suppose we knew he was in real estate,
but so were a lot of other people. Everybody was doing
well. We just had no idea that he owned the whole world."

Indeed, a sense that perhaps his riches were ephemeral
was something that seemed ingrained in the one-time twelve-
dollar-a-week office boy. Despite the millions he was piling
up, Helmsley never ceased pleading poverty. At least, that's
what he tried to make people believe. "I wish I could afford
that" was a litany repeated over and over. Visiting a business associate who had just moved into luxurious new offices, Helmsley looked around, sighed, and said, "I wish I
could afford this." Hearing that an acquaintance was off on
a lengthy cruise, Helmsley said, "I wish I could afford to
do that." Told that a competitor had bought a private plane,
Helmsley said, "I wish I could afford that." Meeting one
of his executives who, having closed a major deal, celebrated by having a suit custom-made, Helmsley examined
him, asked how much the suit cost, and when told, said, "I
wish I could afford that." He went on to claim he had only
a couple of suits and they were forty-dollar off-the-rack
ones. And he said these things with such sincerity that if
the listeners hadn't known him they might almost have believed him.

But behind this sincerity, this implication of poverty, lay
something else, a deeply held conviction that the one true
value of money was to make more money. A close friend
of Helmsley's once persuaded him to visit an art exhibit at
a leading Manhattan gallery. As they wandered from painting

to painting, Helmsley seemed particularly taken by one, and kept returning to it. "So buy it, Harry," his friend said finally. "You like it. You can afford it. It will give you pleasure to have it."

Helmsley reacted with shock. He shook his head. He said, "Oh, no, I would never enjoy it then, knowing my money wasn't making more money." (Helmsley may have known real estate, but it was apparent he had little appreciation of the state of the art market.)

So Harry Helmsley, if a resident of the suburbs, was not really a part of it. It was a place to keep his wife, a place to return to at the end of a long day, if he didn't happen to decide to spend the night at an apartment he kept in the city instead. He didn't even seem to mind the train rides every day. They gave him time to go through papers in bulging briefcases he carried with him, to plan his moves in isolation. His business was his life and his life was his business. "The only time he seemed really alive in those days," says an associate, "was when he was working. The rest of the time it was as though something was missing."

With a single-minded dedication replacing the void at home, without the distraction of an abiding commitment to home and family, he was building his empire, amassing properties and companies, becoming the dominant figure in New York real estate.

"The people who worked for him were his children," the broker Julien Studley has said, "and his heirs were his colleagues." The real estate deal was the be-all and end-all, and he often referred to the successful ones as his "grandchildren." As one competitor put it, "His business was so totally his life that if you didn't know he was married and had a home, you'd have thought he spent twenty-four hours a day in the office doing nothing else."

7

WITH THE ACQUISITION of Brown, Harris, Stevens in 1965, Helmsley moved into the residential market, something he had paid little attention to since his early days as a rent collector for Dwight, Voorhis and Perry. Not one to do things on a small scale since his association with Lawrence Wien, he marched with long and rapid strides toward the profits and perils of landlordism.

In early 1966, he took on the sprawling Garden Bay Manor apartment complex in Queens. A year later, he and Wien joined forces in the purchase of the 691-unit Georgetown Apartments in Washington, D.C., and then he added to his growing stable the 27-building Childs Garden Apartments and the 20-building Windsor Parks complex, both in Queens, and Horizon House, overlooking the Hudson River in Fort Lee, New Jersey. Reaching across the country, he bought the luxury Sierra Towers on the border between Beverly Hills and West Hollywood, with its panoramic view of the city out toward the Pacific. And soon he added an 857-unit garden apartment development in Houston, Texas, and the 3,500-apartment Parkmerced development in San Francisco, bought from Metropolitan Life Insurance Company for $40 million. He was to acquire a lot more.

What he thought was the best, though, was still to come. It was Parkchester.

An island unto itself, a city within the city, Parkchester had been built in 1941 by the Metropolitan Life Insurance Company on 130 acres in a sparsely populated area of the

East Bronx. About the same time, the insurance company constructed several other major developments, one in Harlem, and two, Stuyvesant Town and Peter Cooper Village, east of First Avenue and north of Fourteenth Street in Manhattan. The project in Harlem had been designed to house mainly black employees of the company and, where there were vacancies, other middle-class blacks. Stuyvesant Town was aimed at the white middle class and Peter Cooper at the white upper-middle class; both were bastions surrounded by decaying slums to the south and west.

The biggest of all, and to many the prize, was Parkchester. It was, when built and for more than thirty years, the largest rental complex in the United States. Its population of more than 40,000 lived in about 12,200 apartments of two to seven rooms in fifty-eight buildings from six to thirteen stories high. If they wanted, Parkchester residents never had to leave what might well be called their compound. They had parks and tree-lined walks, playgrounds for the children, a hundred-store shopping center, a 2,000-seat movie theater, a library, a post office, and garage space for 3,500 cars. From the beginning until the mid-1960s, the tenants were Metropolitan Life employees and other white-collar workers. They were very satisfied with the way things were, and they wanted to keep things unchanged. The apartment rents were more than reasonable. The early residents paid from $32 to $71 a month for their apartments, and by 1968, twenty-eight years after the project had opened, they were paying only about $100 a month for the smallest apartment and $165 a month for a three-bedroom, seven-room unit. And Metropolitan Life was a benevolent landlord. As one longtime tenant noted, "The thing about these people is that they've grown old calling an insurance company 'Mother'—Mother Metropolitan will take care of you." Indeed, it did. A large staff made sure that everything in the complex was well maintained, and repairs were done with dispatch.

The tenants were exclusively white—middle-class Irish,

Italians, and Jews. And they were very conservative. (Richard Nixon would carry the district in the 1968 election, while the city was going heavily for Hubert Humphrey, and George Wallace got nearly ten percent of Parkchester's vote.)

By 1968, Parkchester residents were not merely concerned but alarmed at what they imagined as a threat to their way of life. The New York City Commission on Human Rights charged Metropolitan Life with the "deliberate, intentional, systematic, open, and notorious" exclusion of blacks and Puerto Ricans from the development. Between 1940 and 1963, not a single black or Puerto Rican was able to rent an apartment in Parkchester, at least partly because Metropolitan Life gave preference when vacancies occurred to relatives of current tenants, all of whom just happened to be white. Even after 1963, when the civil rights movement was at its most effective, forcing once-recalcitrant landlords to open their doors to minorities, only twenty-five members of those two minorities were able to rent Parkchester apartments despite an average turnover of four hundred apartments a year. But the pressure was building, and it was increasingly obvious to Parkchester residents that in the very near future they would find themselves living next door to black faces and listening to Spanish accents in the public places. It was, in this conservative enclave, a decidedly unwelcome idea. "The thing that's going to ruin this place," said one longtime tenant, "is the blending they're doing, and doing it too rapidly. If they keep a certain type of people, all well and good. But if they let down the barriers, well, you know . . ."

That, then, was a major concern in this bastion of the conservative white middle class. But this threat would soon be overshadowed by Harry Helmsley.

By the middle to late 1960s, Parkchester was becoming a millstone around the neck of Metropolitan Life. The insurance company was confronted on one side by restive tenants determined to keep their enclave lily-white. It was faced on the other side by increasingly militant black and Puerto Rican minorities just as determined to storm that white fortress and cut themselves in for a share of the good life. There was no way Metropolitan Life could win in this situation. The last thing the company wanted was to be considered racist and discriminatory, yet that's precisely what would happen if it continued along the old path or if it bowed to the obvious desires of so many of its Parkchester tenants. If, on the other hand, it agreed to a new, nondiscriminatory policy and opened wide the rental doors, those old tenants might well rise in wrath. Even if city, state, and federal authorities forced such a morally correct and necessary policy on the insurance giant, Metropolitan Life was well aware who would really become the target of the rage of these northern whites who, as the civil rights revolution came home to them, had begun to take on attributes that had once been thought the exclusive province of white Mississippi.

But social problems and racial upheaval were not the only troubles facing Metropolitan Life. There were very real economic ones as well. The tax abatements that had influenced the company to go into major apartment construction in the first place were coming to an end. That meant higher and higher tax bills every year. In addition, while costs of maintaining Parkchester and other developments continued to rise, rents remained frozen as a result of rent controls, and so Parkchester began to look very much as though it would turn from a profit-making investment into a losing one.

The time had come, Metropolitan Life executives reasoned, to get out. "We went into developments when there was a tremendous housing shortage," said one of them. "But now there's a trend away from this and while we have generally had good relations with our tenants, there are differences. And, after all, we are in the insurance business."

Helmsley heard the rumors and went to Wien with the idea of a new Wien-Helmsley syndicate to take over. Initially, Wien was not overly receptive. Though he felt that taking over something on the scale of Parkchester "made great sense economically and as an investment," Peter Malkin says, "Mr. Wien did not want to get directly involved. He felt very much like Metropolitan Life did, that it was very difficult to be successful politically owning residential property in New York City, that the rules and regulations were unreasonable and unfair and that if you tried to get out from underneath the strings by converting the property to cooperative or condominium ownership, there would be all kinds of allegations."

Helmsley didn't see it that way. The Empire State Building had been the jewel of business properties. He saw Parkchester as the jewel of residential properties, one to be seized by a man with his ambitions. "There is," he said, "a certain glamor about buying a city within a city." Besides, he was sure he saw something else. A bitter and outspoken opponent of rent controls since they had been first introduced, he thought that their end was in sight. Politicians would finally see the wisdom of the arguments he and other real estate men had been propounding for years: Controls discouraged new building, discouraged landlords from doing the necessary maintenance to improve their properties or even keep them from deterioration. Rent controls, he argued, eventually harmed everyone, tenant as well as landlord.

Helmsley envisioned a time in the not-too-distant future when rents at Parkchester, and in other residential buildings, would begin to advance to what real estate people called "fair market" levels—i.e., what the traffic would bear. And he envisioned, too, the time when Parkchester would be ripe for conversion to cooperatives. Not only would millions flow from the sale of apartments to tenants, but millions more would be gained from managing the complex even after conversion.

What he ignored were Wien's fears and warnings about political realities. Wien understood, and Helmsley at that moment apparently did not, that there are a lot more tenants who are voters than landlords, and with those in office who want to stay in office, the vote is what counts. Since almost all tenants wanted nothing as much as the continuation of rent control, there was little doubt that despite the landlord opposition, controls would remain.

So it was with some reluctance that Wien was persuaded to join with Helmsley and form a syndicate to relieve Metropolitan Life of what was becoming an onerous burden. On April 17, 1968, they entered into an agreement to buy Parkchester for $90 million, the highest price ever paid for a single piece of property to that time. As usual, Helmsley and Wien personally came up with little of that cost. Together, according to reports, they bought control for less than $9 million, the rest coming from mortgages and limited partners in a syndicate.

Helmsley immediately sought to allay whatever fears Parkchester residents had about a new owner. He talked about preserving the community, said that the changes he intended to make would all be for the better. Parkchester residents were skeptical. They waited with some trepidation to find out what Helmsley would really do. One step nobody had any doubts about was that he would file without delay for a fifteen percent hardship rent increase. Indeed, that is precisely what he did.

And then he made a totally unexpected move and in the process hardened the incipient antipathy that existed toward him. Under Metropolitan Life, the tenants' security deposit of one month's rent, something nearly all landlords require, had been placed in interest-bearing accounts at First National City Bank. Those deposits totaled more than $1.2 million, and every year Metropolitan Life had distributed the interest on those deposits, about four percent, to the tenants. It wasn't much for any individual, only between eight dollars and ten dollars a year, but it was another sign of the insurance company's benevolent attitude. After all, landlords at that time were not required by law to pay interest on security deposits to tenants.

On December 3, 1968, Helmsley and Wien took formal title to Parkchester. (Nobody paid much attention to Lawrence Wien. The man in the forefront was Harry Helmsley; he was the one the people in Parkchester considered the landlord. Questions about Wien usually drew blank expressions.) Less than a month later, Helmsley pulled those security deposits out of First National's interest-bearing accounts and transferred them into accounts that paid no interest at the Bank of Commerce. It just so happened that Helmsley-Spear for years had been a very important customer of the Bank of Commerce, and the bank had granted the firm several very large loans in the recent past. It also just so happened that the bank was a tenant at 60 East Forty-second Street, a building managed by Helmsley-Spear. And it also just so happened that the bank rented space at Parkchester for Helmsley and its lease had no escalation clause, a decidedly unusual state of affairs.

The tenants were outraged. "It was the principle of the thing," said one. "What the hell, ten bucks isn't much, but there was a principle involved. Here was Helmsley telling us what a good landlord he was going to be. Here was Helmsley telling us that he would treat us just as good as Met Life did, even better. And then he goes and steals a few bucks from everybody's pocket."

More than principle was involved, of course. Although ten bucks may not mean much to an individual tenant, it all adds up. What Helmsley had done was make a gift of about fifty thousand dollars a year, the amount of interest the security deposits had been earning, to the Bank of Commerce, at which he was a big customer and from which he was receiving large loans. Further, he was giving himself free use of the million and more dollars in security deposits without having to pay anything for them.

The tenants weren't the only ones who looked askance. New York State Attorney General Louis J. Lefkowitz thought the aroma of the whole thing decidedly rank. Lefkowitz was convinced that if there wasn't a law requiring landlords to keep security deposits in interest-bearing accounts and then distribute the interest to the tenants, there ought to be. He saw in the Helmsley transfer a means to put pressure on the state legislature to pass such a law. But he also saw in the Helmsley action, especially given the real estate broker's long-standing relationship with the new bank, a blatant attempt to defraud the Parkchester residents of money that was rightly theirs.

Lefkowitz filed fraud charges against Helmsley and argued the case in court. This round he lost. "It is quite clear from the statute that the landlord has no obligation to deposit rent security moneys in an interest bearing account," ruled State Supreme Court Justice Joseph Sarafite. "While the action does not invite judicial applause," he added, "neither may respondent's conduct warrant the judicial condemnation sought by the attorney general."

Perhaps not. But the politicians in Albany were impelled to take some action. Bills were introduced in the state legislature in 1970 to require all landlords to place security deposits in interest bearing accounts, notify the tenants of the name and address of the bank in which they have been placed and then each year pay the interest to the tenant. By a vote of 52 to 2 in the state senate, and by 138 to 7 in the state assembly, the bill became law, and the ride Helmsley and other landlords had taken on that gravy train was over.

What Helmsley learned from all this was the reality of tenant power. And that realization obviously convinced him that any hopes he had for an end to rent controls were only idle dreams. (Indeed, twenty years later, rent controls of one kind or another remain in place. The only bone the state legislature ever threw in the direction of the landlords was passage of a so-called "vacancy decontrol" act in 1971 which took those apartments that became empty out of rent control. However, these rents were stabilized at a level about fifteen percent higher than under rent control.) "Wherever you have rent control or rent stabilization," Helmsley would say, "investment ownership is a disaster. Controls have eliminated the possibility of an intelligent investor going in.'' And so he took the step that Parkchester residents, at least some of them, had expected, and feared, from the day he became their landlord. Late in 1972, he announced his intention to convert the development's North Quadrant, containing nearly four thousand apartments in sixteen buildings, or about a third of Parkchester, to condominiums. It was just the first step, everyone knew, in a plan to convert the entire project.

He claimed he was offering the tenants a ''fantastically good deal.'' If they acted within ninety days, they would have exclusive rights to purchase their apartments as condominiums, at prices ranging from $7,400 for the two-room units to $27,200 for the seven-room ones. Further, he said, he was willing to finance up to seventy-five percent of the purchase price at seven percent a year interest, a half point lower than the current mortgage rate at banks. But if the tenants delayed, after ninety days their apartments would be offered to outsiders at a price ten percent higher than the insider price. Still, Helmsley was willing to throw a bone to reluctant tenants, and perhaps ward off possible roadblocks from state and city authorities who were already taking very close looks at the effects cooperative and condominium conversions were having on the middle class. Even if the tenants didn't buy, he wasn't going to throw them out of their homes when another buyer came along, even though as the law stood at the moment, he was entitled to do just that once a building was converted. Those tenants who were still rent controlled, and they were the vast majority, would be allowed to keep their apartments as long as they wanted. Rent-stabilized tenants, on the other hand, of whom there were about three hundred, wouldn't be quite so lucky; they would be allowed to stay only until their leases expired, and then they would be out.

Parkchester residents, Helmsley declared, were being given an opportunity to be part of the wave of the future.

Conversion from rental dwellings to cooperatives and condominiums was the way the city had to go. Thus the plan
for Parkchester presaged "a revolution in New York real
estate. It will help stabilize neighborhoods. The exodus from
the city will be stanched because people will have more
interest in their neighborhoods. This is the only way New
York is going to be saved. I would hope that in twenty years
landlords would be a rarity in New York, that everyone
would own his own home."

Indeed, much of the real estate community seemed ec-
static. Conversion meant a lot more business. "The implications of this are marvelous. The buildings will be kept
better, the tensions between landlord and tenant will be
ended, the tenants will be able to run the project the way
they want to and they will be free to fix up their own apartments," enthused one Helmsley competitor.

His sentiments were echoed by others. Even some politicians found things to praise. "There is no question that
properties are better maintained after conversion," said David Clurman, the assistant attorney general in charge of cooperative and condominium offerings. "In a rental situation,
people just don't care as much. When they own their own
homes, they take an interest in the neighborhood. This is a
means of conserving New York's housing stock." And he
and others congratulated Helmsley on his decision to permit
rent-controlled tenants to remain without fear of eviction
once—and if—the conversion plan was approved.

As for outside buyers? They were waiting anxiously for
the ninety days to pass. "Where else could you find a four-
room apartment at fifty dollars a room?" asked one. Said
another, "I don't know how many other people are buying,
but I'm buying. I think it's a good proposition. With inflation, it can't go down." And yet another: "Look, Metropolitan Life never worried about the wiring or locked doors
or anything else, and these people never complained. Now,
when you talk condominium, they all complain. Why didn't

they complain ten, fifteen, twenty years ago? You know why? They were living on peanuts there. Now they belly-ache.''

If Harry Helmsley found such laudatory effusions heady, the euphoria did not last. He should have known it wouldn't. Although private ownership might be relished by the Man-hattan rich and by the middle class in the suburbs, the mid-dle class in the city at that moment was less than receptive. Helmsley had already tried to co-op several buildings in Manhattan, and the tenants had organized and bitterly fought the attempt. In 1969, for example, he put forward a plan to convert a 142-unit rental apartment building on East Eighty-sixth Street. Shortly before, he and Lawrence Wien had bought the property for $6.5 million. His asking price from the tenants was $8.87 million. Two thirds of the tenants organized, and fought the plan so strenuously that Helmsley and Wien withdrew it and not long after sold the building. This was not an isolated experience. It was repeated again and again when Helmsley announced plans to convert rental apartment buildings into co-ops, invariably at inflated prices.

Thus, to think that in the far reaches of the Bronx, middle- and lower-middle-class residents of Parkchester would leap eagerly at the chance offered by Harry Helmsley to buy was an empty dream.

Helmsley might call it a "fantastically good deal," but the one it was a "fantastically good deal" for was Harry Helmsley. If the conversion went through—which would happen only when thirty-five percent of the tenants agreed to it—he stood to make a killing. The sale price of the North Quadrant, a third of Parkchester, would reap him $55.9 mil-lion, more than half of what he and Wien had paid for the entire Parkchester complex. "That's a very good profit, of course," said one real estate executive in what can only be considered an understatement. "He's got to be counting on an acceleration after the first sales," said another. "If he can get a good capital gain for the first few people who resell their units, word will get around pretty quickly. The rest will be easy.''

And even if all of Parkchester went condominium, Helmsley would continue to reap profits far into the future. What he was selling were the apartments and a share of the common areas—hallways, elevators, sidewalks, and outdoor parking lots. He would retain ownership of the two garages and collect parking fees from those who used them. He would keep the recreation areas because, he said, they were used by all Parkchester residents, though the new owners would pay rent and maintenance fees. Retained as well was the heating plant, which would sell its steam to the residential and other buildings. And his Brown, Harris, Stevens subsidiary would manage the condominium for a $100,000 yearly fee, renewable and renegotiable every three years. Further, until twenty percent of the apartments were sold, Helmsley would have the right to name every one of the twenty-seven members of the board of managers, and as long as he owned forty percent of the apartments, he would still control eleven of those twenty-seven seats. Even when the project went completely condominium, he would still have four seats on the board just as long as he owned even a single apartment.

What it came down to, finally, said one housing expert, was this: ''He's appealing to their greed and to their fear that the neighborhood will change. All he's selling is a profit and a protected community.'' Was that enough? Not likely, in the opinion of other observers. As one said, ''Look at it from the point of view of the guy who lives there. He's a guy who makes $12,000 a year and has been there for eighteen years. His rent isn't bad, and the Bronx is not the best investment in the world. Why should he buy? There's absolutely no reason for anybody to say yes.''

That was precisely how most residents felt:

• ''If you want to buy a co-op,'' said one man who had lived in the North Quadrant since it had opened,

"you can go into a new building. These buildings
are thirty-two years old."

- "Will I buy? Never," said a middle-aged woman.
"We don't have air conditioning, and there aren't
enough closets. If I had money to invest, I'd buy a
newer apartment."
- "God help us," said one tenant. "How long is this
roof going to be over my head?"
- As John Dearie, who would help mobilize and lead
the opposition, said, "You would hear 'ding-dong,
Helmsley conversion plan.' Harry Helmsley became
number one bogeyman."

A universal complaint was that the apartments were over-
priced, which, given the experience of other Helmsley
apartment buildings, was likely. If all went according to his
plan, the apartments would cost far more than the rents that
people were used to paying. The average rent for the controlled apartments was $37 a room, and for the stabilized
apartments, $52 a room. Under the condominium plan, the
new owners would be paying a base maintenance charge of
$22 a room. To that would have to be added interest and
amortization on a mortgage, real estate taxes, and utilities.
Take a typical four-room apartment where the controlled
rent was $140 a month. If Helmsley's offer of a seven per-
cent mortgage and a twenty-five percent down payment was
accepted, that comes to $85 a month. Add in the monthly
charges for maintenance and utilities, about $65, with an-
other $27 in real estate taxes, and the total was nearly $180
a month. And there were fears that even that was an under-
estimate, for once Parkchester was turned into a condominium, it was certain to be reassessed, leading to substantial
increases in real estate taxes.

So community resistance to the Helmsley conversion
mounted. What was needed was a leader. And one emerged.

He was John Dearie. Not only was he a resident of Parkchester, he had been born there in 1940, the year the development opened, had grown up there and lived his entire life
there, except for his four years at Notre Dame. Dearie was
a natural to mobilize what some were coming to think of as
embattled Parkchester. He was tall, ruggedly handsome, articulate, an athlete (All-City in basketball at Manhattan
Prep), a lawyer with a degree from New York University, a
public servant with a job in the United Nations Secretariat,
popular in the community. And he was politically ambitious. Indeed, as the battle against Helmsley gained mo-
mentum, Dearie resigned his place in the United Nations
Secretariat and announced for the Democratic nomination
for the state assembly. He won that nomination and won the
general election in a landslide.

As president of the ten-thousand-member Parkchester
Tenants Association, he and John J. Whalen, the Democratic district leader and head of a newly organized Parkchester Defense Fund, gave voice to the rising tide of
protest. Harry Helmsley already had reason to know Dearie,
for he had been at the forefront of a tenant rent strike over
the fifteen percent hardship rent increase granted Helmsley
by the city's Office of Rent Control, and was in the lead in
the tenants' court battle to overturn that increase. Now,
when he got a look at the four-volume, five-pound encyclo-
pedic proposal Helmsley issued laying out the details of the
conversion ("Maybe they'd rather wait for the movie version," quipped one resident after hefting it), Dearie took
on Helmsley once more. He called the proposal "economically unattractive" and predicted that not more than two
percent of Parkchester tenants would buy. He found a lot to
object to in the volumes. He thought Helmsley's seats on
the board disproportionate. The apartments "were over-
priced," he said, especially considering the difference between what Helmsley had paid for the entire Parkchester
development and what he was asking for just the North
Quadrant. "There was no reason to fight Metropolitan Life

on anything,'' Dearie said. ''Then all of a sudden, instead of paternalistic Metropolitan Life, we've got a real estate guy who's out for the dollar,'' someone trying to sell aging apartments without air conditioning or adequate wiring or a central security system at inflated prices. Metropolitan Life, on the other hand, kept the rents low, the halls and apartments painted and repaired, the grounds well maintained and, as one older tenant put it, ''the kids off the grass.''

What's more, nearly a third of the Parkchester residents were elderly people living on fixed incomes and pensions. They couldn't possibly afford to buy their apartments, even on favorable terms. What conversion would mean for them was living in continual fear that one day they might find themselves without a home, despite all of Helmsley's promises.

Led by Dearie and Whalen, the Parkchester tenants went to war against Harry Helmsley.

They picketed outside Helmsley's home in the luxury Park Lane Hotel, carrying signs that read: ''Harry: Fixed Pensions Can't Afford Condominiums''; ''Harry: You Stole Parkchester from Met Life, Don't Rob Us Now''; ''A Killing in Real Estate Can Be Death to People.''

And they were joined in the picketing by representatives of another Helmsley project a continent away, the Parkmerced development in San Francisco, which he had also bought from Metropolitan Life. Helmsley was in the process of trying to convert that project, too, and was meeting heavy opposition and on the same grounds. ''One third of the people in Parkmerced are old people, and they don't have enough money to buy their apartments,'' a member of the San Francisco Commission on the Aging declared as he showed up to lend his support to the Parkchester pickets.[1]

1. The Parkmerced residents, battling an interloper in San Francisco in New Yorker Harry Helmsley, and with plenty of political clout, won their struggle when the city passed a law limiting the number of apartments that could be converted in any one year; that stymied Helmsley.

The Parkchester opposition filed suit in state supreme court, seeking an injunction to block the conversion plan, calling it a "sham and a fraud."

Initially Helmsley was certain that protests would get nowhere. Though he was selling few of the apartments to insiders, he had still sold about three hundred, mostly to outsiders, in the first few months. And he had the approval of the state attorney general to move forward. And then the state supreme court denied the request for an injunction, noting that at least Helmsley had agreed to protect rent-controlled tenants by not evicting them if they didn't go along with his plan.

Though the tenants immediately moved to appeal Justice Spector's ruling, Helmsley was buoyed enough to take another, and not totally unexpected, step. He announced that he was filing plans with the state attorney general's office for the conversion of the rest of Parkchester to condominiums, once again adding that the conversion would be on the same noneviction basis.

The opposition was incensed that in the middle of court battles challenging the legality of the initial conversion plan for the North Quadrant, Helmsley would try to push through conversion of the South, East, and West quadrants, too, and when they added up the prices, their fury multiplied. Helmsley was asking about $115 million for those newly offered apartments, which would mean that if he were successful in selling the entire Parkchester complex, he would receive in excess of $160 million, or a profit of nearly $70 million on his original $90 million investment.

They protested to the attorney general, whose office had jurisdiction over conversion plans. They filed court actions to block the proposals. And the new assemblyman, John Dearie, introduced legislation co-sponsored by Republican State Senator Roy Goodman of Manhattan that would mandate that there could be no conversion anywhere in the state unless thirty-five percent of the existing tenants approved. (In many cases, landlords had warehoused apartments—that is, refused to rent them, allowing them to remain vacant. This gave them control of an increasing number of apartments in their buildings so that it became ever easier to get the votes of thirty-five percent of the apartments, rather than thirty-five percent of the tenants, to make a conversion plan effective.) The Dearie-Goodman Bill was passed by a large majority, but Harry Helmsley declared that it did not apply to Parkchester. As long as he was willing to let nonbuying tenants keep their apartments without fear of eviction, tenant acceptance of the conversion plan was unnecessary.

The attorney general's office disagreed. For one thing, it felt that the Dearie-Goodman Act did apply. For another, it said it found a number of deficiencies in the plan for total conversion, though it did not spell out just what they were. And, it said, it could not approve the plan while court actions were under way to block even partial conversion.

The tenant opposition was elated, John Dearie calling it "a great victory." He and his followers would continue to pursue their actions against Helmsley in the hope of finally achieving total victory, he said.

Helmsley shrugged it off. All this, he said, was just "the usual course of delays we expect." But he wasn't going to put up with constant delays. "If we have to take some legal actions to force him [the attorney general] to move, we will do so."

Indeed, he did. And initially he was victorious; the appellate division of the state supreme court threw out the tenants' suit seeking to overturn the attorney general's acceptance of the original conversion plan for the North Quadrant. At the same time, the appeals court also ruled that the attorney general could not refuse to consider the plan for total conversion.

The court actions moved upward through the legal system, the tenants winning one round, Helmsley winning the next, until by the spring of 1977, nearly five years after the first announcement of a conversion plan, the last briefs had been filed, the last court arguments heard, and Harry

Helmsley had his victory—of sorts. By a vote of five to two, the New York State Court of Appeals, the state's highest tribunal, overturned the attorney general's ruling that the conversion plan fell within the scope of the Dearie-Goodman law. As long as the developer was willing to forgo eviction of tenants occupying apartments, Dearie-Goodman did not apply.

Helmsley, declaring himself "delighted," said he would now proceed rapidly to turn all of Parkchester into a condominium. As for the opponents, John Dearie tried to put the best face on the inevitable. "We opposed the conversion," he sighed. "Now we are neither for nor against. Our responsibility is to convey the facts on the tenants' rights."

His victory secured, Helmsley set out to heal some of the wounds by going on a renovation campaign around the complex, though the renovations were essentially minor ones, and he named a new, experienced, and popular manager to run things.

But the damage had been done. Parkchester was not what it had been when the affair began. Its old sense of a homogeneous close neighborhood had changed unalterably. More than eighty percent of the old Parkchester renters never did buy their apartments. More than a quarter of them simply gave up and moved after the final court decision. Helmsley, quipped John Dearie, "became a real boon to the moving industry."

Most of the buyers were outsiders, and what Helmsley had originally called his "fantastically good deal" wasn't quite so fantastic for them any longer. The one-bedroom apartment that had been originally marked at $7,500 for insiders, with 75 percent financing available at 7 percent interest, went up to between $13,000 and $18,000, with a 35 percent down payment required and 13.5 percent interest on the 65 percent mortgage. For the outsiders, the price of that two-bedroom apartment was no longer just 10 percent higher; it was 110 percent higher than the original offer, between $23,000 and $33,000.

And the racial composition changed radically. Now the whites became a minority in this once all-white city within a city. If Parkchester remained middle- and lower-middle class, that middle class was increasingly the nonwhite minorities. About half the new buyers were Puerto Ricans and blacks, and even the new renters were 70 percent nonwhite. But these new owners and renters, whatever their color, have proved no more docile than the original battlers had been. They rose in righteous indignation, for instance, when Leona Helmsley, taking an increasingly active role in the affairs of the Helmsley dominions, decided one day in 1985 to fire without warning the security patrol during the middle of labor contract negotiations. Parkchester residents were once more on the march, with picket signs, this time showing up in front of the Helmsley Palace Hotel to shout their rage (to the covert support of hotel employees who grinned and gave thumbs-up encouragement from hotel windows). That march, at least, had an effect, and the security guards were rehired. But the taste that lingered was acrid. And it has grown even more corrosive in the face of a revelation that Helmsley suppressed an engineer's report about major structural defects throughout Parkchester in the condominium prospectus. The result of this has been another lawsuit against Helmsley, which remains unsettled.

And what of the ultimate fate of his efforts to turn Parkchester from a community of renters into a community of owners? That has been anything but a success. In the North Quadrant, only about half the available apartments have ever been sold, and a much larger percentage remains in the other three quadrants, waiting for buyers who have never appeared.

For years, Harry Helmsley had cultivated the image of the gentleman in a profession not noted for gentlemanly dealings. Behind that front, though, lay other, cruder traits that would become increasingly evident as time passed and he amassed ever more money and ever more power. There was arrogance, a certainty that he was always right, a lack of concern for the ideas and needs of those who opposed him. This had been there, if partly concealed, in his dealings with commercial tenants. Many had come to think of him, through experience, not merely as a man who ran an efficient operation but also as one who cut costs to the bone at their expense in order to make big profits. But an office is a daytime thing, escaped when evening arrives. A home is something else, and in his dealings with his Parkchester tenants, he clearly revealed that arrogance and that contempt for others. Increasingly, they, like tenants in other residential buildings under his control, saw him as the epitome of the greedy landlord, unconcerned about their welfare, cutting as many corners as he could to earn bigger and bigger profits, co-oping his buildings at excessive prices and trying to force tenants to bow to his dictates. He was not a slumlord, of course; his buildings were of high quality. But the middle-class tenants who lived in them were coming to think of him as one of New York's greediest and worst landlords.

8

THE DRAMA SURROUNDING the fate of Parkchester was played out in the relative obscurity of the Bronx. For the vast majority of New Yorkers, it was never more than a minor sideshow. Not so the war for Tudor City.

Tudor City is an oasis of quiet charm and grace in the heart of Manhattan, rising on a hill overlooking the East River and the United Nations. Built between 1928 and 1931 by Fred F. French south of what was then the slaughterhouse district, and on which the United Nations headquarters now rests, it was designed as a self-contained sanctuary for the middle class. "This development was planned as a residential community, large enough to create and maintain its own distinctive character," declared a 1939 rental brochure. "It was planned not for millionaires but for people of taste and refinement, people who appreciate the importance of environment."

The thirteen red brick apartment buildings (eleven part of the original development and two added a short time later) span a four-block area from Fortieth to Forty-fourth streets between First and Second avenues. Six of the buildings rise eleven stories, and the rest from fifteen to thirty-two stories, providing about 2,700 apartments for some 7,500 middle- and upper-middle-class residents. Intermixed are four small brownstones, a post office, a library, and a handful of stores. The entire development is done in Tudor style, adorned with a multitude of architectural embellishments: leaded multiple-paned casement windows, stained glass, gar-

goyles, griffins, boars' heads, roses, portcullises, heraldic
arms, and quatrefoils. The buildings are clustered around
four small parks, two public and two private, filled with
trees and benches, that serve as outdoor gathering places
for residents. (At one time there were also an ice skating
rink, tennis courts, and a miniature golf course, but they
are only a memory, and no one is quite certain when they
vanished.) Because of all this, Tudor City has been called
one of the finest large-scale residential projects ever built.
People who rented in Tudor City stayed on and on, their
apartments rent controlled with rents as low as eighty dollars a month for efficiency studio units for those who held
them from time immemorial, and the waiting list of those
seeking apartments was endless, years passing before one
became vacant.

Enter Harry Helmsley. In early 1970, he became Tudor
City's new master, buying it for $36 million. His partner in
the venture this time was not Lawrence Wien but his longtime right-hand man, Alvin Schwartz.

Wien had expressed his reservations about investing in
residential property at the time of the Parkchester purchase,
and he opted out when it came to Tudor City. Indeed, Wien
had for some time been immersing himself increasingly in
the world outside business. He had become very rich, and,
Peter Malkin says, he decided it was time to "give back
much of what he had gotten." He spread his millions around
on "good works," devoting himself to philanthropy. From
this time on, he and Harry Helmsley would take very different roads.

From the late 1960s until his death from cancer at age
eighty-three in December 1988, Wien, though always active
in his law firm, devoted more and more of his energies and
contributed more and more of his fortune to a variety of
educational, international, and, especially, cultural endeavors. He was deeply involved with various aspects of the
United Nations. He became first a trustee and then chairman of the board of trustees of Brandeis University. He

endowed the Wien International Scholarship Program, the largest privately financed foreign scholarship plan in the United States, which every year provides tuition, maintenance, and travel assistance for eighty students from all over the world. A member of the board of trustees of Columbia University as well, he helped endow the Lawrence A. Wien Professor in Real Estate Law, and established a National Scholarship Program at the law school to provide financial assistance to fifteen percent of the students enrolled.

He donated millions to Lincoln Center for the Performing Arts and was vice-chairman of the center's board. He was both a major contributor to and a trustee of the Educational Broadcasting Corporation, which he helped found. In fact, there was hardly a major cultural institution in New York that did not list him as a source of both financial support and personal participation. One outstanding example of his generosity occurred in 1987. There were growing fears in the artistic community over the fate of the eight-story building at 890 Broadway, a nineteenth-century structure containing vast open interior space that the late choreographer and stage director Michael Bennett had established as a rehearsal center for the American Ballet Theater, the Feld Ballet, the Alvin Ailey Dance Company, and other dance, musical, and theatrical organizations. On Bennett's death, there was concern that his estate would be forced to sell the building and its use as an artistic center would come to an end. Wien came to the rescue. He bought the building for $15 million and then offered its artistic tenants such generous terms, and with a donation of $3 million of his own money as their down payment, that within three years, they could easily, he said, "own the building free and clear. . . . I stuck my neck out and the first thing I knew, I'd bought the building. I didn't want it for myself; I wanted it for the ballet companies. I wanted it to be a home for these companies with no rent to pay."

Wien had become, political and artistic leaders said with unanimity, "everybody's favorite angel." At one time he even bought shares in four hundred corporations so that he could pressure corporate management as a stockholder to increase support to charitable, civic, cultural, and educational institutions. Furthermore, he founded the Committee to Increase Corporate Philanthropic Giving, which persuaded corporations to up their donations by about $500 million a year. And, by himself, he gave away hundreds of millions of dollars in an effort to, he once said, repay the country for all it had given him and to enrich the life of the nation and its citizens.

Not so Harry Helmsley. Good works and giving back interested him far less than continuing to build a real estate empire and amass an ever growing personal fortune. So Tudor City was just the next step. Though remaining Helmsley's friend and legal adviser, Wien was little involved in what would become a bitter struggle enmeshing not just tenants and landlord, but city officials, civic leaders, and the press. Without the sometimes cautioning influence of Wien, Helmsley became a public relations man's nightmare. Almost from the day he took control of the complex, he created antagonism. His words and actions, so often arrogant and imperious, mobilized a heated and powerful opposition.

On the surface, and in the public perception, the war was over the fate of two small parks, islands of greenery, gathering places for residents. In reality, though, it was an age-old dispute, real and philosophical, pitting on one side the baronial rights of property owners to do what they will when they will with the property they own, and on the other, the rights of those who live on the land to be secure in their homes even from encroachments by the barons, to protect their homes and their environment.

Hardly had the sale announcement been made before Helmsley pointed to the two small private parks in the enclave, each a mere 100 by 230 feet, flanking Forty-second Street and linked by a wide bridge, called them vacant land, and said he was considering building on them. With that revelation, the battle lines were drawn. For tenants at Tudor City, it seemed confirmation of their worst fears: What Helmsley really planned was to tear down the whole complex and replace it with a so-called $350 million "super block" luxury development hard by the United Nations. For others, it was fear of the irretrievable loss of even a little green open space in a city where open greenery was fast vanishing and what remained must be protected.

Helmsley regarded the issue as a matter of simple economics. "I have a perfect right to build on the park space, and I will do so," he declared. Those parks had an $8 million mortgage, he said, and it wasn't an economically viable proposition for him to maintain them as open space. "If the tenants want open parks, the city should condemn the land and make it into public parkland. In addition to mortgage interest, I pay heavy real estate taxes each year. I can't afford to keep a park. I can't afford to buy a park and pay taxes on it." And so he announced that he was having plans drawn to build two high-rise towers, one of thirty stories and the other of twenty-eight, with 530 luxury apartments, where those parks now stood.

Helmsley's phrasing was, at the very least, unfortunate. In the strictest economic terms, his assertion was probably true. But nobody else saw the fate of those two small islands of green in such narrow terms. The tenants united to fight any encroachment onto their parks. Leading them was a longtime resident and president of Fish and Marvin, a real estate brokerage firm, John P. McKean, who became president of the "Save Our Parks Committee."

"We need to preserve our two existing pocket parks," he asserted. "Indeed, what our city needs is more open parkland, not more steel and concrete monsters." He demanded that the City Planning Commission bar any construction on those small parks, and "if our efforts to obtain such zoning fail, we will go to court and seek an injunction against Mr. Helmsley."

The plaintive pleas of tenants struck a more human note.

"I've lived here for forty-five years," said one eighty-five-year-old woman, "and it would kill the old people if Mr. Helmsley took away our park." Mere mention of Helmsley's name in Tudor City was enough to stir a wave of hisses. To these people he was "Hatchet Harry."

Behind the residents was the support of people who mattered. A half-dozen state legislators from the city announced their intention to introduce bills in Albany to stop Helmsley from building his proposed new high-rises. Public rallies and meetings were held, at which just about every important city office holder, past and current, rose to denounce Harry Helmsley and his scheme. Robert Rickles, the former head of the city's Department of Air Resources, won the cheers of the converted when he declared, "Parks are absolutely essential if we are to save New York." And Edward I. Koch, then a congressman whose district included Tudor City, was incensed. He was throwing his support behind the tenants to "the fullest extent I can. It'll be an outrage if the park is demolished to make way for a high-rise. This matter concerns not only Tudor City but is really a fight for the whole city—that we make it clean and open."[1]

With the lines drawn, Helmsley might have thought to use conciliation. Instead, he proceeded to exacerbate the situation.

On a cold November morning in 1972, Tudor City residents, and soon a pack of reporters, gathered outside the development's eleven-story Essex House to watch as the furniture from the six-room apartment of an ailing eighty-two-

---

1. The strenuous Koch opposition combined with typical Koch hyperbole was the first blow in a barely concealed feud between him and the Helmsleys, Harry and later Leona as well, that lasted from that day on. They declared a truce only when Helmsley supported Koch years later when the then-mayor decided to seek New York's governorship. There were, though, those who saw a certain self-interest behind the Helmsley support; if Koch went to Albany, he would be out of the city and no longer a potential and ever present impediment to the Helmsley ambitions.

year-old woman was unceremoniously carried out and dumped on the sidewalk, and then, several hours later, hauled off in city vans. The lady, who had lived in the apartment for more than thirty years, was being evicted. She owed Helmsley $338, two months' rent. The problem wasn't that she couldn't pay; it was that her niece, who handled her affairs, was also old and ill and, she admitted to onlookers, had been a little careless about paying. By the time she realized what she should have done, it was too late. The landlord had gotten an eviction order, and once it had been executed by the city marshals, nothing could be done legally to stop the ouster. The bewildered old lady, now homeless, was given shelter by her niece.

A spokesman for Helmsley-Spear had little sympathy. The landlord simply did not want her for a tenant any longer. The company had been having "problems" with her; on several occasions in the recent past, her niece had missed rent payments, and so now, as far as Helmsley was concerned, the issue was closed. He could hardly have been more wrong. In the public mind, the image of a little old lady being crushed by the might of one of the city's biggest landlords would linger for a long, long time.

If Helmsley's image was becoming increasingly tarnished, he was still a power to be reckoned with. And so the politicians in city government desperately sought ways to appease both him and the angry residents of Tudor City and a disenchanted public. Late in 1972, the City Planning Commission came up with a variety of alternatives to Helmsley's proposed glass-and-steel towers on the area's small parks. Under one, Helmsley would be given the right to build a forty-six-story tower spanning Forty-second Street, with the two parks spared. A second plan would grant him the right to build a forty-eight-story tower on the northern park, and a new park would be created on a wide platform across Forty-second Street that would link up with the southern park. Still another would grant him the right to build the two towers he wanted to erect and then create a new park on that platform. Yet another would offer an exchange: Helmsley would be given a building-density bonus that would allow him to erect bigger structures on his midtown commercial property than allowed by law in exchange for preservation of the two parks. All these alternatives, the commission said, would be open for public discussion, and after it heard the arguments for and against, it would choose one of them.

Helmsley looked over the options. As far as he was concerned, only the tower over Forty-second Street or two thirty-nine-story towers at either end of the Forty-second Street platform interested him. The idea of giving him a bonus on other properties if he spared the parks was ingenious, he said, but unworkable. "I'm just as interested as the next guy in preserving the parkland," he said. "It's quite a problem."

The commission chose the very one he opposed—the creation of a special park district that would preserve the two parks in return for granting of the twenty percent building bonus on other midtown properties he owned. "This is one of those rare situations in which members of a community have gotten together, not to exclude someone but to save something," a member of the body said.

Helmsley denounced the decision. It was "impractical, unfeasible, inadvisable and unconstitutional," one of his attorneys declared. He would go to court to have it overturned as a violation of property rights "without due process of law."

While the debate over the fate of the tiny parks simmered, Helmsley threw an ingredient into the pot certain to make it boil over. Late in 1973, he filed plans with the state attorney general to convert Essex House into condominiums, quite obviously a prelude to a future attempt to convert the entire complex. Like their counterparts in Parkchester, Tudor City residents immediately announced their opposition. On this issue, at least, the tenants emerged victorious, for a time. Within six months the state legislature passed the

Dearie-Goodman Act, requiring thirty-five percent of tenants in residence to approve an offering before such conversions could become effective. Helmsley had fought its application in Parkchester. At Tudor City, he decided to give in; the conversion plan was put on the shelf, for the time being at least.

A skirmish was over, but the war went on. Helmsley was determined to build his luxury apartments at Tudor City, no matter the cost. Turned away by the political and municipal powers from invading the two small private parks, he would not admit defeat, continued to insist that he had the right to build on that land, and took the city to court to affirm that right. The case dragged on year after year, until finally the court sided with him. The immediate question was, would Helmsley, with his legal victory, arrogantly dismiss all those years of public protest and all the public opinion, and move forward now to demolish the parks?

Then he came up with a new plan of his own. He would be willing, he said early in 1979, to make a swap. Tudor City residents could have their private parks if the city would give him one of its own, a public park at Forty-third Street and First Avenue, directly across from the United Nations. There he would build not two but only a single fifty-story glass-and-steel tower, with 375 luxury apartments, cantilevering over part of Tudor City itself. That modern tower, to be designed by Richard Roth, Jr., of Emery Roth & Sons, might clash sharply with the graceful English country design of Tudor City, but, Helmsley and his architect insisted, would complement the facades of the United Nations Secretariat Building, the United Nations Plaza Hotel, and the United Nations Plaza cooperative apartments to the north. Moreover, the new tower would abut only the twenty-three-story Prospect Tower in Tudor City, which had a virtually blank wall on that side as it was, because the original builder didn't think anyone would want a view of the then-existing slaughterhouses to the north. If the city did not promptly agree to this swap, Helmsley threatened, he would revert to his original one "within a month or so."

"Political blackmail" was what Assemblyman Stephen Sanders, whose district included Tudor City, called the threat. "We should never make urban policy at the point of a gun." If Helmsley actually went ahead, Sanders intended to seek some legal means to block him.

In fact, Helmsley continued to hold off after the month deadline passed, but there was little doubt he did not intend to wait long. In the meantime city officials scrambled for a way out. In the spring of 1979, Robert F. Wagner, Jr., son of the former mayor and then chairman of the City Planning Commission, devised another possible solution. On the corner of First Avenue and Forty-second Street was another city park. What about that park and permission to build the fifty-story structure there in exchange for the Tudor City parks?

The Wagner solution got at least reluctant acceptance from the realtor. Though he "would prefer to build in Tudor City, where the land and location are more suitable," Helmsley said, he would "give serious consideration to the city's proposal" in the interest of ending the long dispute. Helmsley's resistance, though, was more for show than real. If the swap took place, he was getting a real bargain. What the city would get from Helmsley were two parks with 31,000 square feet of space, though Helmsley and not the city would maintain the parks. What the city was giving Helmsley in exchange was a 48,260-square-foot park.

This time resistance came from another quarter. The proffered park contained a playground, and the new proposal "would mean elimination of a heavily used playground, one of the few public recreational areas serving the children and young adults in the neighborhood below 42nd Street," noted the city's parks commissioner, Gordon Davis. "It would be hard to see how we can do away with it." Davis went on to note that he wished someone from the Planning Commission had talked to him before offering this solution.

All the same, a bill was rushed through the state legislature authorizing the exchange, and the city and Helmsley began negotiations over means to implement it. But Helmsley apparently thought the city was dragging its feet. It was time for a showdown. "We pay $1,500 a day in taxes for this land, and we lose almost $1.5 million a year in interest income at present rates," said a Helmsley representative. "Because of the enormous sums involved, the long delays and the bureaucratically inspired litigation, our group has been left with no alternative but to exercise our property rights under the law of the land."

And so without warning, at seven in the morning on Saturday, May 24, 1980, a quiet day in the middle of the long Memorial Day weekend, a Helmsley construction crew suddenly appeared at the northern park and began putting up a plywood fence around it to seal it off for immediate excavation.

John McKean, the head of the tenants' association, was still in bed when his phone rang. A neighbor told him excitedly that a work crew was walling off the park. McKean grabbed a bullhorn, rushed to the nearly deserted streets of the enclave, and began to shatter the stillness of the holiday morning with the alarm. Residents who were still in the city poured out of their apartments and raced to the park. They berated the workmen, urging them to stop. Building the fence without warning was bad enough, but picking a holiday weekend to do it was infinitely worse. A Helmsley representative on the scene shrugged. "There's no difference between now and Tuesday morning," he said, and ordered the work to continue.

The tenants took another course. They began tearing down the fence and hauling away the plywood, piling it up on nearby sidewalks. "It took us a while to catch on that the best way to move the lumber was a water-bucket passalong," said one of the protesters.

The police were summoned, came to the aid of the workers, and removed the angry Tudor City residents. The crew went back to work. By mid-afternoon the park was nearly ringed by the construction fence. But the tenants did not give up. They rushed to court and got a restraining order to prevent any further fence building or excavation. "This is only a breather. The war is not over," declared McKean.

Indeed, it wasn't. At eight the next morning, despite the restraining order, the Helmsley construction crew was back, this time with a bulldozer. About a dozen Tudor City residents sped to the park and formed a human barricade to block the bulldozer. McKean called the cops. The cops arrived, were shown the restraining order, showed it to the workmen, and ordered them to leave. It had all been a mistake, a Helmsley spokesman explained. It had been the result of "an inadvertent lack of knowledge on the part of the construction crew, which was in no way intended to violate the order of the court."

Maybe not, but it wasn't only Tudor City residents who were up in arms about Helmsley's "cheap shot." Congressman William Green, whose district encompassed Tudor City, demanded that the rent authorities act and institute "immediately fifty percent cuts in rent" because of Helmsley's action to "wantonly take away . . . an important amenity" of the area. The chairman of the New York County Republican Committee, Vincent Albano, denounced Helmsley's "sneak attack." And City Councilman Henry Stern, later parks commissioner, was aghast that although Helmsley had a legal right "to make the park a wasteland, what is unbelievable about this is how a leading figure in New York City real estate is so insistent on destroying a small neighborhood open space."

Tudor City residents themselves were not slow in demonstrating their opinion of Harry Helmsley. Graffiti quickly adorned the half-finished fence: "Only God can make a tree, don't take them away"; and "Harry is a creep." Petitions circulated throughout the area demanding action to stop Helmsley. Residents signed without even reading the wording. "I don't have to read it," said one. "All you have to do is walk into this park and you know that it must remain. We have enough buildings and Mr. Helmsley has enough money.''

From its lofty stature at the end of that long weekend, *The New York Times* thought the affair had gone on too long and demanded an immediate resolution. In an editorial it opted for what it called ''triage in Tudor City,'' the swap of parks as proposed by Robert Wagner, Jr. ''The reason a trade must be made at all is that Mr. Helmsley is totally within his rights, no matter how discouraging that may be to those who measure cities by more public values. He did not buy Tudor City for its enlightened design. He bought it for the development potential of the parks. Destroying a park is not admirable policy; it is doing a wrecking job on Mr. Helmsley's image and on his profession's. The loss to the city will be great. But this investment game plan is more important to real estate than civic sensibility. . . . And if Mr. Helmsley wants to show concern for the city that has enriched him, he would help create a substitute. Harry Helmsley Park?''

No matter what kind of solution was put forward it was by now bound to arouse the ire of some vocal and potentially powerful group. And so when an unlikely coalition of city officials, Tudor City residents, and Helmsley moved close to a slightly altered version of Wagner's park swap—the two private Tudor City ones for the larger public park with playground at Forty-second Street and First Avenue and permission for Helmsley to build there a towering fifty-story combination luxury residence and office building, and Helmsley's agreement to immediately remove the construction fence around the Tudor City parks—there was renewed public outrage.

''The United Nations playground . . . is a public playground in an area that is already congested and overbuilt,'' read a letter to *The New York Times*. ''Tudor City residents need their parks, but the other residents of the community, especially the young, require the United Nations playground. Midtown Manhattan is a wasteland as far as youth recreation goes. At this playground, a growing tradition of youth sports is emerging. It should not be destroyed by the proposed swap.''

But John McKean, seeing at last a solution to the problem that had bedeviled him for a decade, responded: ''None of us want to give up any parkland. We have too few parks, too little playground space. We must protect and cherish all of it. If there is another location, another swap without any dislocation of playground space, we're for it. Any playground space taken from First Avenue . . . should be replaced elsewhere. . . . [But] to allow our two parks to be destroyed because Helmsley wants to build on them is just plain wrong. It would be obscene and unthinkable.''

''Faced with the threat by Harry Helmsley to build on the Tudor City parks,'' responded Joanna Battaglia, chairperson of Manhattan's Community Board 6, which took in the area, ''John McKean . . . is apparently willing to sacrifice anything—including a public playground—just so long as it costs him nothing. It costs the rest of the city quite a lot, however, and the issue is not as clear-cut for us as it is for him. The commitment of Mr. McKean to Mr. Helmsley's 'swap' is such that he even attacks a proposed zoning amendment that would save both parks. Mr. McKean fears that this proposal may not be constitutional and that Mr. Helmsley would bulldoze the parks prior to its enactment. . . . There seems to be an unseemly confluence of Mr. McKean's position with that of Mr. Helmsley. I doubt that the long-term interests of the Tudor City tenants, not to mention the city at large, are best served by such an alliance.''

The exchanges grew more heated and the opposition mounted. The Municipal Art Society and the Women's City Club joined in, as did Manhattan Borough President Andrew Stein and the director of the Parks Council, who called it ''blackmail'' to resort to the swap in order to end the controversy about the Tudor City parks.

Helmsley, who knew a good deal when it was offered to him, tried to blunt the opposition. He offered to donate $1 million toward the creation of a new playground somewhere in the area if the swap went through. As critics were quick to point out, that swap was not altruistic. The playground land was not only considerably larger than the parks he would relinquish, but it was also zoned to permit a considerably larger building, which would yield considerably more income.

Others had esthetic objections as well. Helmsley's new tower would not only clash sharply with the architecture of Tudor City, but though its glass facade had been designed by Richard Roth to blend with the nearby United Nations tower, it would rise a mere 225 feet from the Secretariat Building, would surpass it in height, and would destroy what had long been one of the United Nations building's distinguishing features, that it stood alone, the only tall building within blocks.

"In the end," commented *New York Times* architecture critic Paul Goldberger, "this is a battle in which only Mr. Helmsley seems likely to come out ahead. Whether the land-swap idea is considered creative city planning or gimmickry, it involves losses of some open space to the city. And whatever kind of tower is built on whatever site, it will add more construction to an already desperately overburdened midtown Manhattan that needs fewer, not more, skyscrapers."

Nonetheless, after a Helmsley concession to reduce the height of his tower by four stories so that it would be lower than the United Nations Secretariat Building, the City Planning Commission approved the swap. "We felt there was no other option for saving the ambiance of Tudor City," said Herbert Sturz, chairman of the Planning Commission. "There was no happy answer."

The approval by the planning commission, though, did not mean the war was over. Still ahead lay the necessary action by the Board of Estimate, where a three-quarter majority was necessary. That vote was anything but certain. And then Andy Stein, already an opponent, swung into action and just about doomed the whole thing, He had a meeting with Mayor Ed Koch, who had publicly come out in favor of the swap plan, and argued that the city was getting the short end of a very bad deal. The Tudor City parks were worth at most $10 million or $11 million, Stein maintained, while the playground land was worth between $25 million and $40 million. "So, the Mayor said, 'You bring one private developer down here who would pay that price,' " Stein said.

He proceeded to do just that. He put in a call to the builder-developer Donald Trump and set up a meeting with the Mayor. Trump told Koch he would be willing to pay $25 million for the playground-park if the city really wanted to get rid of it. That was enough for Ed Koch. Reversing his previous stand, he said he was now opposed to the deal with Helmsley, and as far as he was concerned, the city was going to keep the playground, not swap it with Helmsley or sell it to Trump. And so another possible solution died.

Were the Tudor City parks doomed, then? Not quite yet. The Planning Commission came up with another swap plan. The Tudor City parks would become public, one donated by Helmsley to the city and the other swapped for a city-owned plot at Fifty-first Street and First Avenue, then the home of the private United Nations School, land the city had been thinking of selling for some time. The plan contained several contingencies—the land was zoned to accommodate a building no higher than thirty stories; Helmsley would have to agree not to build any higher than that, would have to agree not to seek property tax incentives the city was handing out to builders of residential structures, would have to agree to make the building a residential and rental one and not a condominium (there was fear that foreign diplomats, who do not pay city taxes, would gobble up the apartments if they were condominiums because of the close proximity to the U.N.).

Helmsley had no objections, though he did add a caveat. "If this does not work out . . . we reserve the right" to go ahead and build at Tudor City.

The New York Times applauded. Maybe all the delays had been worthwhile, after all, it said in an editorial. "If this plan goes through, the city would get income for its land, Mr. Helmsley would get his new building, the public would get the Tudor City parks, and the issue of the ethics of park swapping would be canceled out. Score one for delay."

Not so fast. The *Times* notwithstanding, opposition surfaced immediately. And it was led by the city's Department of General Services, which happened to be in charge of that land at Fifty-first Street and First Avenue. The land, agency officials declared, was vastly undervalued, and was worth a lot more than the two parks the city would be getting in exchange. They were in favor of simply selling that parcel. "We think it is better for the city to have cash than two parks, in straight dollars and cents," declared Terence Moan, in charge of the department's real property division. "I don't want Trump to walk in if our number is $15 million and say it's really $25 million." No matter what happened, he added, Helmsley would come out "tremendously ahead." The builder would not only have his new site in exchange for one of the parks, but his donation of the second would be tax deductible and he would no longer have to pay taxes on either of the parks.

Helmsley was exasperated. One of his lawyers declared, "We said we would wait a reasonable period of time. I guess at some point it's going to be unreasonable."

That point was fast approaching. After hearing the position espoused by his Department of General Services, the Mayor vetoed the idea. Helmsley responded that he was not only going ahead now with his original plan but he was going to sue the city for $50 million in damages as a result of thwarting his construction plans for more than a decade.

But before he could break ground, the Office of Rent Control stepped in. The parks, it said, were "essential services'' for the rent-controlled tenants, and if Helmsley destroyed them, he would have to compensate the tenants. The Conciliation and Appeals Board handed down a similar ruling that the parks were essential services for the rent-stabilized tenants. Helmsley took the matter to court. The state supreme court turned down his appeal. The parks were ''a communal backyard.''

Helmsley's next move looked like a diversion, though to Tudor City tenants it seemed more an act of retribution for all the trouble they had been causing him for so long. One morning in the spring of 1983, the postmen rang the bells of every apartment in the complex. They had registered letters, with return receipts requested, for the occupants. Inside was an official city form called Demand Form AMO-1A, and it demanded a notarized reply listing just who was living in the apartments. Failure to comply, the notices said, could result in criminal penalties and other sanctions.

These official letters weren't sent by the city, however, but by Harry Helmsley. He was taking advantage of a decision just handed down by the state court of appeals that landlords could evict tenants who share their apartments with people who were not members of their family. The decision was unleashing screams of outrage all over the city. In a time of spiraling rents, apartment sharing had not only become common but for many, especially the young just starting out and the aged at the end of their careers, was the only way they could remain in the city. And this was a time when marriage was no longer necessarily considered essential for those of the opposite sex to live together. The decision, then, was viewed as patently unfair to a large portion of the population. And so both the New York City Council and the state legislature immediately went to work drafting bills that would at least permit tenants to keep roommates. Helmsley acted before those bills could become law. A spokesman for Helmsley-Spear, trying to put the best face on it, said that the forms had been sent out in response to tenant complaints that their mail was often going to the wrong apartments and in "a couple of cases" tenants who had sublet couldn't get back their apartments. "I get many calls from tenants, and letters, that during the night hours, tenants move out and new tenants move in. Finally, it got to the point where we had to do something."

Not only Tudor City residents were incensed. City officials joined the chorus of outrage, and they were in a position to do something about it. Carol Bellamy, then president of the City Council, and Anthony Gliedman, the city's commissioner of housing development, told tenants to put those forms on the shelf and delay answering them. They both noted that nobody in the city government had sent them and there had been no complaints about overcrowding in Tudor City in more than thirty years. The court decision, Gliedman asserted, and the forms Helmsley had taken upon himself to dispatch registered to tenants, "were to protect against overcrowding, they were not to be sent to two people sharing a five-room apartment."

"The forms are intimidating, they're frightening people," John McKean said. "People have been calling me night and day. A lot of people, especially senior citizens on fixed incomes, get together and share the rent. If one has to move out, people will lose their homes and there's no place to go."

The city took Helmsley to court to end what was, at the very least, harassment. Charging that he was misusing those AMO-1A forms, "an abuse of process and a nuisance," it asked the court to enjoin him from   eeding.

The restraining order was obtai.   But a higher state court ruled that Helmsley "has shown a reasonable basis" for sending out the questionnaire because of "rampant subletting and rent gouging by sublessors throughout the project."

If Harry Helmsley had won a small victory, he nevertheless recognized all too clearly that being a residential landlord was not like being a landlord of commercial structures. In a decade and a half, he had realized few of the great profits that he had once imagined, when, like a lobster scavenging the sea bottom, he had greedily ingested every piece of loose residential property he came upon.

He had waged battles not merely at Parkchester and Tudor City. At the luxury twin-towered San Remo on Central Park West, optioned for $12 million, he preached his now-familiar sermon that the city's future salvation (and his own fortune) lay in tenant ownership of apartments. The tenants en masse spurned his offer to sell them their apartments. They were willing to buy, yes, but not at his price of $15 million, which would have given him a $3 million profit on a building he had owned for a very short time. So Helmsley felt he had no course but to turn the building back to its original owner and swallow a $1.25 million loss. A year and a half later, the San Remo went co-op. The price to the tenants: $10 million.

At the 7-building, 2,700-apartment Park West Village complex on Manhattan's Upper West Side, at Fresh Meadows in Queens, with 140 buildings and 3,300 apartments, at apartment buildings all over Manhattan, Washington, San Francisco, Los Angeles, and points in between, his attempts to convert to cooperatives or condominiums created resistance, and often it was over the inflated price he demanded. But there were other issues as well that roiled the relationship between landlord Helmsley and his tenants. Here tenants went on rent strikes. There he found himself accused of refusing to rent to blacks and Hispanics. Here he was charged with discriminating against the elderly. There he was accused of reducing essential services, of seeking to destroy recreational areas. Few Helmsley tenants had a good word to say about their landlord.

It was all too much. By 1984 his taste for residential rental properties had soured. Rental housing, Helmsley declared, "is an impossible business to be in." And so he was going to sell off his portfolio of residential buildings, especially those that were rent-controlled and rent-stabilized, if he could. And the first place he was going to sell was the one that had given him the most trouble and most negative head-lines: Tudor City. "We're fed up with the punishment the tenants are giving us and the city, too," said Helmsley aide and sometime partner, Alvin Schwartz. "The tenants have done everything to embarrass Mr. Helmsley and myself, including picketing." They weren't even going to try to do a co-op or condominium conversion in that enclave them-selves. They had had enough problems at Tudor City with the parks without taking on the tenants in a new arena. "If people make a satisfactory offer," he said, he would con-sider selling the whole area as a single block; if not, he would sell the buildings piecemeal, and then somebody else could fight the battle of the parks. "They are not parks. They are two lots we've been paying taxes on since the year one."

Six of the buildings, four brownstones, and the two parks were sold to Philip Pilevsky, of Philips International, a commercial and residential developer, and Francis Green-berger, of Times Equity, a leading firm in the conversion of rentals to co-ops and condominiums, at an undisclosed price, though one that earned Helmsley a profit. And Harry Helmsley's misadventure in Tudor City came to an end.

Despite his professed desire to abandon the rental resi-dential field, he still owns hundreds of residential proper-ties, more than fifty thousand apartments nationwide. Many he has turned into co-ops and condominiums, which his companies continue to manage for high fees, but the ma-jority are still on the rent rolls.

As for Tudor City, with Helmsley no longer around as the bogeyman to the residents, the new owners immediately an-nounced that the complex was going to be converted into co-ops, at a price that most tenants would not find onerous (and that would earn the new owners a profit of about $100 million). Indeed, the tenants quickly put their money into their Tudor City homes. Even John McKean, who for so long had led the battle against Harry Helmsley, became one of the new owners. He and his wife bought not one but two apartments, the one they lived in and one she had been renting when they met and had sublet after their marriage. "Betty had the foresight," he said, "to know it was very wise to hang on to that apartment."

But equally important for many, the new owners wrote finis to the battle over the parks. They donated the two parks to a public trust, called Tudor City Greens, that would own them for the benefit of the tenants, and endowed the trust with $820,840 for maintenance. "We expect the parks to remain parks," Greenberger said.

The final chapter in the Tudor City saga was written in the late spring of 1988. Harry Helmsley was gone, if not forgotten, enmeshed in new and more serious controversy with far greater consequences for him, when the New York City Landmarks Preservation Commission designated the whole site as a historic district. That meant that within its bounds nothing could be altered without permission of the landmarks panel. And so it will remain, an oasis of gentility on the edge of midtown Manhattan.

9

FOR SOME MEN, control of a residential empire housing hundreds of thousands of people in hundreds of buildings from coast to coast, all with problems and beset with controversies, might have been enough to fill all the hours of the day and all the dreams of power and wealth. But Harry Helmsley would have thought them lesser men.

"You start in the business," he once said, "and you manage and you lease and then all of a sudden you see a property and you think this is a good buy, and you sell it to somebody. Then after you've done that a number of times, you say, 'Why am I selling this to somebody else? He's making so much money, why don't I buy it?' So you put a group together. It might require $10,000 or $20,000 to buy in. Whatever I'm doing now is really the same thing with a couple of noughts added to the end. Deals get bigger as you have more confidence. All of a sudden you are buying apartment houses as well as office buildings and loft buildings. A deal comes along that looks good and you are in the hotel business. And then another opportunity comes along and you are in the construction business."

His dreams and his empire, then, encompassed the world of land and buildings of every kind, and yet it was not enough; still he wanted more.

Some would have thought him spread too thin. But not those who knew him, friends and foes. He was a quick study, grasping every detail in moments. He knew down to the smallest detail everything about every project, every

114

building and property he owned or managed. Nothing escaped him and nothing was done that he didn't know about and approve.

He spread himself widely across his chosen stage, confident that he could handle it all. To that handling he brought the lessons he had learned from Wien and the frugal sense that seemed innate to him in those days: Never use your own money when you can use somebody else's; never stint on rewarding yourself for the work you do; don't listen to criticism; look for bargains; cut your costs to the absolute minimum, and then find more ways to cut the costs.

Thus, when he bought the New York Central Building, looming over Park Avenue just north of Grand Central Station, the contract specified that he had to change the building's name; the New York Central Railroad no longer owned the building and didn't want its name used on it. Helmsley found an ingenious, if miserly, way out. He simply chiseled out the *C* and the *T* from the building's facade and replaced them with a *G* and an *E,* and so the building became the New York General Building. In a pixilated moment years later, Helmsley laughed and explained his ploy. "I'm . . . cheap."

If his methods were parsimonious, his dreams weren't. About the time he moved into residential properties, he decided to become a builder, too. And the myth took root and flourished, carefully nurtured by Helmsley himself and by his public relations counselor Howard Rubenstein, image maker extraordinaire to the politically powerful and the entrepreneurial elite: Harry Helmsley was a master builder, a man who changed city skylines with a multitude of soaring edifices. He was the equal of, if not superior to, the Tishmans and Zeckendorfs and Uris brothers who filled the metropolitan landscape with towers of glass and steel.

In 1965, he bought some property in lower Manhattan, at Broadway and Cedar Street, from the financier Irwin Wolfson (no relation to Herman Wolfson of the Furman-Wolfson Trust), the man who built the PanAm Building. Wolfson had intended to develop that property himself, but he was ill and dying, and so when Helmsley made an offer, Wolfson accepted.

This was the chance for Helmsley to try his hand in the construction game. Skidmore, Owings and Merrill, designer of many of the major skyscrapers, was one of the architectural firms in most demand then, and in testing these waters, Helmsley was not going to take a chance on second-raters. The architects laid out a fifty-two-story ebony tower in the center of a plaza.

The building was ready for tenants in mid-1967. And at first it looked as though Helmsley's ego had won out over common sense. A glut in office space existed in Manhattan at that moment and there was every likelihood that Helmsley's million square feet of rentable space would be hard to fill. But the new builder used all his contacts and all his powers of persuasion, and even offered some very attractive rents, and before long the building was filling up with such tenants as investment bankers Morgan Stanley and Company, the major law firm of Dewey, Ballantine, Bushby, Palmer and Wood (whose senior partner had been, before his death, the former New York governor and two-time losing Republican presidential candidate, Thomas E. Dewey), and Marine Midland Bank, which rented the preponderance of space.

It was a good start and it gave Helmsley the conviction that he could make the same mark here as he had in other areas. And so his ideas grew more grandiose.

Years earlier he had brokered buildings around the commuter railroad stations, convinced then that the boom in suburban housing would mean an equal boom in office renting near the depots from which the commuters poured every morning. He had been right. Now, in mid-1966, he took another look at the same neighborhoods, though from a different perspective. The area around Penn Station, into which commuters from Long Island and New Jersey streamed, was a seedy neighborhood, its only attractions Macy's and Gimbel's. There hadn't been any new construction, office or otherwise, in the area since before the war. The time was ripe, he concluded.

What he had in mind was a building on a grand scale that would soar over the Penn Station area, a magnet drawing upscale corporations that would revitalize that down-at-the-heels district. Called One Penn Plaza, it would rise fifty-seven stories above the street, filling the block from Thirty-third to Thirty-fourth streets between Seventh and Eighth avenues just north of Penn Station. Providing nearly two million square feet of rentable space, it would be the third-largest privately owned building in the city, smaller only than the PanAm Building and a new edifice rising on South Street under the aegis of the Uris brothers. It would also cost more than $100 million.

Even for Harry Helmsley, with all his ambitions and all his assurance, it was too big a project to handle alone. Once again he turned to Lawrence Wien, and Wien agreed to join him in the venture. They leased the land from the Bowery Savings Bank, which owned it, for fifty years at $200 million, or $4 million a year, with several options for lease renewals after the initial half-century. The Bowery, in turn, leased space on the north and south sides of the building to house branches of the bank. Then Helmsley and Wien formed an investment syndicate, Mid-City Associates, with themselves as the general partners, to build and own One Penn Plaza, with Helmsley-Spear in charge of renting and managing the property. With their reputation and with Helmsley's success in his initial construction project, they had little trouble convincing Metropolitan Life and Equitable Life to join them and take on the mortgages. What's more, Ebasco Industries, then in an expansionist mode, with growing divisions in utilities, engineering, construction, chemicals, and consulting services, signed an agreement to buy 40 percent of One Penn Plaza and lease twenty-four floors, more than half the rentable space, for the next twenty-five years.

On April 1, 1969, ground was broken. But before it was finished two and a half years later, Helmsley and Wien began to have nightmares of being stuck with an empty shell. Ebasco had merged into Boise Cascade Corporation, and Boise Cascade wanted no part of the deal. At a cost of $30 million to $40 million, it canceled Ebasco's agreement. The buyout at least made the cancellation easier to swallow, though money is not a tenant and does not fill empty space. And almost simultaneously a recession in the office-leasing market struck. The city was inundated with new office towers—downtown in the financial district, uptown along the Avenue of the Americas, Park Avenue, and Third Avenue—and all of these were considered more prestigious locations than the Penn Station area. By the time One Penn Plaza opened in late 1971, more than 1.4 million of its nearly 2 million square feet remained empty, and even the millions paid by Boise Cascade and the major tax abatements granted by the city[1] could not totally allay the gloom.

For One Penn Plaza, then, the crucial question was how to attract tenants. Major corporations and others who might rent several floors just weren't interested in that neighborhood or that building, didn't, in fact, seem much interested in any neighborhood or any building.

Helmsley found another way. He slashed rents. Originally, he had intended to charge ten dollars or eleven dollars

1. Relief from paying taxes was something builders and owners had long claimed was an essential incentive to build and renovate properties. City fathers in a number of municipalities agreed, and so in the years following World War II, it became a common practice to grant abatements on real estate taxes, sometimes full abatements for decades, sometimes partial abatements that declined as time passed.

Such abatements have been eagerly accepted by the real estate industry, of course, and declared essential by many civic leaders to foster urban growth and renewal, but they have also come under increasingly sharp attack, especially from heavily taxed homeowners who have been forced to bear an ever larger tax burden. Moreover, all too often what is built is not much-needed low- and middle-income housing, but rather luxury housing and monumental corporate headquarters.

a square foot; he marked them down to eight dollars and nine dollars a square foot. Then he lured small businessmen and professionals by carving up a number of the floors into offices to suit their needs. Within a few years the building was 85 percent rented, three quarters of this total housing what Helmsley-Spear called "small-space tenants." And as the building filled, the rents rose, to what they had originally been slated to go for, and beyond.

So One Penn Plaza, despite its uncertain beginnings, turned out to be another Helmsley triumph. And it opened the way for an upgrading of the neighborhood, bringing in other new towers, a new Madison Square Garden, and, much later, the Javits Convention Center to the west, near the Hudson River.

Now Harry Helmsley was an established, prominent, and successful builder, in addition to everything else. The opportunities to advance ever further in this field seemed to be there. But most he let slip away. He had a chance in 1972, for instance, to get in on the ground floor on the grandiose dream of Nelson Rockefeller for a nearly self-contained city in lower Manhattan, to be called Battery Park City. But when mortgage money was hard to find and if he went ahead he would have to risk his own capital, he backed out.

In truth, Helmsley's reputation as a builder of office towers on the grand scale, so cultivated by himself and his publicity men, abetted by the press and believed by the public, was inflated. There is little to show for it save for those first structures in lower Manhattan, and One Penn Plaza. There were many plans and many projects, all surrounded by glowing promises, but there was little fulfillment.

10

BUT THEN THERE were his hotels.

At first, he bought. In 1958, Helmsley heard that the St. Moritz Hotel was up for sale. The price: just over $3 million. It was a hotel with an international reputation and an international feeling, a building of elegance and refinement. Built in 1931, its opulence and ornamental touches in the art deco manner, and its 775 rooms on thirty-three floors with a sweeping vista across Central Park from its corner on Central Park South and the Avenue of the Americas, made it one of the city's meccas for visitors. Its restaurant, Café de la Paix, had a French ambiance, and its Rumpelmayer's was a treat for generations of children who savored the ice cream and pastry concoctions and gazed in awe at the multitude of stuffed animals that looked down on them. Helmsley wanted it. He brought the news to Lawrence Wien, for these were the heady days when their partnership was flourishing. The lawyer heard him out but was reluctant to make a move in that direction. "He didn't like to operate hotels," Peter Malkin says. "His idea was really more of investments in real estate rather than operating a business, and a hotel is more of a business than real estate."

It was not the first time, nor would it be the last, that Lawrence Wien had examined a Helmsley prospect, explored all the ramifications, and then decided to pass. On most such occasions, Helmsley had bowed to the Wien instinct, looked for and found buyers elsewhere, and did not become personally involved beyond brokering the sale, for he had learned that more often than not Wien's intuitions were well grounded. This time, however, Helmsley did not give in, was enthusiastic enough about the hotel's potential as an investment to persuade Wien to go along, form a syndicate, and make the purchase.

"What happened," Malkin says, "was that Mr. Wien bought the land and the building and then he carved it up into three positions which he sold initially to Chase Manhattan Bank and then leased it back. The master lease was owned by St. Moritz Hotel Associates, which was a partnership of Mr. Wien and myself. And then an operating sublease was granted to a corporation owned by Mr. Helmsley, because Mr. Wien didn't want anything to do with operating that hotel." Helmsley did; even then he was beginning to see possibilities in the hotel world. This was his foothold.

The St. Moritz, then, was the first. Hardly had the deal been closed before Helmsley had another for Wien's inspection. In Westbury, on Long Island, Roosevelt Raceway had recently opened and the bettors were flocking to it for a chance to put their money on the trotters. Foresighted developers began to see the prospects in the area around the track for shopping centers and other large buildings, the raceway being the lure whose patrons would spill over and enrich others in the environs. A new shopping center was being carved out adjacent to the track. One of its major structures was to be an $8 million, 204-room hotel called the Island Inn. Helmsley called it to Wien's attention, and Wien quickly saw the profit potential in an investment in a hotel near a racetrack that operated in the evenings. The two men formed a partnership and proceeded to buy a sixty-two-year lease on the Island Inn, paying $300,000 in annual rent plus 30 percent of everything they took in room rentals over $800,000. It looked like, and it proved, a sure winner, safer and more profitable than anything running around the oval down the street.

Over the next years, mainly on his own, Helmsley picked

up the Carlton House and a couple of other established inns in Manhattan.

Then, in 1967, even as he was conceiving his plans for One Penn Plaza, he announced he was going to build a hotel of his own, a forty-six-story edifice on Central Park South. He had bought the land at a good price, Helmsley said, and at first he wasn't sure what he wanted to do with it. After debating several alternatives, he opted for a hotel.

"I think Harry decided to build it," says a man who has done much business with him over the years, "because he wanted a penthouse *pied-à-terre,* and he thought, 'Why not own the floors down below, too, and make some money in the process?' "

But who needed a new luxury hotel at that moment? There hadn't been a new posh inn built in Manhattan in nearly a decade, and with what seemed good reason. The guns-and-butter philosophy preached by President Lyndon Johnson—that the country could afford to fight the war in Vietnam without damage to the domestic economy—was leading to inflation and stagnation, and if a recession had not yet set in, most economists felt that it wouldn't be long before it did. New York City was already suffering, and the suffering would be a lot worse. Conventioneers who had once flocked to the city were now shunning it, and those who did appear were appearing in fewer numbers. Room occupancy rates at hotels were declining, down to less than 70 percent, and sinking fast.

Despite all the gloomy forecasts, and despite the refusal of one of his favorite sources of money, Metropolitan Life, to back his new project, Helmsley persevered. This time he put up out of his own pocket a good portion of the $30 million cost and found investors willing to come across with the rest; if Harry Helmsley was actually putting his own money into something for a change, then perhaps he was on to something after all, they reasoned.

He was not even deterred when his announced choice of a name for his new hotel, the Park Lane, drew an angry response. From 1927 until 1965, there had been a Park Lane Hotel in Manhattan. It had been a dignified, architecturally gracious 488-room hotel on Park Avenue between Forty-eighth and Forty-ninth streets. Many of the residents made their homes there, living in large suites. The service was superb and the ambiance resembled a private club. It was swept away in the building boom that changed Park Avenue from a boulevard of old, graceful structures into a showplace for some of the best, and worst, examples of postwar sheer-wall Bauhaus functionalism. To have the name of Park Lane attached to another hotel, and one that might well be just another characterless behemoth, seemed outrageous. But nothing could stop Helmsley from calling his hotel just that, for Realty Hotels, which had owned the original Park Lane, had let its control of the name lapse when it was sold. So the name was there for the taking, and Helmsley took it.

To the surprise of many—"He will take a schlock property and run it as a schlock property forever," is one critic's opinion—Helmsley determined to do things right at the Park Lane. He hired Emery Roth and Sons, who had designed the old St. Moritz Hotel, to draw up the plans. He hired the internationally famous decorator, Tom Lee, Ltd., to plan the interiors. He spared no expense to make the hotel a showplace. And a showplace it was. When it opened in April 1971, a critic for *The New York Times* hailed it as "an asset to Central Park South."

Everything was in good, if expensive, taste. The small lobby was adorned with travertine marble and illuminated by huge crystal chandeliers. This lavishness was continued in the crystal fixtures lighting the corridors, and Italian marble tops on the dressing tables in the bathrooms of the individual rooms. There were only sixteen rooms to a floor, and the rooms were not only large by the contemporary hotel standards, but soundproofed by layers of acoustic material and gypsum blocks behind five-inch-thick walls. Not venetian blinds but draw curtains and roller shades covered the tinted glass windows. Every room had two closets, and both could be opened only with the particular room's door key; neither the maid's nor the master key would fit. Tom Lee designed thirteen different color schemes for the rooms, featuring a variety of flocked wallpaper, quilted bedspreads, and a lot more.

The sense of exclusivity extended beyond all this, though. For the same room rates as any luxury hotel in the city, guests were greeted by multilingual concierges. They need not fear being jostled in the lobby or the elevators by roistering conventioneers, for discounts were not offered to lure tourists en masse, and the largest meeting room could hold only 150 people. Initially there were no ballrooms, convention halls, or hospitality suites, though a later remodeling did add a large ballroom.

The Park Lane, then, was a triumph. It was celebrated by critics, and that celebration drew the out-of-towners, domestic and foreign, in increasing numbers. Even while other hotels around the city were saddled with empty rooms, the Park Lane was filled almost from the day it opened, and the profits from it filled Helmsley's coffers.

And with its building Helmsley got his penthouse *pied-à-terre,* two floors on top of the hotel, complete with swimming pool. An old associate remembers that soon after the hotel opened, he was invited to that penthouse early one evening to discuss business. The first things he noticed were the carpets rolled up against the wall, canvas draped across the furniture, pools of water on the floor and over everything, water dripping from the ceiling. "After I went to work this morning," Helmsley told him, "they turned the valves on to fill the pool upstairs. The guy who installed it guaranteed there was no danger that it would overflow." He laughed. "What the hell. He's going to pay for the damage."

When everything was finally ready in the penthouse, Eve Green Helmsley, Harry's wife of nearly thirty-five years, invited some of the women she played tennis with at the Sleepy Hollow Country Club to lunch at the new hotel and to take a look at Harry's penthouse. She took them on a tour, showed them the solarium, the swimming pool, the spacious rooms, the wraparound terrace, the fabulous view. As she led them to the door, she said, "This is the first and only time you'll see this place, girls. Harry and I are getting a divorce."

Harry Helmsley, at age sixty-two, had found the love of his life.

Part Three
Leona

11

LEONA MINDY ROBERTS was what she called herself. She was born Lena Rosenthal, but Lena, a common girl's name among Polish immigrants, soon gave way to Leona. Everything else about her origins is open to dispute, for with a deliberate calculation, she has shrouded her early life in obscurity, sometimes telling one story, sometimes another, trying always to hide much, reveal little. The truth lies somewhere in all the stories. Perhaps the clues to the real person lie not in which particular version may be true but in all of them, in the fact that she has found it essential to invent so many.

A careful sifting through the stories and what records are available reveals a history along these lines: She was born on July 4, 1919, though into the 1980s, it constantly grew later. Most often, she has simply refused to give her birth date, though when pressed, she coyly admits, year after year, to being fifty-nine—eternally.

She has always maintained that she was born in Brooklyn. But there is some evidence to show that she was actually born in High Falls, a small town west of Poughkeepsie in New York's Ulster County. That, at least, is what it says on the birth certificate she filed with the courts years later when she officially changed her last name from Rosenthal to Roberts.

She was one of four children. She had two sisters, Sandra and Sylvia, and a brother, Alvin. She often claimed that her father, an immigrant from Poland named Morris Rosenthal, was a successful manufacturer of ladies' hats, or, sometimes, of caps for the military, but, like Harry Helmsley's father, he was more likely a millinery salesman, and not an especially successful one, for the family was peripatetic, arriving in Brooklyn from High Falls when she was a small child and changing addresses constantly, from Coney Island to Bensonhurst, back and forth, at least five times, perhaps more, before she was thirteen.

She has said her family "was very, very close," but the closeness seemed to have been mainly with her father, a gentle man who suffered from heart disease and died before she was twenty. With her mother, Ida, who like her father, was an immigrant from Poland, there was constant tension and frequent battles. And there was friction between Leona and her two sisters that deepened over the years; from the time she was in her twenties, her relations with Sylvia were so fractious that thereafter they rarely spoke or saw each other except at times of family crisis, and she refused to attend Sylvia's funeral when that sister died in the early 1980s; with Sandra, there were repeated breaks followed by reconciliations. When Sandra died, also early in the 1980s, it was apparently at a moment of alienation, because Leona stayed away from her funeral, too. With her younger brother Alvin, whose early years were marked by serious illnesses, she was protective and domineering; much later, she gave him a job as an executive in the Helmsley hotel chain.

She was a good student in school, something the records do indicate; her reports from Seth Low Junior High School in Brooklyn say she had "extraordinary talent in English and communication subjects." She has said she graduated from Abraham Lincoln High School in Brooklyn, but school officials, going through the records, say she dropped out long before graduation; they were told her family was moving to Gloversville in upstate New York, but there is no record that such a move was ever made.

The stories she has told of the next years, after she left high school, have varied so widely and conflicted so radically that it is impossible to say what actually occurred or what she really did. She says she took on the name Leona Mindy Roberts, though sometimes calling herself Lee Roberts, Leni Roberts, or Mindy Roberts. That seems certain. But that's about all.

She claims that she became a model, a Chesterfield cigarette girl. She may have—cigarette advertisements of the time used sketches of models drawn from photographs—but the cigarette maker has no record or photographs in its files of a model named Leona or Lee or Leni or Mindy Roberts, which may prove nothing, since it can't find the records or photographs of some of the models it knows for certain posed for those ads. Whether she was really a cigarette girl, then, no one but Leona would know for sure, but that she had a fondness for cigarettes is patent—until the mid-1980s, she was a three-pack-a-day chain smoker.

She also claims that after high school she spent two years at Hunter College, a New York City public institution then considered one of the most outstanding public women's schools in the country. But Hunter, while dedicated to educating the daughters of the poor, accepted only the most promising high school graduates and turned most of them into teachers. The school has no record of a Leona Rosenthal or Roberts as a student in the late 1930s.

What is certain is that in 1938, she married a lawyer named Leo Panzirer, ten or eleven years her senior. He had known her from the old days in Coney Island, and had begun to court her soon after she turned sixteen or seventeen. She was nineteen when they married.

In 1940 the Panzirers had a son, Jay Robert, Leona's only child.

The marriage was not a success, though, and by the end of the decade they were divorced. (Leona has never talked about the marriage, and Panzirer adamantly refuses to say anything at all about his former wife—"I haven't seen her in years and I don't know anything about her except what I read in the papers, and I'm not going to talk about what she was like back then. That's ancient history.'')

Just what she did after the divorce, dependent on minimal alimony and child support, and with her family refusing to help, is as unclear as almost everything else about this time. But there are indications that she worked for a time as a saleswoman in a department store, then got a job as a clerk or secretary with a garment manufacturer named Joseph Lubin. Lubin was attracted to her and she reciprocated, and they soon married. This marriage worked no better than the one to Panzirer. Leona and Lubin fought constantly, and after a few years were divorced. Within a year they married again and before long were divorced. The year was 1962, and once more she was on her own with few funds. She was in her forties, too old to go back to modeling for cigarettes, if, indeed, she ever had. But she was tough, resourceful and attractive, if a little overweight, and she was ambitious. Someone suggested that she try real estate. For a woman without a college education, without experience, in her forties, it was a natural, as many women in similar circumstances have discovered. For Leona Mindy Roberts, it was the perfect answer.

12

SHE BEGAN AS a receptionist at Pease and Elliman, one of
the prestigious residential brokerage firms. It was a start,
but only a start. Leona Roberts had no intention of remaining behind the front desk while others were renting or selling apartments and raking in the commissions. She was sure
she could show and sell better than anyone. After a couple
of months she talked the bosses into letting her handle a
few small clients. It wasn't long before the word around
Pease and Elliman was, according to one fellow broker,
"Don't turn your back on Leona Roberts." She was, they
said, not above taking another broker's clients if he happened to be otherwise occupied, nor was she above steering
someone else's clients to a property she controlled and on
which she would earn the commission. "Leona was out for
Leona. It was as simple as that. Nobody else even came in
second place."

She succeeded well enough so that before long she was
selling co-ops and condominiums, and then was handling
the highly lucrative conversion of rental apartments into co-
ops and condos. At this point, another side of her emerged.
People in rent-controlled or rent-stabilized apartments more
often than not resisted buying, as we have seen. Leona knew
how to put heavy pressure on, though, warning them that if
they didn't agree to buy, she had other buyers ready to put
their money on the line. Arguing, some would say threatening, she became very good at persuading people to buy
now before it was too late, before they were out on the street

and somebody else was living in what had been their apartment.

And she had very good instincts. She could be a tiger or she could be a pussycat, depending on the situation. She sensed just how far she could push her clients, both buyers and sellers, and when to back off. She could show an apartment and before she was finished have the clients convinced it was just what they had been looking for all along. Equally, she could persuade a landlord or a seller that certain renovations were absolutely essential if the apartment was going to move, and in the process convince him that the idea had been his in the first place. "You had to see Leona in action to believe it," says a former colleague. "She could have shown the Mayor a bench in Central Park and had him believing it was better than Gracie Mansion."

She could sell, and she had that something else that lifts a salesperson above the ordinary, that leads to great success. She had the ability to sense what people were really after. Unlike many brokers, she did not waste their time by showing them a dozen apartments they wouldn't possibly accept, in the hope that at the end, out of exhaustion and resignation, they would take one that earned a higher commission. Rather, she would steer her clients with some dispatch to one she sensed they would take with little resistance, and though the price might be higher then they had hoped, and the apartment not all they had specified, it would be close enough.

"We'd been looking for an apartment for months," remembers one woman. "We must have been to a dozen brokers and we told them precisely what we wanted, and none of them showed us anything that came even close. It was the most frustrating experience. They took us all over the Upper East Side and they showed us these truly dreadful dumps and then they would try to convince us they were really charming and a steal at the price, and that with only a little work, they'd be just what we wanted. Then a friend told us about Leona Roberts. We sat down and talked to her for about an hour, explaining just what we needed and where we wanted to be. She was patient and charming and she said she couldn't promise anything, but she'd see what she could do. The very next day she called and said she had something that might interest us. She met us there and she took us around and said she was sure she could convince the landlord to make whatever alterations we wanted. She didn't hurry us at all. I think we must have spent the whole afternoon with her. We didn't even have to look at another apartment. After she'd explained everything and what the landlord would do, we knew it was perfect. We took it, and it was. And we've been happy here all these years. I don't care what people say about her now. If we needed another apartment and she was still in business, I wouldn't think of going to anyone else."

As much as anything, she was entranced by making the deal, setting up people in just the right way so the sale could be concluded on the best terms. The money was important, certainly, but she also gloried in the power of manipulating clients to go her way.

All of this was fed by an insatiable desire for more. "People are going to know Leona Roberts," she told a fellow broker one day.

"People in the business already know you, Leona," he replied.

"No," she said. "I mean everybody. Everybody's going to know the name Leona Roberts."

She said it with such conviction that he was convinced she was deadly serious, and he was even persuaded that if anyone could make that come true, she was the person.

After only a few years in the business, she became a vice-president of Pease and Elliman, earning a salary and commissions in six figures. She bought herself a penthouse apartment at 77 West Fifty-fifth Street, close to Fifth Avenue, and furnished it lavishly. She went out and bought two mink coats and closets full of expensive clothes and shoes.

She had, it seemed, just about every material object she could want. It was not enough. She had higher aspirations.

In 1968 she persuaded her employers to set up a new division, called Sutton and Towne Residential, with herself as president, to handle cooperatives and conversions on Manhattan's Upper East Side. She did so well in her new job that, she would later boast, "During three months in 1968 I earned $450,000 in commissions."

More important, within the next year she came to the attention of a real estate competitor whom, she would later claim, she had managed to best in several deals. His name was Harry Helmsley. She would say, "Harry heard of my reputation and he told one of his executives, 'Whoever she is, get her.' When he finally called me, I told him, 'You can't afford me. I'm in a bad bracket now.' Finally he gave me a deal I couldn't refuse. He said I could have an interest in a building he planned to buy, the Imperial House.[1] When he told me that, I said, 'Swear with your eyes that you're telling the truth.' He blinked a few times and I thought, 'This big mogul is blinking his eyes at me like that.' I knew I liked him right away."

That's one way she tells it. She has also, on occasion, told another story with more romance to it. She went to a real estate dinner, was introduced to him, and soon they moved onto the dance floor together, and while the band played, "Raindrops Keep Falling on My Head," Helmsley crooned into her ear, making up his own words to the tune. She knew then he was the man for her.

There's yet another story, not quite as colorful nor quite so filled with romance and the aura of love at first sight as the ones Leona has re-created. This one claims there was

1. Located on Sixty-ninth Street on Manhattan's East Side, Imperial House was once considered the epitome of a postwar large-scale luxury apartment building. Helmsley's efforts to buy it failed, and so the interest in it promised to Leona Roberts came to nothing. It was one of the few promises he made her that didn't pay off for her.

nothing accidental about the meeting, claims the lead was taken not by Harry Helmsley but by a Machiavellian Leona Roberts. She knew about Harry Helmsley, as did everybody in real estate, for he was the biggest man in the business. With her eye always on the main chance, she decided the place to be was with Helmsley. So she went to Leon Spear, to whom she had sold a Park Avenue apartment. He was a member of the Spear family, the Spear in Helmsley-Spear. Not only that, his brother-in-law was Alvin Schwartz. Leona asked and he agreed to arrange an introduction. She was at her best at that first meeting, and impressed Helmsley, both as a woman and a business person. It was the beginning.

At one time or another, Harry Helmsley has heard all the versions of their first meeting. He has never given his own version of that fateful encounter.

However Harry Helmsley and Leona Roberts met, the outcome was the offer of a job as senior vice-president of Brown, Harris, Stevens, at a salary of a half a million dollars a year, fifty thousand dollars more than she was making as president of Sutton and Towne. She had come a long way since she had started as a low-paid receptionist in a real estate office less than a decade before.

She was past fifty when she accepted Helmsley's offer, though she did not look her age. Few even knew what it was, any more than they knew that she was a grandmother.

Life had not been easy for her only child, Jay Robert Panzirer. His first years were spent in a household filled with quarreling, and his parents were divorced before he was ten. In the ensuing years he and his mother had moved constantly from apartment to apartment in the Bronx as Leona married and divorced, and then married and divorced a third time. And through these years, he was raised by a mother often forced to scratch for survival. A volatile woman, she dominated her son. She was fiercely protective—some who saw them together later said overprotective—sometimes loving, always demanding, rarely forgiving, seldom satisfied, setting impossible standards for him. (It was a pattern evident, as well, in her relationship with the other males in her life for whom she had deep feelings—her brother Alvin and Harry Helmsley.) Jay responded often with resentment and a barely controlled seething rebellion, though usually he endured in petulant silence. A fellow junior high school student remembers that he ran with a wild crowd, though this display of perverse independence vanished in the presence of his mother. Even when he was grown up, their relationship never seemed to advance much beyond that of teenager bristling at his domineering mother. A close friend in later years says, "When he was around her, one thing that stood out about him was a sense of, 'Oh, Mom, leave me alone.' "

He developed a flair for design, perhaps learned from his stepfather, Joseph Lubin, and after attending the Philadelphia Textile Institute, he went to work in New York's garment industry as a fabric designer. About 1963 he met and married a girl from Brooklyn named Myrna Binowitz. To friends, it appeared a good match, though Leona Roberts told them that they were both too young and too financially insecure. But for once Jay showed independence in the face of his mother's demands, and they married over her objections. Leona blamed Myrna, not Jay, for what she thought was a rash decision, and relations between them were always cool.

They were not married long before Myrna became pregnant. The child was stillborn. She became pregnant again, and this time had a miscarriage. Finally, in 1967 she gave birth to their first child, a son they named Craig. Leona did all the right things. She showed up at the hospital bearing gifts and, if still cool toward her daughter-in-law, seemed delighted with her new grandson. She attended the Jewish *bris,* looking "beautiful and very self-confident," remembers a friend of the Panzirers. She visited the baby at home, bearing the usual gifts, acting the proud grandmother.

In 1969 Jay and Myrna had a second son, David, and a year later, a daughter, Meegan.

For all the outward sheen of business success and assurance, those who saw Leona Roberts in the home of her son thought something very amiss in her private life. Invariably she arrived alone and did not fit in easily. And the father of one of Myrna's closest friends recalls a time when Leona, perhaps having had too much to drink before her visit, came on to him very strong, and before the evening was through, to his surprise and shock, she tried to get him to go to bed with her. They had only just met, and his wife was with him. At first he thought it must be a joke. But when he turned her down, she was furious.

In these years she was careful to keep her personal and professional lives separate. She talked about her grandchildren rarely, and many people did not know she had one, let alone three. Privately she wanted to advance Jay's career, but the way she would do it was at a distance. As long as Jay and his children were around, they would mark her of a certain age, for they would call attention to her status as grandmother. In fact, whenever she was with Jay in public, when she took him to dinner or somewhere else, he had to agree never to call her "Mother," but Aunt Lee or Aunt Leona, or just plain Lee or Leona.

Then the opportunity came to help and, at the same time, remove him and his family from close proximity. As an increasingly important figure in the Helmsley organization, and in Harry Helmsley's life, she was able to get Jay a job as design coordinator with a Helmsley division in Ohio. And so Jay, Myrna, and their three children moved far from friends and family, far from interfering with the youthful and unencumbered image Leona Roberts was projecting.

Jay's work required him to travel a great deal around Ohio and neighboring states, but Myrna thought little about his long absences. They seemed to be happy, he was making more money than ever, and she was busy raising their three small children. And then one day after they had been in

Ohio for a few years, she would later tell her closest friend,
the doorbell rang. A woman about her age was standing
outside. She seemed a nice attractive person.

And then the stranger asked, "Is Jay Panzirer here?"
Myrna looked at her and said, "He lives here. Why?"

"I'm looking for him. I'm Mrs. Panzirer."

"You can't be," Myrna Panzirer said, stunned. "I'm
Mrs. Panzirer."

In that instant she understood her husband's absences and
sometimes odd behavior, understood what lay behind the
enigmatic telephone calls he sometimes received. As the
two Mrs. Panzirers compared notes, they discovered there
were other absences for which neither could find an adequate explanation. They came to the conclusion, though they
found no absolute proof, that there was probably at least
one more Mrs. Jay Panzirer.

It was the end of the marriage of Jay Robert Panzirer and
Myrna Binowitz. Myrna threw him out and filed for divorce, though she did not cite bigamy, or polygamy, as the
grounds. In fact, except to very close friends, she has never
talked about the reasons for the breakup of the marriage.
For a time she was stranded in Ohio with her children, with
no funds, no friends, no family, no way out. Her very rich
mother-in-law, Mrs. Harry Helmsley by this time, refused
to come to her aid, or to help her grandchildren. In fact,
Leona blamed not Jay but Myrna for all that had happened.
Everything had always been Myrna's fault. Some years
would pass before she would reestablish any kind of relationship with her grandchildren, though as they grew older,
she saw less and less of them, mentioned them hardly at
all. They were, some people said, too cruel reminders of
her own advancing age.

Eventually Myrna found her way back to New York,
picked up the pieces of her life, and remarried. But the scars
remain and to this day she will not talk to outsiders about
anything to do with that past.

As for Jay Panzirer, he, too, left Ohio, moving to California. There, still with his mother's aid from a distance, he set up shop buying supplies for hotels, especially those owned by the Helmsley organization. And he married again. In 1976, his wife, Ruth, gave birth to a son named Walter, after Harry Helmsley's brother who had died two years earlier. But, though he played golf and tennis, his health was not good. He suffered from arrhythmia, a serious condition that interrupts the rhythm of the heart and grows progressively worse. Through the late 1970s he had three heart attacks and spent nearly a year in the hospital after one. And his marriage to Ruth was failing.

By 1979 he was a bachelor once more and living in Orlando, Florida. Through the influence of his mother, he was working full-time for the Helmsleys, as head of the subsidiary, Deco Purchasing and Distributing, the central purchasing agency for the organization's buildings and hotels.

13

BOTH LEONA AND Harry have said it was love at first sight. Harry Helmsley, a man in his sixties, was swept away like a teenage boy in the throes of first love. Leona, a woman in her fifties, was captivated, consumed by emotions she was to say she had never felt before.

There are the cynics who claim that she had set out on a deliberate, calculated campaign to woo and win him, that passion had nothing to do with it and his billions everything. But those who have seen them together, at the beginning and over the years, say the cynics are wrong. "You only had to look at them together," says a woman who was once their friend, "and you knew. There was that kind of glow that you could never mistake. Harry was madly in love with her, and Leona was just as much in love with him. Maybe his money had something to do with it at the beginning. Who knows? But, remember, she wasn't exactly poor herself. If you ask me, or anyone who knew them, it was a real love match."

There were, of course, the obvious things that drew Harry Helmsley. Leona was very different from his wife. Eve Helmsley was quiet and reserved, she was well educated, and she was a lady. Nobody ever accused Leona of being a lady, and she certainly was neither quiet nor reserved. On the contrary, she was brash, capricious, and given to sudden and often violent temperamental outbursts. Eve was a housewife who cared little about the business world and so shared little and understood less of her husband's obsession

142

with his career. Leona was a success in the very business
that Harry had made his life; she shared a thirst for it that
he could recognize and appreciate, and so they could talk
easily and naturally about what mattered to both. But Harry
Helmsley might have found that in a dozen other women,
as Leona might have found it in other men. Passion was
something else, unable to be defined but equally unable to
be ignored.

So all-consuming was their passion that it could not long
be kept a secret, and they did not even try. Harry began to
spend more nights away from his suburban home, at the
apartment he kept for himself in the St. Moritz, and he
could often be seen going into the building on West Fifty-
fifth street where Leona lived. They dined out together in
small, out-of-the-way, candle-lit restaurants, and held hands
across the tables. Leona went on a campaign to make herself even more alluring to Harry. She had put on some
weight over the previous years, so now she went on a diet
and slimmed down, turning herself into the slim woman the
public would come to recognize. "I lost a pound a day for
twenty days. Twenty pounds I lost for Harry, and I kept it
off," she once told an interviewer. She went to specialists
and tried a number of esoteric remedies to tighten her face,
improve her complexion, strip away the dead skin, make
her more youthful.

And Harry Helmsley, who had offered her a job, a high
position, and a large salary in his empire, offered her a
share in his life, his fortune, and his future.

In so doing, Helmsley shed the encumbrances of his past.
He did so without regret. The cost of the shedding would
be high, but he was sure that whatever the cost, it would
not be too high.

He and his wife, Eve Green Helmsley, separated in 1971,
after nearly thirty-three years of marriage. It came at a moment of singular triumph for him, the opening of his Park
Lane, a hotel immediately celebrated as a tasteful addition

to the New York skyline. It would be a home for Leona, not Eve.

So Helmsley abandoned the suburbs, for which he cared little anyway, and initially moved into his apartment at the St. Moritz, leaving Eve in possession of the house. Within a year they were divorced. He gave her $7 million in cash, cars, the Briarcliff Manor home, and all the material possessions in it that they had collected over the years. She in turn quickly sold the house for $135,000, several times its original cost, and moved into an apartment at Helmsley's Carlton House Hotel, where she paid no rent. There she remained for a time, moved on to Florida where she had friends, stayed a short while, and then settled into a wealthy retirement community in New Jersey, where she still lives. According to people who have seen her since the divorce, she is not bitter. About Leona, she has said only, "I don't know her. But I hear she's hated."

The courtship that had been, if not clandestine at least not flouted in the months before the separation, now became open. Harry and Leona were together constantly, dining more often in expensively fashionable and exclusive restaurants than in the ones that had been the scenes of their earlier rendezvous, attending affairs to dance the nights away.

And then in the summer of 1972, Harry Helmsley and Leona Mindy Rosenthal Panzirer Lubin Roberts were married.

A decade later, during a generally uncritical, even flattering interview on *60 Minutes*, Mike Wallace would ask her gently, "Did you marry Harry Helmsley for his money?"

Leona Helmsley laughed and in her gravelly, Brooklyn-accented voice, replied, "Harry Helmsley married me for my money. I gave him all my money. I had one million dollars of my own. That I had earned, as a broker. I was the best in the field. That's why he went after me. But when I married Harry, really, a lot of people probably did think along those lines. So why not? I don't get paid. I don't draw a salary. . . . He gives me titles. No money.''

Wallace turned to Harry Helmsley and asked, ''Why don't you pay her a salary?''

''When I get her for nothing, why should I?'' he laughed. ''I'm telling you the truth. What am I going to pay her for? She'd put it in my bank account anyhow. Then I'd have to pay taxes on it, because she'd be earning it. What's mine is hers. It's not a question of do I pay her. She has . . . she owns everything I have. And I own everything she has.''

''She told me she gave you a million dollars,'' Wallace said.

''Oh, that was in the old days, when a million dollars was a million dollars,'' Helmsley replied, and both he and Leona laughed loudly.

True, by the summer of 1972, Leona Helmsley had earned her million and more. And when she married Harry Helmsley, she began to back away from her active life as a broker, as senior vice-president of Brown, Harris, Stevens. In some ways, it was just as well that she did.

She had been specializing in the highly profitable conversion of rental buildings, as she had been doing at Sutton and Towne, and she had done very well. Then, in late 1971, she attempted to co-op a twenty-story rent-stabilized Sutton Place building, at 345 East Fifty-sixth Street. When the 172 tenants read the prospectus, they were outraged. She was asking from $15,000 for a studio apartment to $85,000 for a three-room penthouse, with monthly maintenance ranging from $120 to $682. In sum, the price she was asking for the building was on the order of $10 million, more than $6 million above, or nearly three times, the $3,775,000 assessed value of the property.

The tenants resisted, and when Leona realized that she had nowhere near the thirty-five percent, or sixty-one tenants, required under the law, she began to put on the pressure.

''We were getting calls constantly,'' remembers one couple, "and so was everybody else. We had no interest in buying then. We were very happy with the rent we were paying, and we didn't have all that much extra money to put down. Besides, we thought the prices she was asking were just way out of line. I imagine today those apartments are worth a lot more than what we might have paid, so looking back, perhaps we should have scraped up the money and bought, but nobody knew the apartment market was going to boom like it did later. Right then there was a recession and we were hearing stories about a lot of people buying apartments in very good buildings at distressed prices. So we didn't think we ought to have to pay two or three times what we all thought the apartments in our building were really worth. Nearly everybody we talked to agreed. And then those calls started to come. She was making them herself, Leona Roberts. She wasn't even polite. She used the coarsest and the nastiest language you ever heard. She threatened that if we didn't sign the agreement to buy, we'd be . . . and the words she used were—we'd be out on our ass and it would serve us damn right. Only what she said and the way she said it was a lot worse than that. She told us she had three outside buyers ready and waiting to purchase our apartment at the outsiders' prices, which was, I think, ten or twenty percent higher. The last couple of calls she said she had all the signatures she needed from tenants to put the conversion into effect, and she had so many outsiders just dying to buy apartments in the building that if we didn't sign on the dotted line within forty-eight hours, we'd better start packing. That was what she was telling everyone. It was absolutely terrifying. Here was this woman telling us we were going to lose our homes if we didn't do exactly what she wanted.''

They had reason, indeed, to be afraid. Brown, Harris, Stevens filed a ''declaration of effectiveness'' with the attorney general's office, asserting that sixty-five tenants or their successors had agreed to the conversion plan, and so those remaining tenants who had not bought had a choice only to buy or get out.

But some of the tenants not only didn't like Leona Roberts' tactics at all, they were also sure they smelled something very peculiar in the declaration that so many others had agreed to her terms. They went to Attorney General Louis Lefkowitz and complained. Lefkowitz in turn investigated and what his office found was enough to send authorities to the state supreme court to block the conversion, on the grounds that "fraudulent practices" were being used. The investigation, the attorney general said, showed that on at least eleven occasions the tenants were "fraudulently coerced" into buying on the "false representations" that outsiders had already contracted to buy their apartments.

"The major perpetrator of these fraudulent acts and practices," the court papers filed by Lefkowitz declared, "was and is the defendant Leona Roberts." And it was Leona herself, and not Brown, Harris, Stevens, who was cited as the defendant in the action.

Leona reacted with righteous indignation. The charges, her lawyer declared, were false, and had been trumped up by the attorney general and his staff as a publicity stunt in an effort to gain public attention by acting against a successful and well-known target, Leona Roberts, and her even more successful and renowned boss, Harry Helmsley. What was worse was that the case was being tried, and so prejudiced, by press releases and press conferences that were being reported in the newspapers and on television. The attorney general had even gone so far as to unconscionably release Leona's home address, which led to her being "inundated for several days with a steady stream of obscenities" in anonymous phone calls.

State Supreme Court Justice Jacob Markowitz agreed with the attorney general. Leona Roberts had, indeed, he said, committed "fraudulent acts." As a result, he barred the conversion of the building, ordered the owners to return all the money they had collected from tenants as full or partial payments, and directed the owners to offer new three-year leases conforming to the rent-stabilization law to the tenants.

Had anyone wanted to press further, Leona Roberts could have been taken before the Real Estate Licensing Board. What she had done was a serious transgression not only of accepted practices but also of the profession's rules and regulations, so her real estate license could be either suspended or revoked. Indeed, her license to act as a broker had been temporarily suspended while the court considered the attorney general's suit, though her attorney managed to get the suspension lifted after forty-eight hours, and as a result, she was able to continue working on more than a dozen other conversions.

Once Judge Markowitz handed down his ruling, however, her career in real estate was in real jeopardy. State authorities decided to begin proceedings toward the end of stripping her of her license permanently. Her attorney apparently persuaded her that the wisest course was to act before the state did by voluntarily turning in that license. Thus, since the state would not have moved against her, there would be nothing to prevent her from applying for a new license sometime in the future, should she so desire.

But by that time her license no longer held much interest for her. She had suffered damaged pride and a sullied reputation, true, but she had little reason to hold on to the license or to gain a new one other than for a chance to repair them. That was hardly reason enough. For she was backing away from the business anyway, because Leona Roberts was about to change her name to Leona Helmsley.

"I've heard people say Harry would forgive her anything," says a man who has esteemed Helmsley for years. "They're wrong. Harry never forgave her anything. Because he never thought there was anything to forgive. As far as Harry was concerned, anything she did was all right and anything she wanted she deserved."

14

So they married, and Leona Roberts, high-powered real estate broker, "the best in the business," as she had called herself, became Leona Helmsley, whose business now became the care, protection, and enhancement of Harry Helmsley, who became the creation of myths and legends: Harry Helmsley as public man basking in the spotlight, as *bon vivant,* as man-about-town, as fun-loving party-goer, as king of the dance floor, as friend of the famous and powerful, with Leona Helmsley traveling at his side.

Suddenly, Harry Helmsley, who for more than forty years had been married to his business, whose business had been his occupation and his preoccupation, who had had time for little else, and his new bride were part of that set of the "beautiful people." Three or four times a week, they danced the nights away, cheek to cheek, Harry crooning ballads into Leona's ear. They accepted any and every invitation just so long as there was a band and a dance floor. Harry had always liked to dance; it had been the one thing he and Eve had in common. But this was something different. When he was on the floor with Leona, there was a new sense of unity, as though they knew instinctively what each would do, and there was spring in his step and the years seemed to fall away,

And every March 4, Leona threw a ball of her own to celebrate Harry's birthday. It was her way, she proclaimed, of showing the world that she was "just wild about Harry." So sure was she that everybody else was, too, that she named those affairs the "I'm Just Wild About Harry" birthday parties. The two hundred invitations were eagerly sought, and few were ever turned down. The guest lists read like a who's who of American rich and famous: presidents of Wall Street investment firms and leading banks, mayors and governors, senators and congressmen; trendsetters in the arts and entertainment; even the Roman Catholic cardinal of the New York archdiocese. "Cardinal Cooke," she would boast, "calls us the best team in Manhattan. And we're not even Catholics." Those Leona thought of as enemies or rivals were barred from the celebrations, of course. Mayor Ed Koch, for instance. For a time, Donald and Ivana Trump. Her list was a long one.

The celebrations always began up in the Helmsley's aerie on top of the Park Lane. As guests stepped off the elevator, they were greeted by a butler who pinned on their lapels a large, brightly colored pin proclaiming, "I'm Just Wild About Harry." He himself was always at the center with his own pin, "I'm Harry." After cocktails and hors d'oeuvres and mounds of imported caviar served freely around the gardenia-strewn and multicolored lit pool-in-the-sky, the party would adjourn to the Park Lane's ballroom. Awaiting them there was a lavish banquet at tables adorned with centerpieces commemorating the love of Harry and Leona. The year of Helmsley's seventy-fifth birthday, for instance, in the middle of every table was a pair of miniature dolls, eighteen pairs in all, each twelve inches tall, representing famous couples, real and fictitious, of history—John Smith and Pocahontas, Antony and Cleopatra, Rhett Butler and Scarlett O'Hara, Louis XV and Madame DuBarry, Tarzan and Jane, Napoleon and Josephine, Pinkerton and Madame Butterfly, L'il Abner and Daisie May, Cinderella and Prince Charming, Romeo and Juliet, Fred Astaire and Ginger Rogers, the King and Queen of Hearts, Fay Wray and King Kong, Adam and Eve (complete to fig leaves, Eve barebreasted), and more. All were as exact replicas as research could make them—except for the faces. On top of every

male doll was the visage of Harry Helmsley, and on top of
every female the features of Leona.

As she celebrated him, so he celebrated her. He was forever telling her how brilliant and beautiful she was. "My
husband likes to tell me I look like Ava Gardner when she
was young," Leona would tell an interviewer, though she
herself thought she photographed more "like Jackie Kennedy, or Anne Bancroft in *The Graduate.*" And together
they boasted to almost anyone who would listen of their
sexual prowess, of their love life together, as though no one
else could approach the ecstasy they achieved.

In 1977, as July 4, her birthday, approached, the story
goes that she turned to Harry and said, "So, what are you
going to do for me this year?" His reply: "Wait and see."
And on her birthday the lights that bathed the Empire State
Building were no longer white. He had changed them to red,
white, and blue, an ostentatious public display of his affection.

She would later say, "The only thing that Harry ever indulged me with is sheep," referring to the four sheep that
would later roam the grounds of their estate in Greenwich.
In fact, he denied her nothing. She had an outsized appetite
for designer clothes, many made for her by Julia Creations.
"She's fabulous," Leona would say. "She has the taste of
a Paris designer. I want her to be recognized." To that end,
she ensconced Julia in a suite at the Helmsley-controlled
Graybar Building. As for shoes, she had pair after pair. If
not quite on the scale of Imelda Marcos, the collection was
impressive, nevertheless. To accommodate her steadily
mounting accumulation, she took over another suite in the
Park Lane and turned it into closets.

He bought a jet and gave her free hand at redecorating it
to her own taste, which is what she did, sparing no cost.
The entire interior, from bulkheads to ashtrays and seat
buckles, was coated with gold leaf.

He gave her diamonds and rubies, emeralds and sap-
phires, rings and bracelets, necklaces and pins. The Park

Lane penthouse was adorned with paintings by Dufy and
Pissarro, collections of jade, and Steuben glass, a sixteenth-
century Buddha, a custom-made Scalamandré carpet. And
more and more and more.

And in public, their abiding love and admiration for each
other was constantly on display, in deed and word. "The
best thing I ever did," Helmsley has said, "was marry her."

"I'm bright, but he's brilliant," she crooned. "I have
never heard a bad word about this man in my life. He is an
honorable man. Good looking. Cute. The sexiest. A good
sense of humor and tremendously romantic, and he's my
best friend. Every day I get up and turn to him and I say,
'Today is a good day because I'm with you.' "

It all seemed idyllic, as though nothing could ever jar the
eternal honeymoon. But there was a dark episode, too.

In November 1973, married only a little more than a year
then, Harry and Leona Helmsley jetted down to Palm Beach
to spend the Thanksgiving holidays in their Palm Beach
Towers penthouse, a luxury condominium he had developed
overlooking Lake Worth. On Saturday evening, November
24, instead of going out on the town to pursue their passion
for dancing, they spent a quiet evening at home and, according to Helmsley, went to bed about 11:30. About two
hours later, he would say, "we were suddenly awakened by
someone in the room leaning over my wife." Leona began
to scream and struggle, and the intruder clamped something
over her nose and mouth to smother her. "I struck out at
this person, she did, too, and knocked this person down.
I'm not sure whether it was a man or a woman. Obviously
it looked like a prelude to a robbery. When we chased her
or him, we got stabbed. My wife got stabbed in the chest
and I got stabbed in the arm. The person fled and I called
the switchboard and the girl got me an ambulance."

The police and the ambulance responded. Both the
Helmsleys were rushed to Good Samaritan Hospital in Palm
Beach. Harry was treated for a minor wound in the right

Harry and Leona Helmsley took special pleasure in a night on the town, particularly if there was a dance floor and a band. (Marina Garnien, Black Star)

An early photo of Leona Mindy Rosenthal Panzirer Lubin, before she added Helmsley. (AP/Wide World Photos)

Lawrence Wien, friend and partner of Harry Helmsley, perhaps the strongest business influence on him. Behind him, the Empire State Building which Wien bought, and gave to Helmsley to run. (*The New York Times*)

Harry Helmsley wanted to build skyscrapers on park land when he bought Tudor City. The residents let Helmsley know just how they felt— and many observers agreed. (Chester Higgins Jr., *The New York Times*)

The Helmsleys launched a new advertising campaign to celebrate the renaming of their hotels— and the ascension of the Queen to rule them. (AP/Wide World Photos)

A pool in the sky was a feature of the Helmsley penthouse in their Park Lane Hotel. (Joyce Pupkeen, *The New York Times*)

Dunellen Hall, The Helmsleys' weekend retreat, included a ballroom as well as indoor and outdoor pools, visible behind the house. (Sygma)

The Helmsleys' troubles begin, as they are arraigned on income tax evasion charges, along with two top aides. Front row, from the left, seated: Joseph Licari, Frank Turco, Leona Helmsley. In front of her sits Harry Helmsley, with attorney Gerald Feffer to his right. (AP/Wide World Photos)

A grim and ill Harry Helmsley on his way to court in the grips of two law enforcement officials. (AP/Wide World Photos)

An uncharacteristically drab and distraught Leona Helmsley leaves court with her attorneys and bodyguard. (AP/Wide World Photos)

Frank Turco, once Leona Helmsley's right-hand man. (AP/Wide World Photos)

Judge John M. Walker, who presided at Leona Helmsley's trial. (AP/Wide World Photos)

Joseph Licari, once Harry Helmsley's chief aide.

James DeVita, Assistant United States Attorney, in charge of the prosecution.

Leona Helmsley, beset by a media army, leaves federal court after her conviction. (Michael Schwartz, *New York Post*)

forearm and released. Leona, however, was not quite so lucky. The knife had penetrated her chest, and while the hospital said she was in satisfactory condition, she was held in intensive care for three days, and then released on November 28.

The police investigation turned up little. Nothing had been taken from the penthouse. There was no sign of forced entry. The weapon, a twelve-inch kitchen knife that was part of the Helmsley apartment's cutlery, was found on the building's grounds below the Helmsley's bedroom window. There were no suspects, neither Helmsley able to identify anyone, and no one was ever arrested.

But a cloud hovers over the entire incident. Police and court records in Palm Beach have disappeared and Palm Beach authorities say they have only the haziest recollection of the episode. There are, however, some neighbors of the Helmsleys who have a recollection of those days. There are stories that spread widely through the winter playground of the wealthy in the ensuing days that there had been a long delay between the moment of the attack and the call down to the switchboard, that it had not been instantaneous, as Helmsley said.

And there was the story that the Helmsleys, particularly Leona, were sure the attacker had been either one of their employees or a family member of one of those employees. "They were after jewelry," Leona has asserted positively.

"We all heard that explanation," says one of their neighbors, "and we heard that they knew exactly who it was, only they didn't want to press charges because they felt sorry for the people and they didn't want a scandal. But, you know, somehow it just didn't sound quite right and we always wondered just what did happen."

Unlike many of his fellow real estate and construction magnates, his name appeared on nothing he owned. "Harry Helmsley would never have named a building for himself in

his life,'' Leona said, praising his modesty. "You don't
puff.''

In 1978 that changed. The man once content to reside in
the shadows was now a public man. For the first time his
name was carved on the facade of an edifice. The New York
Central Building, which he had frugally changed to The
New York General Building, he now refurbished, gilding its
clock and ornamentation in gold leaf, illuminating its spire
in emulation of the Empire State Building. And then he
renamed it The Helmsley Building. "I thought,'' said
Leona, whose influence on him had become decisive, "that
was a suitable mark for him.''

Indeed, even *The New York Times* had nothing but praise.
"Now it is The Helmsley Building,'' the paper said in an
editorial, "restored by Harry Helmsley, the real estate developer, to its original quality. . . . Modernists who for
years spurned the building's fruity classicism now genuflect
before the richness of its materials and details. With a newly
illuminated top, the building joins the architectural light
show of eccentric spires that is New York's crowning glory.''

But there was increasing evidence, too, that the darker
impulses in Harry Helmsley—the greed, the arrogance, the
overweening ego—always there but held at least partly in
check, were now being given free rein under Leona's influence. The one-time rent collector who had hounded the poor
in Hells Kitchen was in a position now, with all his riches
and all his power, to hound and prey on anyone, and he did.

These were the years when the situation at Parkchester
and Tudor City and elsewhere was becoming steadily exacerbated as Helmsley took an ever more intransigent stance
toward the demands of his tenants. He had never been
known for subtlety, or for the ability to bend in the face of
pressure, public or private. But before the arrival of Leona,
though he had sometimes raged in private, his public posture had usually been that of the gentleman willing at least
to listen to arguments. Now he was showing a different face,
a more unyielding one that exuded, to the dismay of his

public relations people charged with enhancing his image, a public-be-damned manner.

This now was the Harry Helmsley who would tell the people in Tudor City and the public at large, "I can't afford a park."

This now was the Harry Helmsley who, when questioned about the plight of New York's middle class in the face of spiraling apartment costs and rents and a shortage of affordable housing, could snap, "There's always trailers down South and used housing, though not in the best areas. This is what a lot of people are going to have to get used to."

But not for Harry and Leona Helmsley. The middle class might be relegated to trailer parks. The Helmsleys would have palaces.

One night in 1974, Leona has said, "Harry came home and he said, 'What do you think of the Villard Houses for a hotel?' I said, 'You're crazy.' He said, 'Come and look.' I did. I said, 'Harry, it's a *palace!*' "

15

LEONA HELMSLEY WAS right. The Villard Houses were, indeed, a palace. A High Renaissance palace, to be precise. A visitor from Rome would have been struck immediately by the resemblance to the Cancelleria, built between 1483 and 1511 and attributed to the great Renaissance architect Bramante, and with good reason: The Villard Houses had been modeled after Bramante's masterwork.

The houses were one of the irreplaceable treasures in a city whose past was vanishing under the onslaught of the wrecker's ball, replaced by sterile, monolithic Bauhaus clones.

Actually six brownstone mansions joined in a U-shape around an interior central courtyard, the Villard Houses were built between 1882 and 1886 on the Madison Avenue block front from Fiftieth to Fifty-first Streets for the financier, railroad promoter, and sometime journalist Henry Villard. The first major work of the renowned architectural firm McKim, Mead and White, they marked the beginning of a Renaissance revival in American architecture, a departure from the then prevalent romantic and Romanesque styles. In reality, the mansions were not designed by any of the famed partners, Charles Follen McKim, William Rutherford Mead, or Stanford White,[1] but by a draftsman named Joseph Wells,

---

1. White's own architectural masterpieces have been overshadowed by the romantic legend surrounding his murder (ironically in the old Madi-

a modest man who later turned down an offer of a partnership in the firm, saying he found enough fulfillment at his
drawing board.

Whatever the vagaries of history, the firm created nothing
less than a monument to grace and good taste. And its status
as a priceless landmark was recognized by both the New
York City Landmarks Preservation Commission and the National Register of Historic Places. Not only the exterior design was hailed, though. Grand and graceful as it was, it
was more than matched by the interior.

The critic Brendan Gill, who was chairman of the Landmarks Conservancy, a private group dedicated to preserving
the city's design legacy, called the interior ''the richest and
handsomest set of rooms for entertainment then in existence
in New York and perhaps in the entire country.'' Morrison
Heckscher, curator of the American Wing of the Metropolitan Museum of Art and president of the New York Chapter
of the Society of Architectural Historians, said the south
wing contained ''without question the finest late nineteenth
century interiors left in New York of national importance.''
And hailed by all was the famous richly gilded Gold Room
with its two huge murals by John LaFarge, called *Drama*
and *Music*.

Those rooms moreover were filled with an aura of those
who had wandered through them over the years. After Villard's death in 1900, they were the home until 1931 of Mr.
and Mrs. Whitelaw Reid, the publisher of the *New York
Herald Tribune* and later Ambassador to the Court of St.
James's. After the Reids departed in 1931, new owners took
over parts of the buildings, among them Joseph P. Kennedy,
who later sold his Villard holdings to the publishing company Random House, which used it as its headquarters. In
1948, the remaining sections of the Villard Houses became
the property of the New York Archdiocese of the Roman

son Square Garden, which he had designed) by Henry Kendall Thaw, the
husband of White's mistress, Evelyn Nesbitt.

Catholic Church; the rear of its St. Patrick's Cathedral rises directly across Madison Avenue. For the next twenty-five years the houses would serve as executive offices for the archdiocese. And so on any given day in offices on one side of the central courtyard one might have found Francis Cardinal Spellman or Bishop Fulton J. Sheen, and in offices across the courtyard, Random House's publisher, Bennett Cerf, talking to such Nobel Prize winners as William Faulkner or Eugene O'Neill, or going over the galleys of the first American editions of James Joyce's *Ulysses* or Marcel Proust's *Remembrance of Things Past.*

In 1971 Random House, having merged with several other publishing companies and having grown severalfold, found its quarters in Villard Houses too small. Accordingly, it sold its holdings to the archdiocese and moved into larger and more modern offices in a new skyscraper a few blocks away.

And then the archdiocese itself found that it, too, had outgrown Villard Houses and the buildings abutting them to the east. It built a new twenty-story edifice on First Avenue and moved its offices there.

The question, then, was what to do with the now vacant landmark. The buildings, of course, had inestimable value as architectural gems. But for those concerned with business and not art, what was far more valuable were the air rights above the Villard Houses and the church-owned buildings behind.

In 1974 the archdiocese found what it considered a solution to its problems: Harry Helmsley. He was anxious to take the entire package, buildings and air rights, off the archdiocese's hands, especially when all of it would cost him a mere $1 million for a ninety-nine-year lease. He knew precisely what he would do with them once they were in his pocket. He would build a hotel, a palace soaring at least fifty stories. It would be for Leona.

Ever since his initial foray into hotels, the purchase of the St. Moritz, he had thought hotels an extraordinarily fertile field, one well worth cultivating. Lawrence Wien might have hesitations, but Harry Helmsley had none, especially as his troubles at Parkchester, Tudor City, Parkmerced, and other residential and business properties began to multiply. Hotels were a different proposition altogether. Instead of troublemaking tenants who stayed on year after year in price-stabilized apartments, hotel guests rented rooms for only short terms, paid whatever the market would bear, and rarely complained.

The world of hotels, then, was for him. He already had in his portfolio the St. Moritz, the Carlton House, and his special pride and joy, the Park Lane. A year earlier, in 1973, he had tried to buy the renowned Plaza Hotel, offering $7 million in cash and the assumption of the existing $11 million mortgage to the then-owner, Sonesta International Hotels. At first Sonesta seemed willing, but then complications arose and the deal fell through.[2] Now, instead of buying, he would build the hotel of his, and his wife's, dreams.

But what would become of Villard Houses once they fell into his hands? They might have an intrinsic value for posterity far beyond their material worth, but to retain them and build his palace around them would be, he thought, not merely difficult but very expensive. What he wanted was simply to turn them into rubble and start anew. But that might not be practical, might even be impossible, given the buildings' status as landmarks. An uproar was sure to result when any such plans became public.

He would instead try to save some of the buildings, for,

---

2. Two years later, in 1975, the Plaza was sold, to Harry Mullikin and his Westin Hotel chain. Mullikin spent an estimated $200 million renovating and refurbishing the hotel over the next decade, then, in 1987, sold it, along with the rest of his Westin chain, to a group of investors, headed by Robert M. Bass, a Fort Worth oilman, and Hiroyoshi Aoki, head of a Japanese construction company. The price for the Plaza alone: $250 million. The investors, though, held the Plaza for less than a year. In 1988 they sold it to Helmsley's archrival, Donald Trump, for $400 million, more than twenty times the price that Helmsley might have bought it for in 1973.

after all, "the Villard interiors are absolutely stunning and I would love to use them for some of the hotel's banquet facilities." As for the rest, he couldn't really say, because "the project is still at the drawing-board stage," on the easels of his favorite architect, Richard Roth, who had designed the Park Lane. "I think," he was to say, "it is important that you have an architect that realizes you are a commercial developer, as I am. In the final analysis, if the building doesn't make a profit the architect hasn't served you. I've seen many a monument that is a monument to the architect but a disaster for the developer." Few doubted what he meant. If Harry Helmsley had his way, the Villard Houses, or at least most of them, would pass into history. The original sketches revealed just what Helmsley wanted— a sheer-walled glass tower.

Helmsley was not going to get his way, though, not if those who cared about the past had anything to say about it. After one look at the Helmsley-inspired drawings, the screams of outrage rose to a crescendo. The way Helmsley and his architect envisioned the new hotel, the back section of the Villard Houses would be sliced off and razed. Only the facade facing the Madison Avenue courtyard would remain, serving as an entrance to a characterless fifty-two-story tower that would rise behind it. The tower's piers would run vertically, a sharp contrast to the horizontals of the old mansions, and would be sheathed in travertine, a material used at Lincoln Center and so thought by some to bestow instant class to any building. In this case, however, travertine would certainly not enhance the Villard Houses' brownstone exterior. And atop the tower, as atop the Park Lane, would be arches, which led some critics to call the whole thing merely an overblown Park Lane, and others to liken it to a McDonald's in the sky. Those arches, architectural critic Paul Goldberger derided, seemed "an attempt to be pretty at a scale that is not very hospitable to prettiness."

Bizarre as many found the exterior designs, even more grotesque did they find the plans for the interiors. Helmsley and Roth wanted to cover a main floor in travertine, a decidedly flat surface that would sharply clash with the texture of the Villard facade being retained as an entrance. And then they were simply going to gut the entire Villard interiors, claiming it was just too difficult, despite Helmsley's original public expressions, to work them into their scheme. As for the two sides of the Villard U, they would merely be detached, have no connection with the new hotel, and be rented out separately to the highest bidders.

It was appalling. "If New York cannot find a better way to preserve the Villard Houses than the current plan for a new hotel that would amputate them in part and ignore the rest, then all that much-touted talent in the fields of art and finance that this city is supposed to have is a myth," stormed *The New York Times*. "A plan of this poverty of imagination and paucity of standards cannot be the only course. . . . It seems obvious that some of the city's great minds had better start coming out of their boiserie (if there is any) in its banks, law offices, and cultural institutions to find the answers. Square footage may be the ultimate beauty in real estate, but that is a limited measure of a city's soul."

In January 1975 the city's Landmarks Preservation Commission, which had to give its approval before any changes in a landmark building could be made, told Helmsley that while it would give him the right to use the air space to build a hotel on the site, he had better go back to the drawing board and come up with something that did not do so much damage to these priceless structures.

So Helmsley and Roth went back to the drawing board, and four months later came up with a new set of plans, which they were sure would be just right. Gone were the Park Lane arches on top. Gone, too, were those vertical travertine piers; in their place was a smooth bronze-colored facade with horizontal accents that would supposedly be in harmony with the Villard design. And on the side streets, Fiftieth and Fifty-first, at the base of the tower, were three four-story arched windows encased in dark stone, theoretically as complements to the arched windows of the Villard Houses.

The exterior was an improvement. Anything would have been. But in the new design, the interior would still be almost entirely gutted, including the famed and revered Gold Room. Even a last-ditch proposal, offered with sighs of resignation, to save it by turning it into a bar had been spurned by Helmsley. The Gold Room was on a different level from the hotel lobby, he said, and so the idea of joining it to the lobby with stairs "would not work because you can walk down into a bar, but you can't walk up going out of it." To which one observer replied, "Then build an escalator."

Helmsley's facetious explanation was no more acceptable than his plans. Once more *The New York Times* took umbrage. "The city cannot afford to settle for this kind of willful failure and conceptual bankruptcy; the architectural and environmental costs are too great. The 'new' solution remains no solution at all. It should go back to the drawing board."

And the newspaper's architecture critic, Ada Louise Huxtable, one of the most respected voices in the field, devastated the design and those who had promulgated it in a long critique that was at once scornful and melancholic.

> All this, including the demolition of the spectacular Gold Room of the south wing, is to be done in the name of the economic efficiency of a hotel plan that offers no indication of anything better than the standardized, overreaching mediocrity that goes under today's "luxury" label. . . .
>
> Nobody except Mr. Helmsley and Mr. Roth seems to feel that the Gold Room is expendable. The double-height, barrel-vaulted, balconied room with its La-Farge murals, sculptured wall detail and generous gold leaf is unequivocally magnificent; it is also the last of its kind in New York. It is easy to visualize the kind of impoverished design that will replace it. The dec-

orating clichés of the modern American hotel are vacuous, pretentious and immutable.

In fact, it is hard to figure out what anyone has been doing in the four months between the first and second versions submitted to the Landmarks Commission. The current proposal has a new and less offensive tower, but it is far worse along the side streets with overstated arches in fake brownstone to "match" the Renaissance Villard facades, and the Gold Room is still scheduled for demolition. By any measure except computerized investment design, the results are a wretched failure. . . .

Any architect worth his salt knows that this is not an insoluble problem unless someone wants it to be insoluble. Nor does the matter of protecting the old while building the new provide insurmountable costs or engineering considerations. After examining plans and elevations, the AIA [American Institute of Architects] suggested solutions. "How often," the architects asked, "can a new structure so easily annex so distinguished a space?"

The impression that remains is that the hotel "experts" find it easier to stick relentlessly with stock solutions than to make the different levels work within their economic game plan. There is a brand of hotel gnomes, turned out by hotel schools, supplied with a stock of formulas that is currently defacing the country, and the world. The fact that the hotel might gain immeasurably in beauty, quality and individuality, and this could ultimately be an economic asset, is apparently beyond the comprehension or concern of anyone involved. . . .

One comes reluctantly to some inevitable conclusions. The architect, whatever his restrictions, has done an appallingly bad job. The developer, whatever his intentions, is inflexibly wedded to formulas that he evidently will not relinquish or modify for values that he fails to perceive. He will not, in short, invest money or creativity in a superior solution. No calculations are being made in terms of image, quality and civic pride—which can also be a profitable formula. It is, alas, a state of mind. And it determines the state of the city, as well.

After that double-barrelled blast from the city's most powerful architectural opinion maker, a blast echoed by a legion of other influential voices, including the Catholic archdiocese, which came under heavy pressure from large and important contributors to do something to save the Gold Room at the very least, Helmsley had no choice but to return once more to that drawing board. The new plans emerged in September 1975, and lo and behold, the Gold Room was saved, to become part of the hotel's public space as a cocktail lounge. There were other changes, too, some of them greeted with sighs of relief. The two wings would no longer be detached and rented separately; now they would be saved and become part of the hotel, with at least some of the preserved rooms open to the public.

"To Mr. Helmsley," now wrote a mollified Huxtable, "for these extra efforts, we raise a glass. (Considering that the 1886 Villard Houses are mint Age of Elegance McKim, Mead and White, it has to be vintage champagne.)"

The bitter battle was now over. The final Helmsley plans were approved by the Landmarks Commission with only a single dissent, from Commissioner Chester Rapkin, who, while acknowledging that the Villard Houses had "the gross misfortune of occupying one of the most valuable sites in the city," said he was opposing the Helmsley plan in the hope of drawing public attention to "the fact that we are standing by while our precious architectural heritage is being destroyed by the onslaught of the market."

So Leona and Harry's Palace, all fifty-one stories, all thousand-plus rooms, was to become a reality. And it would be, he promised, not just a hotel but the greatest hotel in the world. He wanted construction to begin without delay. He was going to put up some of the estimated $65 million construction cost himself, he said (the estimate would quickly go up to $73 million, and before long go up again and again), and he would go out and look for investors to provide the rest.

To raise that necessary money, Helmsley turned to the tried-and-true formula perfected by Lawrence Wien. He set up a syndicate, with himself as the general partner. But even using that formula, money was not easy to come by in 1978, at least not at home. Inflation was beginning to gallop, and spiraling interest rates were making domestic investors leery and drying up once available sources. Moreover, some had hesitations about going into a deal with Harry Helmsley. The widow of the vice-president of a major insurance company, a man charged with investing the hundreds of millions of dollars available to his firm, remembers Helmsley assiduously courting her husband whenever they met, taking him aside for long conversations, even calling on occasion at home. Though Helmsley had approached him in the past with investment deals, and he had listened to the proposals, he had always hesitated and then decided against. This time, though, there was no hesitation. He spurned every Helmsley approach and one evening told his wife, "Putting money with Harry Helmsley is just too great a risk. He's probably the last guy I'd want to be partners with."

Still, foreigners were beginning to buy into America, lured by what they saw as potential bargains in a country where inflation was driving prices ever higher. And so Helmsley found his limited partners abroad. The French investment bankers LePercq, de Neuflize and Company brought together a group of European money interests, "big hitters," one lawyer calls them, and they agreed to put $16.5 million into the Palace as limited partners, with the possibility of throwing in another $6.5 million if legitimate costs ran higher than the Helmsley budget then proposed, in exchange for fifty percent of the profits. That left $56.5 million still to be raised. Helmsley himself anted up $6.5 million, hardly the major personal stake he had implied he would make. For the $50 million balance, he turned to the mortgage market and found takers, lured at least possibly by a stroke of good fortune. The New York City Industrial and Commercial Incentives Board gave him a tax abatement, meaning that even before construction began he was being relieved of an estimated $200,000 in taxes on the Villard Houses blockfront and once the Palace was built, the initial abatement would amount to an estimated $1.5 million, fifty percent of the taxes that might be due, with the abatement declining in stages until the full taxes were due after ten years. That tax relief, of course, was not just a stroke of generosity on the part of the city authorities. Helmsley had said that with taxes what they were and costs rising steadily, he might have to abandon the whole project if he didn't get that abatement.

Late in 1978 construction on the Palace began. No expense would be spared to make it, as Helmsley promised, "the greatest hotel in the world." And during the two and a half years of construction, Leona Helmsley would emerge from the shadows to take her place as a power in her own right, a queen, on the throne beside her husband.

It had been apparent to those who had seen her since her marriage in 1972 that while she gloried in her new prominence as the wife of Harry Helmsley, still she was not satisfied to remain merely his helpmate. She was too ambitious for that, too covetous of power. The world of selling real estate no longer interested her; she had outgrown it. So, where better to establish her own kingdom than in a palace, or, more specifically, *the* Palace?

Helmsley, who would deny her nothing, did not deny her this. It would be her job to make the Palace all they had dreamed, and forget the cost. To help her, he turned to Sarah Lee, head of Tom Lee, Ltd., and the widow of its founder, Tom Lee, a man who had won Helmsley's admiration with his interiors for the Park Lane.

Despite those marital ties, Sarah Lee was anything but a logical choice to take on such an awesome undertaking. Until her husband's death in an automobile accident in 1971, when she was suddenly thrust into the leadership of his then-leaderless company, she had never done interior design. She had worked in magazine publishing, copyediting at *Vogue*, editing at *Harper's Bazaar,* and running *House Beautiful* as editor-in-chief. She had by necessity learned on the job, guided by the experienced staff at Tom Lee, Ltd. "Mr. Helmsley asked me when he gave me the job what I'd done like this. I said, 'Nothing. I don't think anyone has.' He loved my honesty. He said, 'I guess you'd better do it.''

Leona Helmsley offered no objections then. But she did not know Sarah Lee. Had she, Helmsley might well have gone in a different direction. From almost the day they began work, the two women acted as though the other had some deadly contagious infection. "Let's just say Sarah Lee and I don't have any love for each other,'' Leona Helmsley would say later. "She made me mad. She piggybacked my husband. She took this job and got forty other jobs because she had the Palace." And Sarah Lee would say with a touch of sarcasm, "She should be called Leona the Magnificent. She really wants total opulence, and I think she's going to have it.''

When Harry and Leona had said they would spare no expense in creating a palace, they had meant it. Sarah Lee had not realized just how much they meant it, or how completely Leona would be in control of every aspect to ensure it. When it came to designing the hotel dining room, for instance, Leona vetoed Sarah Lee's plan, which she thought too modest, and insisted that the walls be covered in Florentine silk and the woodwork rubbed in silver. In addition, Lee says she designed a single-tiered canopy that resembled a giant tiered bird cage for the Fiftieth Street entrance. (Leona disputes the claim, saying the canopy was designed by a committee.) The Helmsleys looked at it and asked how much one tier cost. She told them $100,000. The Helmsleys said they'd take two.

And so it went. Sarah Lee would come up with a design, and then Leona would lard it or change it completely. The situation finally reached a crisis over Lee's designs for the bedrooms. Leona hated them, thought the colors too bright, the furnishings too obvious, the embellishments not classy enough. She complained to Harry and offered to do some model rooms herself and have Sarah Lee do some and then let Harry choose the best. Leona's rooms were in light pastel colors, the two bergère chairs in every room upholstered in velvet or cord, the night tables and dressers oversized and covered with marble, the headboards of the king-sized beds sculpted wood, adorned with gold and silver and upholstered, the bedspreads quilted cotton or satin; the bathrooms were huge, marbled, and to ensure the comfort and enjoyment of the guests, contained trays with a lint remover, two toothbrushes, bottles of shampoo, moisturizer, colognes, shaving lotion, shoehorn, sewing kit, bottles of Saratoga water and glasses, and special soaps. Everything was sumptuous, everything expensive, everything outsized. Lee's rooms were somewhat more modest. Leona won the contest, of course; it was one she knew she could not lose.

So, Leona was given the power to design all the bedrooms in the Palace. Lee was given more menial jobs. All the same, the friction did not end, but grew ever worse. Finally, as work on the Palace was nearing the end, in a rage Leona accused Lee of not showing her the rug purchased for the hotel lobby, and then sued the decorator. "I had shown her the rug three times," Lee insisted. Then, in one of those grandiose shows of Leona Helmsley power, she fired Lee on the day before the hotel was to open and rescinded her invitation to the grand opening-night party she was throwing for three hundred "close" friends. Lee would tell one interviewer that was all right with her because she hadn't intended to go to the party anyway, that months before she had accepted an invitation to a gala in Los Angeles for the very same night. To another reporter, though, she said, when she got the news, "I went to bed and cried for days."

And then it was done. On September 15, 1980, the Helmsley Palace, "the most magnificent hotel to open in New York in a century," according to its own press release, was ready to receive its first guests. Or at least to accept its first guests, if not quite ready. "The grand opening had been set for a long time," explained the reservations manager, "and we really couldn't put it off." There was scaffolding everywhere as workmen, piling up the overtime, tried frantically to finish the job. From the twenty-third to the fifty-first floors, none of the rooms was ready. Rates for rooms on floors ten to twenty-two had been marked down for these first days from $120 a night to $96.50, though even there things were not quite as they might have been. The housekeeper on one floor, for instance, was seen fiddling with a lock on the room where all her tools were stored. She couldn't get it open, no matter how hard she tried, "and I have all the passkeys," she complained. And down below, everything was still in a state of confusion. None of the Villard House rooms was ready, nor were most of the other public attractions. The only place to get a meal or a drink was in the bar. Still, the hotel was in business at last.

Soon the scaffolding was down, the workmen departed, the room rates back to what the Helmsleys proclaimed as the highest in the city (from $120 for a single room to $480 a night for a two-bedroom suite, with the price for a suite in the penthouse "available on request"), and the curious were flocking through the portals to goggle at what the Helmsleys had wrought, and, perhaps, in hopes of getting a glimpse of the lady whose notoriety was rapidly becoming legend.

There was, indeed, plenty to admire, at least inside. The exterior, whose soaring curtain wall rose directly behind the

Villard Houses, was nothing less than an example of monumental mediocrity, an eyesore. But the interiors seemed to justify all the battles and what Helmsley claimed was an additional $10 million pricetag. Everything that had been saved had been cleaned and repaired with meticulous and scrupulous thoroughness. The eye was dazzled by the beauty and splendor of the frescoes, and all the Tiffany and La-Farge and St. Gaudens art. The oval-shaped ballroom, replete with nineteenth-century paintings hung between decorated pilasters, was far beyond the usual pedestrian hotel modern. The grand staircase was a sight to behold, especially since it led to the saved—despite Helmsley's resistance—and restored Gold Room, from whose balcony musicians played at tea time. The old dining room with its carved mahogany polished to a gleaming satin had been turned into a magnificent bar. The lobby walls gleamed with red Verona marble, and on the entrance balcony there was a St. Gaudens mantel in matching marble that some critics called the sculptural equal of a larger and more elaborate one in the garden court of the Metropolitan Museum of Art's American Wing. And now Harry Helmsley would stand in the lobby, look around, and say, with pride and no recollection of his own efforts in the past, "What started as a commercial venture ended as a work of art."

16

NO ONE GLORIED in the triumph more than the Helmsleys. Harry boasted that he had created a work of art that would turn a handsome profit. For her part, Leona was Queen of the Palace. More than that, she was Empress, ruler of all the Helmsley hotels.

For now there was a burgeoning chain. Even as the Palace was rising, the Helmsleys were carving an expanded place for themselves as hoteliers. The first outward grasp was barely noticed. At the end of 1978 they reached outside Manhattan and picked up the twenty-five motels known as the Hospitality Motor Inns, then owned by Standard Oil Company of Ohio. The cost was a mere $36 million. But now the Helmsleys were in the hotel business in the East, the South, and the Midwest.

Much more the subject of comment was their decision to build yet another hotel in the heart of Manhattan just a year later. The fiscal crisis that had held New York City in peril was coming to an end. Tourists and conventioneers, who had shunned the Big Apple, not only because of its expensive accommodations and outrageous restaurant prices but equally because of fears that it was dangerous to walk the streets, were returning, not in a trickle but in a torrent. New York, with all its glittering enticements, had become a magnet once more. After years of empty hotel rooms, luxury and first-class ones were suddenly at a premium, and there was an accelerating demand for still more.

By the late 1970s the tourist business was booming as

never before. Before the end of the decade, more than 17.5 million people, including more than 2 million foreigners, would be spending their money annually in New York's watering holes, hotels, theaters, and other attractions, more than double the number at the beginning of the decade. The boom showed no sign of leveling off, but rather every indication of a continued upward spiral. Conventioneers, who provided about twenty percent of the hotel income, were back in record numbers, more than 4.5 million of them, nearly double the number in 1973. "In the mid-1970s, we were all saying New York could not go above 850 conventions because all the hotel and conventions sites were filled," said Bjorn Hanson, the manager of Lavanthol and Horwath, an international consulting and accounting firm which specialized in hotels. "But last year [1979] we had 910 major conventions and they're still coming."

All those tourists had to have places to stay, but as the influx turned into a flood, those good places were becoming harder to find. In 1946 there had been about two hundred thousand hotel rooms in the city. Twenty-five years later, only half that number remained, and even at this level the occupancy rate barely reached above sixty-five percent, which meant that many a hotel was teetering on the edge. Indeed, when the Royal Manhattan on Eighth Avenue in the heart of the theater district went under and was about to be auctioned off, Cecil Day, head of Days Inns of America, spurned a proposal that he take it over and turn it into a good budget-priced inn. Maybe the city could use one, he said, but he had little confidence in New York's future and he doubted whether anyone else did, either.

Harry Helmsley had built his Park Lane in the middle of this crisis of confidence and had made a success of it. But that was an exception. Then came the turnaround. Hotel occupancy rates soared, reaching 73.3 percent in 1977, climbing to 78.5 percent a year later, and nearing 85 percent by 1979. "The magic mark in the hotel business is 75 percent occupancy," said one expert, "and when it rises higher than that, everybody's eyes light up and there's a flurry of refurbishing and building.'' In order to spur this construction, the city began offering those 50 percent real estate tax abatements to anyone who would build new hotels. They would not only provide places for the visitors to stay but would also guarantee thousands of new jobs in an industry that had been losing jobs steadily for years. Those jobs might be low-paying ones for the most part, but they were jobs nevertheless.[1]

The takers of those generous city tax breaks lined up. For starters, the Milford chain did what Cecil Day wouldn't do, took over the Royal Manhattan, and transformed it into the thousand-room Milford Plaza. Times Square was also getting an even bigger hotel, a 2,200-room Marriott-Marquis, brainchild of Atlanta architect-developers. The New York Hilton was adding 1,200 rooms to its already huge inn on the Avenue of the Americas. Hilton International, in what some saw as a gamble and others called a foresighted move sure to pay off, had a twenty-two-story, 825-room hotel, the Vista International New York, rising in lower Manhattan, hard by the World Trade Center and Wall Street, the first new hotel in the downtown area in decades. Donald Trump, a man whose ego was equaled only by his grandiose plans and accomplishments, acquired the spot next to and above Grand Central Terminal, where the decaying Commodore Hotel had once stood, and at a cost of $100 million built his ornate thirty-story, 1,400-room Grand Hyatt New York. Fifteen blocks north, just off Fifth Avenue, the deluxe Park-

1. During the previous decade, membership in the Hotel, Motel and Club Employees Union, Local 6, of the A.F.L-C.I.O. had fallen from thirty-five thousand to just over twenty thousand. With the turnaround, membership was on the rise once more. Pay for most hotel workers, of course, hardly put them in the higher income brackets. ''The industry pays miserably,'' one expert noted. All the same, these jobs, which required little or no skill and little or no ability to speak or understand English, were a route into the economic mainstream for the immigrants flocking into New York from Latin America, Asia, and elsewhere.

er Meridien rose, with 600 rooms for transients and 100 apartments for permanent residents. And it was just a beginning.

Harry Helmsley was not one to be left in the rear. He had the Palace on the rise. And he had something else, too. A block east of Trump's Grand Hyatt and a few blocks west of Helmsley's embattled Tudor City stood an abandoned New York vocational high school site. The site was up for grabs and Helmsley grabbed it in late 1978. On it, he announced, he would build another new hotel, if not quite in the same class with the Palace, still a decidedly upscale one. It would rise thirty-eight stories, would contain about eight hundred rooms, and would cost $42 million, most of which Helmsley said he himself would provide, for a change. Designed by Helmsley's favorite architect, Emery Roth and Sons, it would celebrate the union of Harry and Leona Helmsley, the first names of Harry and Leona. But Leona thought to call it the Harlee (for she was sometimes called Lee) would be just too "déclassé." So she decreed that the name should end with a "y," and so it did and so the name of the hotel became Harley. (That name, though, would adorn the hotel for only a short time. By 1985 it became the New York Helmsley, another building named after the man who only a few years before would, as his wife said, have thought it "puffing" to put his name on a facade.)

And who was chosen to rule the Harley and the Helmsley Palace and all those other hotels and motels that were coming under the Helmsley aegis? Not some experienced boniface, but Leona Helmsley herself. In June 1980, on the eve of the opening of the Helmsley Palace and the Harley, Harry Helmsley decided it was time to reward his wife publicly for all the good work she had done. He named her president of all the Helmsley-owned and -controlled hotels in and out of New York. "It was Harry's idea," she said modestly. "He thinks I work hard. He thinks I deserve it. He said I was so involved in the business I might as well be president and he'd be chairman. He said the best thing about it was that the board of directors meeting was over when we got out of bed.''

And with that, the legend was born. The name Leona Helmsley would soon be as synonymous with luxury hotels as Frank Perdue with chickens and Aunt Jemima with pancakes. Until then the public at large had known her, if she was known at all, as the wife of Harry Helmsley, the real estate tycoon. All that was now to change.

Joyce Berber, president of the advertising agency Berber Silverstein and Partners, was hired to develop a campaign to sell the Helmsley Palace by selling Leona Helmsley. Following Leona about the hotel, Berber watched her turn from informative guide into raging imperious virago. Oblivious to all, or perhaps with a calculated deliberateness, Leona launched into one of what soon would become familiar tirades, screaming at maids and others about beds that were not made just the way she wanted, about towels that were too thin, accepting no excuses, using language, as the song goes, ''that would make a sailor blush.''

It was the inspiration Berber needed, and once she had it, she knew she had a campaign. Leona Helmsley was the Queen, and her hotel was ''the only Palace in the world where the Queen stands guard.'' The initial conception might have come easily, but transformation from seed to reality was not painless. Nothing was done without Leona's approval, and her approval was hard-won. There was hardly a planning meeting that she did not attend, regard the ads being laid out, and proceed to put forth ideas she was certain were better. Everyone quickly perceived that what she ordered had better be done. ''She was always very specific about what she wanted, about what she liked and didn't like,'' says one of her later ad executives, ''and she was sure her ideas were the best.'' Adds another in the ever changing parade of Helmsley ad managers, ''She comes on as extremely forthright, but that sometimes turns into brutality. She's icy, without compassion, she is remorseless and pitiless.''

Soon the ads spewed forth, filling page after page, week after week, month after month in the classiest glossy magazines, in newspapers, everywhere. Berber was responsible for the first series, though always with Leona Helmsley looking over her shoulder. Then, as was her wont, Leona fired her, then rehired her a short time later, and then summarily fired her once more upon discovering that Berber had taken on the account of Donald Trump. Not only was she fired for that venal infraction, but Leona tried to evict the agency from its $6,930-a-month suite of offices in the Helmsley Palace. Berber was not disturbed. "We took a calculated risk when we took on the Trump account. But every single day we're glad we did. We just can't get over what a likable, decent type of person he is. She was nice to us, but you don't want to stand by and watch her tyrannize the peons."

The image that emerged should be familiar to all. Leona Helmsley in gold lamé gown, diamond tiara crowning her head, poses beside the grand staircase leading to the ornate lobby of the Helmsley Palace, or in a long red skirt and low-cut black top with huge puffed sleeves—the Queen standing guard. It was just the beginning. Later, a smiling Leona Helmsley, wearing a high-necked white blouse under black, strands of precious gems around her neck, would stand before a background of some famous palace somewhere in the world: "In India, it's the Taj Mahal. In New York, it's the Helmsley Palace." "In Denmark, it's Rosenbourg. In New York, it's the Helmsley Palace." "In Spain, it's the Alhambra. In New York, it's the Helmsley Palace." "In Scotland, it's Balmoral. In New York, it's the Helmsley Palace."

But merely being the Queen of the Palace was not enough. She would, as well, be celebrated in another series of ads as empress of all the Helmsley hotels. The gracious ruler with impeccable taste catered to every need and whim of her guests, down to the most minute detail. Head-and-shoulder shots of Leona in a pastel suit with heavily padded shoulders, a smile frozen on a face so heavily retouched it looked unreal, were superimposed on a background of a hotel bedroom, bathroom, public room. You people out there, the ad stated, would think these rooms were immaculate, but not Leona Helmsley. She knows what's amiss and she does something about it because "being perfect is what our hotel is all about."

Then Leona appeared in a red suit with a huge black tie, seated at her desk in her office in the Park Lane Hotel, examining her mail and penning an answer.[2] The letter from Leona Helmsley, president of the Helmsley Hotels, was displayed boldly across the page just beneath her picture.

To a couple who just had a new baby:

> Congratulations and thank you for the birth announcement. I doubt, however, whether I can attribute the conception of your baby to the amenities in your suite as you mentioned in your letter.
>
> This time Mother Nature deserves the credit. May I humbly suggest that you name the baby "Lane" to celebrate a night you'll always remember.

Or, to a couple who had lost a valuable pin:

> Thank you for telling me how delighted you were to pick up the phone as soon as you returned home to learn that we found your wife's new $58,000 pin— before either of you even realized you'd lost it. Edith,

2. At one point, she claimed to receive more than two thousand letters a week from people who had stayed at her hotels, mainly from those who wanted only to express their appreciation for the wonderful treatment they had received. She said that she read them all and answered most, a feat that boggles the mind. Even if she were a speed reader and dictator, at a rate of five minutes to read and answer each letter, she would have needed just about an entire week, twenty-four hours a day, just to keep abreast of the correspondence.

the day maid, discovered it in your room and called
our security people, who, in turn, called you.

I'm relieved that your visit to New York had a happy
ending, and hope you'll be staying with us again soon.
Considering all the places in New York where you
could have lost your pin, we're pleased it was on the
floor of your room—though I never thought I'd have
to apologize for our thick carpeting.

A great many people found those ads in keeping with
Leona's growing reputation for the brazen and tasteless.
Classy they weren't. Open to parody and satire they
were, as the columnist Russell Baker was quick to demonstrate, writing to an imaginary house guest:

Dear Mr. Kegmore: You will be surprised to find
that you lost a sock during your New York visit, and
delighted to hear that we will be mailing it under separate cover as soon as it returns from the laundry.
When I think of all the places in New York where you
might have lost a sock, I'm pleased that you selected
our living room, though I never thought I'd have to
apologize for the commodious size of our sofa cush-
ions.

Others thought the ads nothing to laugh about, especially
those with a stake in the Helmsley Hotels. At one point, the
limited partners in the Helmsley Palace complained about
them to their attorney, said they were embarrassing and
asked if he could put an stop to them. He couldn't, he explained. They had other, far more serious problems to deal
with, and, besides, the Helmsleys had the right to promote
the hotel as they thought best, without interference.

"I never wanted to do all this," she would protest coyly.
"It was the ad agency's idea. I only agreed after Harry gave
his approval." In some quarters, including those of some
of her ad agencies, her protest was viewed with skepticism.

Still, egotistic and crass as the ads might be, they did the job they were designed to do. They propelled Leona Helmsley into the spotlight, made her famous in her own right, made her admired by some and the envy of many. And they helped make her hotels a success.[3] Some in the hotel business who were appalled by her style nevertheless praised the results she got, though a number were quick to point out that the Helmsley hotels spent far more per room in advertising than anybody else. Others noted that while many of the Helmsley-run inns operated at the profitable seventy-five percent or higher occupancy rate, they were mainly the ones in which the Helmsleys had the highest personal stake and did not have to share much of the income with limited partners. The hotels in which limited partners had put up most of the money did not fare quite so well. Even the Helmsley Palace, after the initial influx of curiosity seekers, hovered under seventy percent occupancy, though the Helmsleys claimed it was nevertheless a money-maker, its outlandish rates more than compensating for the empty spaces.

3. There were, at one time, it was claimed, forty-seven hotels in the chain. Over the years some were sold off, and by the beginning of 1989, there were twenty-three headed by Leona Helmsley and a number of others outside her immediate jurisdiction, if not control. Those for which she claimed direct responsibility included: in Manhattan, the Helmsley Palace, Helmsley Park Lane, and New York Helmsley, which were built by the Helmsleys, as well the refurbished and modernized Helmsley Carlton House, Helmsley Middletowne, and Helmsley Windsor; the Sheraton-Huntsville in Alabama; the Harley of Hartford/Springfield in Connecticut; the Harley of Orlando, the Colonial Plaza Inn-Orlando, and the Harley Sandcastle of Sarasota in Florida; the Harley of Atlanta in Georgia; the Harley of Lexington in Kentucky; the Harley of Grand Rapids and the Harley of Lansing in Michigan; the Harley of St. Louis in Missouri; the Harley of Cincinnati, the Harley of Cleveland-Airport West, the Harley of Cleveland-East, the Harley of Cleveland-South, and the Harley of Columbus in Ohio; the Harley of Pittsburgh in Pennsylvania; and the Sheraton Inn and Conference Center in Wisconsin.

So, as she had predicted years before, Leona Roberts, now Leona Helmsley, had become rich and famous, admired and envied. She was more than a mere innkeeper. She was a Queen, a gracious hostess concerned about the comfort and well-being of her guests, who might stop them in the lobby, or drop in on them in their rooms to make sure everything was as they wanted and she demanded. She might write to them when they departed, call them unexpectedly at their homes, always solicitous and caring. If powerful friends needed a place to stay in an emergency, she would open her doors to them. Thus, when former mayor Robert F. Wagner and his wife Phyllis, who had become friends of the Helmsleys, found themselves temporarily homeless after fire damaged their East Sixty-second Street apartment, Leone put them up in a $1,250-a-night suite at the Helmsley Palace, on her, for nearly a month, until repairs were completed.

Yes, everybody now knew Leona.

17

LEONA HELMSLEY HAD always had a darker side, though, witnessed by those who had come within her orbit, but now, with all the wealth and power of the Helmsley empire at her command, it emerged full-blown, its shape increasingly grotesque.

A benevolent monarch she might be with the transients who passed through her hotels as visitors. But for those who worked for her, she was an autocrat who brooked no argument, who tolerated no fault or mistake, however small. What once might have been barely tolerated as the idiosyncrasies of a driven woman were magnified, given free rein. "It's fun," she would say. "I think I'm an empress."

An empress who demanded absolute perfection from those who served her. "You have to expect that people who work for you will do a good job," says a former executive at the Park Lane. "Everybody makes mistakes now and then. But with her, if you screwed up once, she treated you like garbage. She never complimented anyone. You don't develop loyalty that way, but I don't think she cared." As a result, the turnover rate of employees at the Helmsley hotels has been far higher than anywhere else in the industry. People came and went as through a revolving door, some fired, for cause or on a whim, some quitting in disgust. "Regardless of how much money somebody pays you," says one of the latter, "there's only so much screaming and cursing and all the rest you can take." In fact, the only consolation was, as a one-time employee noted, "If you last six months working for her you can get a job anywhere because people figure you must be the best.''

And the stories, some perhaps apocryphal, most apparently true, of her tyrannical behavior, which some would say had the earmarks of deepening paranoia, began to multiply. One didn't have to be a psychoanalyst to see the signs. ''She never trusted anyone, she was suspicious of everyone, she thought everyone was out to use her and to get her,'' says a former associate. ''And the richer and more powerful she got, the worse it got.'' Says another: ''She can exude such warmth and love you feel you are being embraced by this rich, glamorous, sexy lady. Then, in an instant, she can turn so vicious and verbally violent that you are left flabbergasted.'' And still another: ''I've stood there when she's been screaming at people who an hour before were 'honey' and 'darling, here's some chicken soup and go see my doctor.' ''

It became nearly impossible during these years to go anywhere without hearing stories, multitudes of them, about the exploits of Leona Helmsley. Some were repeated so often that they became Leona-clichés. What disturbed many observers was how obviously the lady relished venting her power and instilling fear. She would display her rapid mood swings before reporters, interviewers, curious onlookers, anyone.

- Leona on an unexpected inspection tour enters a room, spots a crease in a bedspread, a piece of lint on the floor or dresser, a crooked lampshade, anything. She screams imprecations, obscenities: ''The maid's a slob. Get her out of here. Out! Out!'' And then explains, ''You're dealing with people who don't live here, whose name isn't on the building, who get away with what they can. I give them reasons to want to get away with less. If something is wrong the first time, I ask them to change it, the second time I ask an octave higher, the third time I ask the person if they want me to do it, the fourth time, if things aren't absolutely right, they're fired.'' About one particular maid she had verbally battered, she explained, ''She's one of my best employees today. And you'll never see that again, not in her rooms. Maybe someone else's, but not in hers.''

- Leona marches into the hotel dining room or kitchen, notices a busboy, a waiter, an assistant chef, anyone, turns violent and shouts, ''You, with the dirty fingernails, you're fired.''
- A man who once worked in the Park Lane restaurant remembers that she would often sit down and order something that was not on the menu. ''People were afraid to tell her we didn't have it, or that she couldn't have something. They would run out to the nearest store and buy it and run back with it and the chef would prepare it, and then she would scream at them because it took so long. She had a bad mouth, a very bad mouth, and she used a lot of foul language. A couple of times she even fired people because they took so long getting her something we didn't have. She had the attitude that she had so much money and so much power, she could see no reason why she couldn't have something she wanted, and if people didn't like the way she was, she wasn't going to change, she was going to change them.''
- At an afternoon tea one time, Leona was served by a recently hired young waiter who trembled in the presence of the fearsome lady. She noticed the rattling cups in his hand. ''What's the matter with you?'' she shouted, threateningly. ''Nothing, nothing, Mrs. Helmsley.'' As she glared, her voice rose

so everyone in the room could hear: "Get him out
of here!"

• Leona, hearing that a secretary who had spilled
something on her dress had dared send it to the
Helmsley Palace dry cleaner, raged that the woman
had cheated her, and fired her on the spot, though
she had worked for the Helmsley organization for
eight years.

• Leona, leading a reporter on an inspection tour of
the hotel kitchen, lashed out at the help because
loaves of bread were not covered and there was garbage on the floor where plates were being scraped.
Turning to the reporter, she said with a laugh, "In
the beginning, security wouldn't allow me in here.
There are knives, and phew, they hated me. There
was enormous turnover. Now my boys love me. They
have pride in working for us, and they make bigger
tips." Love, though, may not be precisely the word
Helmsley workers would use.

• On one occasion, Leona chased an executive down
the corridor after he told her he was quitting. To the
amazement and horror of the secretaries and other
executives, she screamed, "How dare you walk out
on me? I'm Mrs. Harry Helmsley. I'm Leona Helmsley."

If people quitting incensed her, firing them was,
on the other hand, an indisputable pleasure. "Harry's oldest and dearest employees," says one who
quit, "mostly men who had been with him for thirty
or forty years, she would pick at them and pick at
them until Harry would say, 'Yes, Leona, I will fire
them.' She was remorseless, a bird of prey."

The story that was current, with some evidence to

back it, was that anyone who had been with the Helmsleys long enough to collect on his or her pension program was in imminent danger of incurring wrath and being summarily fired. "She told me once," says a competitor, "that she needs fresh blood every year and a half or so."

- Employees trembled with fear when summoned to her office, one remembering that as she stood outside the door, she was "saying 'Hail Mary, full of grace, please let her not yell at me.' "

- At the end of a luncheon interview with a reporter, Leona became enraged when the waiter came with the check not enclosed in the customary leather folder. "Find it," she shouted, "or you'll be looking for another job."

- Leona moved the general manager of the Park Lane, where he had earned the reputation as one of the best hotel managers in the business, and installed him as general manager of the Helmsley Palace. But when he called, while on a vacation cruise, to wish her a happy birthday, she shrieked at him over the ship-to-shore phone that he was fired, giving no reason except that she wanted him gone.

- Leona, at one of her "I'm Just Wild About Harry" balls, was listening, smiling, nodding in agreement as a friend told a joke. When he finished, though, she glared at him, snarling, "I don't find that funny at all," and threw a glass of red wine across the front of his tuxedo.

- Leona was spotted at another party standing in the corner giving the finger to a man with whom she had recently had an argument over a business deal.

- Leona walked up to a competitor at one of her parties, broke into his conversation, and ranted at him, to the shock and embarrassment of scores of onlookers, accusing him of "doing business" while her guest.

• Leona, furious that Donald Trump and his wife, Ivana, with their own new showy hotels and flamboyant lifestyle, were stealing headlines and praise from the Helmsleys, and that Ivana was aiming to supplant her as Queen of the hotel world, feuded publicly with them and barred them from her "I'm Just Wild About Harry" parties. (Trump himself, though, denies that there was ever a feud. In 1988, he said Ivana and Leona get along and he considers Harry Helmsley "a good man and wonderful businessman." His opinion of Harry hasn't changed but about Leona he and his wife now have nothing good to say.)

• Leona gave beepers to her chauffeurs so that wherever they were, they would come racing when she wanted them. Beeping one on a Sunday morning, she became furious when he took some time answering. When she demanded to know where he was, and why he had delayed, he explained, "I'm in church, Mrs. Helmsley." Leona fired back, "You work for me now. You don't go to church."

• Leona coyly told Mike Wallace during her twenty-minute stint on *60 Minutes* that "the only thing Harry ever indulged me with is sheep." Waving her hand across the wide lawn of her Greenwich estate toward the four animals, she said with apparent affection, "One is Bo, one is Peep, one is Baa, one is Baa-Baa. Come here, Bo, it's your mother." Soon after Wallace and his CBS camera crew departed, though, she ordered the flock slaughtered and the chops distributed among the estate's servants.

- Leona, who incessantly roamed the Park Lane, constantly ordered new painting, new wallpaper, new furnishings, new everything, and hang the cost. Explaining why the Park Lane's manager and decorator had quit over an argument about carpeting, she said, "I thought the new carpet in the dining room should be as good as the old one was. They wanted something that would have saved three thousand dollars." Maybe so, but someone who had overheard part of that argument says, "Nobody in his right mind would have stayed after the language she used, not if they wanted to retain a vestige of self-respect."

The same woman who had no qualms about spending fortunes on her hotels, or herself, though, showed a distinctly miserly side as well. She was always trying to cut corners and save a few dollars here and there. It emerged full-blown in the events that surrounded the renovations at Dunnellen Hall in Greenwich, but precedents had already been established.

The most notorious came in 1986 when it was revealed that she had gone out of her way to avoid paying New York sales taxes on hundreds of thousands of dollars' worth of jewelry she bought at the exclusive Van Cleef and Arpels store on Fifth Avenue. Documents and testimony before a grand jury that indicted store executives for participating in a scheme to help customers (none of whom was indicted or even called to testify) evade the sales taxes detailed just what she had done and how. A regular Van Cleef and Arpels customer, Leona Helmsley had spent more than $485,000 on jewelry on just two purchases in 1980 and 1981, on which sales taxes of more than $40,000 were due. She made eight other large purchases later, the records showed. On every occasion the salesman said that she had told him, "I don't have to pay sales tax since I have a residence in Connecticut." She then walked out with the jewels while empty boxes were sent to an out-of-state address she provided. Another time, according to the salesman, she had laughed when she ordered him to ignore the sales tax and said, "That's how the rich get richer." Why didn't she pay sales tax? "She fully believed that the price she was paying for the jewelry was inclusive of sales tax," her lawyer said. "She had no idea at all that they [the store executives] were not paying any taxes that were due." And though she did have a residence in Connecticut (this was, however, before the purchase of Dunnellen Hall), she conceded that her legal residence was New York City. And so, caught, her excuses notwithstanding, she reached into her pocket and came up with the back taxes.

There were stories, too, though charges were never brought, that what she had done at Van Cleef and Arpels was a practice she had followed in the exclusive shops where she was a valued client all over New York. Remembers a woman who once worked as a salesperson at one of those shops, "One day I was writing up the sales slip for things she had bought. It wasn't all that much, just a few hundred dollars. I started adding in the sales tax, and when she saw what I was doing, she started screaming. They must have heard her all over Fifth Avenue. She used absolutely the vilest language you ever heard. She threatened to have my job. All because I was figuring that she owed maybe twenty or twenty-five dollars in sales tax. I couldn't believe it. Somebody else in the store told me she did that all the time if anybody tried to charge her sales tax. The thing to do was just forget it and put down some out-of-state address. We sent out the empty boxes, of course, but whatever she bought we had to send by messenger to her office or over to the Park Lane."

Oh well, some people said, everybody tries to get out of

paying sales taxes if they can. She just happened to get caught that one time. There are worse things.

Indeed. In the mid-1980s Harry Helmsley fell ill, seriously enough for him to be hospitalized. "We've never been apart for one night," he recalled later. "Even when I had to go to the hospital, she raised hell, made them bring in another bed so she could be in the same room with me. I liked it. It's a very comfortable feeling to know someone cares that much." Leona, of course, was no nurse, and if her husband had to be in the hospital, he had to have the best nurses round the clock. One of those private nurses remembers that week very well. She was ordered about constantly, peremptorily, her every move criticized. She was dispatched on errands far outside her normal duties. It was one of the most difficult nursing assignments she had ever undertaken.

When the day came for Harry to be discharged, Leona called the nurse aside, asked for her bill, which was something less than a thousand dollars, a pittance for people of the Helmsleys' station, and said she would send a check off immediately to cover it. Weeks went by and no check arrived. Perhaps Mrs. Helmsley, busy woman that she was, had simply forgotten. The nurse called the Helmsley offices to inquire. Leona's secretary heard her out, told her Mrs. Helmsley was a very busy woman and would get around to the payment when she had a moment.

Mrs. Helmsley apparently was so busy she kept not getting around to it. Two months went by, three, four, and no check arrived. In despair the nurse called again and asked when she might expect payment. After a lengthy pause, she was put on hold. Finally, the secretary came back on the phone. "Mrs. Helmsley says," she told the nurse, "that if you ever bother her about this matter again, she will make certain you never work in your profession again." She hung up. Shaken, intimidated by this bald use of Helmsley power, the nurse decided the wisest course was to let the matter drop.

Where was Harry Helmsley all this time, while his wife was spreading her power so widely, leaving fear wherever she went? He was watching it all. "He absolutely adores her," says someone who knows them both well. "It's apparent that as far as he's concerned, she can do no wrong. He gets a kick out of her. He thinks she's feisty. She adds spice to his life and he loves that, so she can do anything she wants and he'd never say nay."

There is another view, though perhaps a complementary one. "She gives the appearance that she does whatever she wants . . . as long as Harry wants it."

Indeed. They are a well-matched pair.

18

THE DECADE OF the 1980s was an age of unparalleled greed. This was a time when the amassing of millions, even billions, by any means at the expense of anyone was celebrated as a virtue, and the public flaunting of that wealth and the power that came with it was a natural concomitant. The ruling motif was more, ever more. The Helmsleys were in their element, symbols of an era.

But for all their notoriety and all their lavish and arrogant ways, their personal lifestyle could not conceal the dry rot in the foundation of the Helmsley edifice, any more than the arrant materialism of so many could hide the malignancy that was eating into the heart of the entire society. That decay had been there, gnawing slowly and steadily into the timbers. What had once seemed a solid structure began to show signs of crumbling.

For years, Harry Helmsley had gotten away with shoddy maintenance on the buildings he owned, controlled, or managed, ignoring complaints with his old standby, "I'm frugal. I don't throw money around." As his attention turned increasingly toward hotels, and his preoccupation ever more with Leona, the condition of his other properties deteriorated steadily. Tenants complained about chipped and cracked lobby floors and walls, about peeling paint, about reduced service, and more. Even on the first building he had named for himself, the Helmsley Building on Park Avenue, the gold leaf was scaling, the brass was dull and turning green, and graffiti were left on the walls.

With a growing frequency in the 1980s, Helmsley buildings became the targets of a steady progression of legal
complaints and lawsuits filed by disgruntled tenants, twenty
or thirty times as many as were filed against other large
business and residential landlords in the city. And investors
in Helmsley properties, too, began to sour on their partnerships with him.

Rewarding himself with profits, even outsized ones, was
one thing. He had been doing that for a long time. Now,
however, he no longer made any pretense, even boasted
about it. Did he ask more on apartment conversions than
the apartments were worth on the market? Did he cut services even below bare minimum in order to increase his
profits? Did he take disproportionate shares of profits when
buildings were sold? Did he play both ends, collecting broker's commissions from sellers when he headed a syndicate
of buyers and, at the same time, acted as the broker? Did
he do all these things, and more? He was hardly even de-
fensive. "I've been rich and I've been poor," he was fond
of saying in these later days. "Rich is better. I live the way
I am. I find I have more fun living that way. And I don't
harm anyone. Just because I'm in the real estate business
doesn't make me an ogre any more than if I were a used-
car salesman." It was, perhaps, a revealing analogy, given
the reputation of and public attitude toward used-car salesmen—and landlords.

But it was an attitude that was certain to lead to conflict.
In 1980, for instance, Wien and Helmsley decided to sell
the Equitable Building on Broadway in the financial district,
which a Wien syndicate, with Wien and Helmsley as general
partners and Helmsley as the broker, had bought in 1958.
Helmsley quickly found a buyer willing to come up with
$60 million for the property, and the sale was handled by
his Charles F. Noyes subsidiary. The limited partners in the
syndicate bristled when they found that Noyes's commission
was $2.5 million and Helmsley himself was taking an ad-
ditional 5 percent of the profits from the sale over and above

the share he got as a partner. They brought suit. Helmsley and Wien won, the judge ruling that since the limited partners had signed a form indirectly authorizing both the brokerage contract and the commission, their suit was without legal grounds.

Another group of limited partners sued a few years later, in 1983, when Wien and Helmsley sold the St. Moritz Hotel to Donald Trump for $31 million. Helmsley-Spear was the exclusive broker for the sale, and in addition to its commission, which was somewhat higher than usual, Helmsley cut himself in for another 5 percent of the proceeds. Once again the court ruled for Wien and Helmsley. Though the limited partners had not gotten all they might have out of the deal, the judge said, the general partners, Wien and Helmsley in this case, had no obligation to tell their limited partners why they were doing something. Their obligation was only to inform them of what they were doing.

Helmsley would not get his way, however, with his limited partners in that monument to himself and his wife, the Helmsley Palace Hotel.

The hotel was supposed to have cost $73 million to build. That was the estimate Helmsley presented to LePerq, de Neuflize and Company when he persuaded the French investment bankers to organize a syndicate of limited partners who would put up at most $23 million toward the cost (the other $50 million coming from a mortgage arranged with Helmsley's favorite lender, Metropolitan Life). In exchange for that stake and 50 percent of the hotel's profits, Helmsley would build, he promised them, the Eighth Wonder of the World, the greatest hotel on the face of the earth.

But the hotel didn't cost $73 million. By the time Harry and Leona Helmsley got through spreading the money around on all the changes they wanted and all the luxuries they thought essentials, the Helmsley Palace came in for more than $120 million. Faced with this rather substantial overrun, Helmsley turned around and demanded that the LePerq syndicate come across with another $20 million, nearly double its original investment, to cover those additional costs.

"He was used to dealing with disparate groups of limited partners," says a lawyer familiar with Helmsley, "large groups who individually put up minimal amounts of money, or at least not really substantial amounts, that added up to the total. The only thing they had in common was the investment. So he probably told himself, 'They're not going to fight me. They never do. They always give in because they don't have any choice.' He was counting on the old divide-and-conquer rule."

It didn't work out quite that way this time. LePerq had put together a small group of large investors, and they were not about to capitulate without a fight. They took the position that Helmsley had told them he had this great deal, that he had this extremely valuable piece of prime property that he had practically stolen from the New York archdiocese, and to build this magnificent structure all he needed was $17.5 million, or maybe another $5.5 million beyond that if costs went higher. Now he was telling them that he had spent so much more because that was what he had to spend on this jewel of a creation, and because he had spent it, they had to come up with half of that additional cost.

No way, LePerq responded. If Helmsley wanted to spend that much extra money, close to $50 million more, that was his problem and his responsibility. They went to Gerald Fields, a partner in the law firm of Battle, Fowler, Jaffin and Kheel, explained the situation, and asked him to take on their case.

Fields' first step was to ask for the Palace books to see just where the money had gone and was going. What his accountants discovered gave him pause. Harry Helmsley, it seemed, had been playing a few games to enrich himself at the expense of his limited partners, games that were, at the very least, "improper."

To do all the buying of furniture, fixtures, equipment, and other supplies, not just for the Palace but for all the other

Helmsley-owned and -controlled hotels and buildings, he had set up Deco Purchasing and Distributing Company as a wholly owned subsidiary in Orlando, Florida, and installed as its head Leona's son, Jay Panzirer, who had by then split from his wife, Ruth, and moved to the Florida city. Deco and Panzirer bought and bought, and billed and billed. How much of a commission they received depended, though, on just how much of a stake the Helmsleys had in the buildings Deco was supplying. According to Jay Panzirer's new wife, who would soon have large reasons to want to sing songs about the way the Helmsleys, Harry and Leona, did business, "If a building was owned one hundred percent Helmsley, Deco sold materials to it at one price. That price would increase as the percentage of Mr. Helmsley's stake in the building decreased." In the hotel business, a supplier's commission is generally in the neighborhood of 5 percent; when it came to the Helmsley Palace, Deco was collecting 20 percent.

The discovery of Helmsley's use of Deco led Fields and his accountants into a detailed examination of the entire convoluted operation of the Palace, and revelations about just how Helmsley managed to turn everything to his own advantage, and the disadvantage of the limited partners.

The LePerq syndicate had assumed, as it had every right to, that when it put its money into Helmsley's hands, the result would be a fully equipped hotel ready to welcome its first guests. But that wasn't the way Helmsley did things. The books, for instance, showed that among the $40 million in cost overruns, half of which the partnership was going to pay if Helmsley had his way, there was a $2 million item labeled "repair and maintenance account." What those repairs and maintenance were, it turned out, were opulent chandeliers and wall sconces for the public areas and bathrooms, costing $42,381; gold and silver detailing and another new chandelier for the Trianon dining room, at a cost of $112,714—the Helmsleys had been "very disappointed" with the looks of the room until these new additions—and a few other luxuries, ad infinitum. If Helmsley wanted to spend money on that kind of embellishment, that was all right with LePerq, just so long as the money came out of Helmsley's pocket and not theirs. That he had spent and committed far beyond his original estimate was, they maintained, his problem, not theirs. Further, they were sure, after going through the records, that he hadn't even contributed the original money to the partnership that he had promised. It was, they maintained, time for him to start taking some financial responsibility and risk, and stop looking to others to bear the whole burden.

Equally disturbing were the managing companies Helmsley had set up to run the hotel, which were charging fees that would surely eat into whatever profits the limited partners might expect in the future. He had set up, for instance, Supervisory Management Corporation as the entity that would actually run the hotel. And then he had the Palace enter into an agreement with a company called 9179 Equities Associates, which happened to be a partnership of Helmsley himself and Supervisory Management, to lease telephone equipment for six years at $31,116 a month and computers at another $11,182 a month.

He had set up yet another company, Basic Estates, Inc., from which the hotel leased for a period of three and a half years television sets, television stands, and refrigerators costing respectively $19,745, $1,731, and $1,865 a month for the Palace's rooms. When someone took a calculator and did some figuring, the results were distressing, to say the least. One Helmsley-owned company, for instance, was buying television sets in massive lots, paying, according to experts in the field, less than $300 a set. Then that company was leasing those sets to the Palace, and thus to the syndicate, for about $20 a month each, or nearly $800 a set over the term of the lease, a rather substantial profit going into Helmsley's coffers and out of the potential profits of the investors.

While the going rate for office space in prime locations

in New York was in the neighborhood of $40 a square foot, Helmsley leased from Supervisory Management 7,787 square feet of office space for himself and Leona on the Palace's fifth floor at $15 a square foot for inside offices without windows and $25 a square foot for offices with windows; the term of the lease was for ten years and there were no escalation clauses.

Harry Helmsley was thus playing decidedly conflicting roles. He was, with a very limited outlay of his own money, the general partner in one company, the Helmsley Palace Hotel, which owned the hotel, and thus was entitled to share equally with the limited partners in whatever profits the company earned. He also owned the company that operated the hotel, and its hefty fees cut into the profits he would have to share with his partners. He also owned various other companies supplying goods and services, whose high prices and excessive commissions sharply reduced potential profits of the hotel itself though pouring more money into his pockets. In essence, then, whatever the hotel might earn, it was a no-lose proposition for him and a no-win one for his partners.

He might well have practiced the same kind of duplicity on the partners in his other properties, especially those that had been largely financed by syndicate money, but others in the past had rarely challenged him. With LePerq, though, he was up against a very different kind of partner. LePerq had no intention of brooking such practices, no matter how often used, ingrained, and tolerated.

Not only was LePerq determined to fight Helmsley's demand for more money, they were also going to sue him for what they considered, at the very least, unethical practices in the hotel operations.

Helmsley, of course, was not unaware that his partners were looking askance at his demand for more money, nor was he ignorant of what they must be finding as they went through the books. He moved to head them off in the summer of 1981.

First, he invited them all on a private tour of the Helmsley Palace to see for themselves what he had wrought with their money, and then to a luncheon to celebrate it all.

Gerald Fields met that morning with the partners at LePerq's New York office on Park Avenue to plan strategy, how to deal with what would obviously be a prearranged "praise Harry" show at the Palace that day, and how and when to proceed with legal actions against Helmsley. The general view was that they would listen without emotion, and would not join what was certainly going to be a display of unadulterated adulation. When the meeting was over, the group walked the few blocks over to the Palace.

It was a show, indeed. The Helmsleys, Harry and Leona, were waiting for them, surrounded by a bevy of sycophants. The partners were taken on the grand tour, and the Helmsleys and their dependents oohed and aahed over the marvels. The partners, for the most part, kept silent, their faces and demeanor revealing nothing.

Then it was on to the luncheon. "We sat down for lunch at a horseshoe-shaped table," Fields says. "Harry was at one end, Leona next to him, and they were surrounded by their yes-men. The partners were down one side and I was at the very foot. All through lunch he would look at me, as though he was wondering who I was and what I was doing there. He knew." The meal was lavish, and when the dishes had been cleared and coffee served, Helmsley rose to make a speech. He welcomed his guests, the limited partners, and then, referring to his demand that they come up with another $20 million, he said, "I've heard that a number of the investors are unhappy with my request. They're ungrateful. I am building the world's finest hotel. I am a fair man and I will not be had."

When Helmsley was through, disciple after disciple leaped to his feet to proclaim Helmsley a prince of a man, second to none, a creator of wonders, in one of which they were now sitting. As the show went on and on, Fields began to grow concerned that all the praise might have a deleterious

effect on the determination of his clients. Helmsley kept
looking toward the group of partners, obviously hoping that
at least one would rise and join the chorus. At what seemed
a crucial moment, one of the LePerq executives motioned.
Helmsley recognized him. He got to his feet. Helmsley
waited. Everyone waited. The executive tossed off a non
sequitur that deflated those expectations. In an instant the
limited partners were all rising and heading from the room.
The lunch was over.

Then Helmsley knew for certain that he was in for a lawsuit. Having little taste for a courtroom, he took a different
tack. Under the terms of the partnership agreement, he and
the limited partners had the right to appeal to a panel of
arbitrators to resolve differences. Helmsley did just that. On
May 25, 1982, he filed for arbitration of his demand for the
additional $20 million from the syndicate. The next day,
Fields filed a lawsuit against Helmsley, charging the builder
with "self-dealing and other improper activities."
Among the allegations:

1. Helmsley improperly charged numerous items in
   excess of $2 million to the Partnership as operating
   expenses . . . which should have been paid for by
   Helmsley as part of his obligation to furnish a complete fully equipped hotel or as part of expenses
   attributable to other Helmsley properties
2. Helmsley improperly caused the Partnership to enter into lease agreements with affiliated entities for
   certain equipment necessary for initial equipping
   and operation of the Palace Hotel
3. Helmsley failed to contribute his required working
   capital to the Partnership
4. Helmsley entered into a lease . . . for 7,787 rentable square feet of office space on the fifth floor of
   the Palace at an unfair rate

5. Several improper acts [were] undertaken by Helmsley as general partner of the Partnership including
his retention of Deco, his affiliate, to purchase all
operating supplies for the Palace at excessive commission rates . . . and his selection of his personal
auditors as auditors for the Palace.

The lawyers for both sides met, as lawyers will, and
agreed to forgo a lawsuit and let the American Arbitration
Association decide the matter.

Since Helmsley had filed for arbitration of his monetary
demand first, his was the first side heard, then LePerq's
counterarguments. The three-lawyer panel of Robert P. Pat-
terson, Jr., Richard E. Keresey, and James D. Zirin, distinguished and respected lawyers all, didn't take long to rule
that Helmsley had no right to ask his limited partners for
any more money.

Fields and the LePerq group had that victory. It was not
enough. After the arbitrators' decision was in, Helmsley's
lawyers approached Fields and said, "You won. You won
big. You aren't really going any further, are you?" Fields
told them he certainly was, and handed them another copy
of the charges he had filed. Reluctantly, Helmsley agreed to
do something about the Deco commissions, cutting them
from 20 percent to 10 percent. But that was as far as he
would go.

So they went back to the arbitrators, this time to adjudi-
cate the LePerq claims against Harry Helmsley. For twenty
days in the spring and summer of 1983, the three attorney-
judges listened to the arguments and took testimony.

One of Gerald Fields' concerns as those hearings began
was that Helmsley would claim he was such a busy man,
controlling such a vast empire with so many aspects, that
he couldn't possibly be aware of everything done by his
subordinates. So Fields moved quickly to counter such an
assertion. His opening remarks to the arbitration panel were

larded with glowing comments about Helmsley's attention to detail, no matter how minute, his control of every aspect of his empire. "I talked about him as a truly outstanding man of real estate," he says, "how he knew everything that was going on everywhere, how nobody who worked for him did anything without his knowing about it, and how he always knew exactly what he himself was doing. I really laid it on. And then he turned out to be the best witness we had, and the worst witness for himself. When it came his turn to testify, his lawyer asked him, 'What do you think of Mr. Fields' characterization of you in his opening remarks?' I'm sure he thought Helmsley would be modest and protest that I'd reached too far. Instead, Helmsley rather preened and said, 'That's a modest statement.' I knew then that this was going to be a lot easier than I dreamed."

His task was made even easier by Leona Helmsley. Under Fields' questioning, she was evasive, searching for ways not to answer potentially damaging questions, and, he remembers, "trying to ooze charm. She thought she was being cute. She misjudged the audience." This was no jury of ordinary citizens who might be impressed by her reputation or won over by her pose of helpless female. She turned aside one of Fields' questions with a coquettish, "Mr. Helmsley tells me I'm pretty." The judges were three hard-nosed lawyers who had seen all the courtroom tricks used by witnesses a lot more experienced at the game than Leona Helmsley.

In October 1983, the arbitration panel handed down its decision. It was a nearly total victory for Fields and the LePerq group:

- Helmsley was ordered to pay the Palace Hotel partnership $757,616 of what the limited partners had called his "fraudulent" $2 million charges for "repair and maintenance."
- He was not entitled to charge the Palace and the

partners for the leasing and renting of various computers, telephones, television sets, television stands, refrigerators, and other items, and he was ordered to return nearly $2 million that had been collected by his various subsidiaries under those leases. The leases were ordered canceled, which meant an additional $2.2 million saving for the partners.

- He was ordered to pay the Palace and the partners $235,202, the difference over a two-year period between the rent he had been paying on the Palace office space and the fair market rental value of that space, and in the future he would have to pay a fair market rental. Not only that, the lease would also now provide that he be charged for increases in real estate taxes, increases in the pay of porters, and that the electricity he used in the offices, which had been figured in as part of the rental, be metered. Those changes in the office leases would bring in about $2.2 million.

- Deco was ordered to refund to the Palace and the partnership all fees it had collected in excess of 5 percent, which meant a payment to the hotel and the partners immediately of about $600,000 and a savings of over $2.8 million in future commissions.

- Helmsley was ordered to get rid of the auditors who had been keeping the books and replace them with new ones acceptable to the limited partners.

- In a final blow, Helmsley was ordered to pay the arbitrators' fees and expenses and the first three days' expenses of the American Arbitration Association and 60 percent of the remaining expenses, which meant a cost to Helmsley of $135,575 for having the dispute arbitrated.

• The only balm to Helmsley was the decision by the arbitrators to dismiss the LePerq claim that he hadn't put up his share of the money.

In all, it was a bitter defeat. Harry Helmsley, the master builder, the real estate and hotel giant who had for so long gotten his way, who had ridden without thought over all those who had tried to stop him, had been humiliated.

19

THERE WERE TWO very different men in Leona Helmsley's life. First and foremost there was her husband, Harry. And then there was her son, Jay Panzirer.

However one might view his means of achieving success, Harry Helmsley was the most important man in his field, one of the richest men in America, a man with outsized ambitions and unyielding determination, a self-sufficient man.

Jay Panzirer was a man of limited ambitions and few successes, a man who walked through life and left little mark of his passing, a man dominated by and dependent on his overbearing mother.

He was in Florida now, settled into an expensive ranch-style home in one of Orlando's better neighborhoods, complete with live-in housekeeper, gardener, pool man, handyman, and day maid. The house did not belong to him, though, but to Deco Purchasing and Distributing Company. It was one of the perks of running the Helmsley-owned supply firm for his mother and Harry Helmsley, buying all the necessaries to furnish the vast Helmsley properties, taking orders, doing as he was told.

Showing initiative was not for Jay Panzirer. He learned the hard way that it was not only not expected of him, it was not wanted, and if he tried the result would surely be trouble—for him. It happened once, early in 1980. Panzirer decided to boost Deco's business by going out and winning new accounts, hotels that were not owned or controlled by the Helmsleys. He reasoned that if he could do this, Deco would grow and everybody would profit. He might have had a second reason, as well. He had just married again and perhaps he thought a little show of independent enterprise might impress his new bride.

Whatever the reason, Harry Helmsley didn't see it Panzirer's way. Deco was his own private preserve, and he wanted to keep it that way. Dealing with outsiders might well call some of its practices—the high prices it charged and the commission it received from Helmsley hotels, for instance—into question. And so when he learned that Panzirer was in the midst of those negotiations, he and Leona rushed to Orlando. In a rage he confronted Panzirer, ordering him to break off the dealings immediately. Panzirer sought support and protection from his mother. This only served to make Helmsley angrier. He turned on both mother and son, and raged, ''One more time and you're both out!''

Mimi Doyle, who had just become Jay Panzirer's latest wife, remembers the scene vividly. ''This was the only time,'' she says, ''I've ever seen Harry stand up to Leona.''

Panzirer and Mimi Doyle had met at a party celebrating the opening of the Helmsleys' new Harley of Orlando hotel in July 1979. She had arrived in Orlando seven years earlier from the New York suburbs, where she had been raised in an upper-middle-class Irish Catholic family. Divorced and with no children of her own, she was supporting herself as a sales representative for a local FM radio station. Noticing her at that opening night gala, Panzirer sent over a bottle of champagne—Dom Perignon 1966, she remembers. Within a month they were engaged to be married. She backed out. He persisted. She accepted another proposal and in January 1980 they were married.

Along with her new husband came a ready-made family. Panzirer's oldest child, Craig, approaching adolescence and, like many children his age from broken families, in conflict with his mother, moved in with his father and his wife. Moreover, though his previous marriages had ended badly,

neither Myrna, by then happily remarried and living in the
New York area, nor Ruth, still in California, placed many
obstacles in the way of Panzirer's other three children visiting now and then, when he asked. Both felt it would have
been unfair to the children if they prevented them from
knowing their father. And then, as a friend of Myrna's says,
looming in the background was their grandmother, Leona
Helmsley. She adored her only son. He was her heir. If she
had had little to do with her grandchildren over the years,
still there must have been the unspoken consideration that
his children, should she come to know them, might one day
come into their share.

From all indications, the marriage of Mimi Doyle and Jay
Panzirer was a happy one. "We had both been married before," Mimi says, "and had finally found something that
made us both very happy. Jay and I were virtually never
apart. When he was in the office, he was calling me five
and six times a day. We would have lunch together regularly. About the only thing he did that I didn't join in was
play golf on Saturday afternoon. We were in tennis leagues
together. We went to charity balls and parties, traveled regularly all over the country." Indeed, they became a prominent part of the Orlando social scene.

If Harry Helmsley was distant with his stepson and Mimi,
that was understandable. Jay, after all, was little more than
an errand boy. And Jay was a rival for Leona's attention and
affection. Because of his wife, Harry might give the younger
man a good-paying job, but affection or even respect was
another matter entirely.

As for Leona, who had disliked her previous daughters-
in-law, she seemed taken with the blonde, attractive Mimi
Doyle. She showered Mimi with gifts, telling her, "You've
made my son very happy, which makes me joyous." Writing to her, she effused, "If I could pluck a star from the
sky, I would give it to you." Perhaps not a star, but everything else. "If I bought a pair of shoes that I liked," Mimi
says, "she'd buy me more in every color." And not just

shoes. Leona bought sterling silver, a tapestry, expensive furnishings, and knickknacks of all kinds. Among the precious jewels and diamonds, she gave Mimi a twenty-four-karat topaz ring set in white, pink, and yellow gold and encrusted with 136 diamonds, costing eighteen thousand dollars at the Fifth Avenue jeweler Buccelatti, to celebrate the *bar mitzvah* of her grandson, Craig. She and Mimi were alone in Leona's Park Lane dressing room, Mimi remembers. "She was having her hair done, makeup done, that sort of thing. She said, 'I have something for you,' and she went into the closet. In the closet, she had a vault. She came out with the ring. She handed me the ring." At that reception following the *bar mitzvah,* Leona grabbed Mimi's hand, held it up to show the ring to an Orlando newspaper reporter and photographer, and boasted that she had just made this expensive gift to her daughter-in-law.

There were visits back and forth. The Helmsleys flew the Panzirers to New York for the opening of the Helmsley Palace. When the Helmsleys stayed at their condominium in Palm Beach, which was usually every other weekend, the Panzirers were invited over for dinner, and the Helmsleys traveled to Orlando to see them. The two couples even went together, with grandchildren, to Sea World and Disney World. "No bodyguards," Mimi says. "These were relatively normal folks." There are even photographs taken in New York and in Florida of a warmly affectionate Leona with her grandchildren, though Mimi and others say that Leona displayed little affection or concern for any of those grandchildren. Not only were they a reminder of her own advancing years, but, like so many children, they refused to give her the unquestioning devotion she expected and instead spoke their minds. In one incident, she turned to her youngest grandchild, Wally, and asked coyly, "Who's the prettiest girl in all the world?" Wally naturally responded, "Mommy." Leona went into a tirade, shouting at him, "That's nonsense, I'm the prettiest girl in the world."

She was so filled with fury that Wally, then only six, burst into tears.

The family harmony, however tenuous, was brief. Jay Panzirer was not well. Arrhythmia is a degenerative, irreversible heart disease. He had already been hospitalized twice for lengthy periods as a result, and his condition was worsening. Early in 1982 he flew to Boston to see a heart specialist. The report was not good. His heart was deteriorating rapidly, and little could be done. He returned to Orlando to resume a normal life for as long as he could. On Wednesday, March 31, during a business lunch at the Orlando Harley, he complained that he was not feeling well, excused himself, and went to a room in the hotel to lie down for a while. When he did not reappear, someone went to look for him. He was on the floor of the room, beside the bed. He had had another heart attack, this one so massive that it had apparently hurled him from the bed onto the floor. He was dead.

"One of the most difficult things I had to do," Mimi says, "was tell his mother that her son was dead." The Helmsleys were en route in their private jet to Palm Beach for a long weekend when Mimi called. "I got Harry and I told him. Then I told Leona. She broke down and screamed." She also, according to someone on board, turned to an assistant and screamed, "Don't let them print how old he was."

The death of a child, no matter at what age, is one of the most traumatic experiences anyone can undergo. Children are supposed to survive their parents. A parent's hopes and dreams are invested in the child. In this, Leona Helmsley was no different from anyone else. No matter how well informed of her son's condition, she was not prepared for his death and she was of a moment stripped of him, stricken, bereft.

There are stages of grief. First comes denial. It didn't happen, it couldn't have happened, not to my child. Then

there is rage, a savage and unthinking striking out at everyone and everything in search of someone to blame. Why are
you, who cannot be compared with my child, still alive? In
this Leona was no different from anyone else who has lost
a child, and so much of what she did in the period that
followed, though exceptional in its cruelty, is at least par-
tially understandable as part of the pattern of mourning.

She was stoic at the funeral in Orlando. When it was
over, she said she wanted his body flown to New York for
a memorial service and burial at Woodlawn Cemetery. Mimi
agreed, though she would have preferred burial in Orlando.
Leona, Harry, Mimi, Craig, and other mourners boarded
the Helmsleys' jet for the flight back to New York, but the
casket would not fit through the cargo doors of the jet. Harry
Helmsley quickly arranged for the shipment of the casket in
a commercial plane. For some strange and unexplained reason, he listed himself on the death certificate as Jay Panzirer's father.

After the services, friends and relatives returned to the
Helmsley suite at the Park Lane. Gathered were Leona,
Harry, and Mimi; Jay Panzirer's four children, Craig, David, Meegan, and Wally; Leona's surviving sister, Sylvia
(who died a short time later); and her brother, Alvin Rosenthal, who worked as an executive for the Helmsley organization; Mimi's mother and brother, John, an aide to
Connecticut's then-senator Lowell Weicker; and a few others.

The atmosphere, as it always is on such occasions, was
strained, people fumbling to find something comforting to
say. Suddenly the rage that had been building within Leona
as her son's death became real to her erupted. She turned
on Mimi. "I will destroy you," she said icily. Then she
turned on her grandson Craig. "You killed your father,"
she accused.

Craig became hysterical. (Seven years later he still would
not talk with strangers about his grandmother or his father,
saying only, "We don't want to be involved.") Even as

Mimi tried to comfort him, Mimi's mother gathered her and the children and hurried them away.

A few days later, Mimi and Craig Panzirer returned to the Orlando home she had shared with Jay for a little more than two years. Almost immediately she learned that Leona's threats were not idle. She and Craig and the other children, those close to Jay, had become targets for retribution. She was served with an eviction notice. Deco, which owned the house, wanted it back and wanted her out, without delay. She immediately called Helmsley, who happened to be at the Orlando Harley, and he soon appeared at the house.

"I asked Harry why he was doing this. And he explained to me, quite in detail, that the house was worth X amount of dollars and he could sell it for X amount of dollars and realize such and such a profit. He said he could no longer afford to amortize the cost of leasing the house to Jay against Jay's salary. His last comment was, 'So you can see I need the money.' "

Mimi pleaded with him, if not for her sake then for Craig's. It was April, and Craig was in his last year in junior high school. Less than two months remained before his graduation, and it would be too cruel to force him to move then, especially after the shock of his father's death. Helmsley bent just a little. They could stay in the house, he said, until Craig's graduation, then they would have to go. "But," says Mimi, "they sent someone in to do a complete inventory of my house, including my underwear. There's a list on file somewhere of the number of bras and panties, the sizes and colors."

It was just the beginning. Jay Panzirer's estate was a tangled web. For years he had neglected to make a will, and only on his return from Boston with the news of his deteriorating condition had he finally gotten around to having his lawyer draw up a document leaving the proceeds from his estate to Mimi and Craig, his oldest son. An appointment was made for Jay to come in and sign it, but he died before that date could be kept. Thus, with no legal will, he was considered to have died intestate. Under Florida law, that meant that whatever he had should be divided, after payment of just debts, half to his widow and the rest equally among his four children.

But the Helmsleys didn't see it that way. Not long after Helmsley's eviction notice Mimi got another legal paper from the Helmsleys. This one was a demand for payment of the cost of shipping Jay Panzirer's body from Orlando to New York and an additional $1,419 for the expense of the New York funeral.

The court papers piled one on another in quick succession. Leona claimed that Jay had borrowed $100,000 from her in mid-1980 to buy a share of stock in the Helmsley Palace, and she sued his estate for that principal plus interest.

Then Leona went after a $67,233 money market account with Shearson-American Express. The day after her son's death, the account was put in Mimi's name when a document containing Panzirer's notarized signature was presented to the brokerage house. The Helmsleys charged that Jay Panzirer's signature had been forged. Though Shearson executives, the notary, and friends all said that Jay had arranged the transfer a week before his death, the Helmsleys hired a handwriting expert to back them up and sued to grab it.

Helmsley's company, Deco, sued to recover $37,500 paid to Panzirer's consulting firm, JRP Associates; the money, it said, was an advance against salary and fees, and since he had died before he could perform the services for which the money was earmarked, the money must be returned.

Leona sued again and again, to get back sterling silver, paintings, a video recorder, a backgammon table, loose diamonds she said Mimi had stolen from the couple's safe deposit box, even a quilt she said belonged to her as part of the furnishings of the Orlando home. She even sued to recover the Buccelatti topaz ring, asserting it had been a loan, not a gift.

For the next five years the lawsuits dragged on and on, decisions in one court appealed to the next level of the legal system.

Leona won her suit to recover the $100,000 plus interest she said her son had borrowed from her. The court awarded her $146,092.

On the suit alleging forgery in the transfer of the money market account, the Helmsleys won on technical grounds in a lower court, but then the decision was reversed on appeal.

Mimi won the first round in Deco's suit for the return of prepaid salary and fees, and then lost when Deco appealed. Mimi was thus forced to dip into the money market account to come up with the money to repay Deco. And Deco even seized her DeLorean car and had it auctioned off. In one of life's ironies, the man who bought it, a construction executive from Kentucky, met Mimi and later married her.

The courts refused to honor the Helmsley demand that Mimi pay the cost of shipping her husband's body to New York or the funeral there.

Leona was forced to withdraw her suit to recover the topaz ring when Mimi's lawyers produced the photograph of Leona holding Mimi's hand, ring prominently displayed, and describing it as a gift.

Another claim was filed by Jay's second wife, Ruth Panzirer, for $3,900 in alimony payments that had not been paid after his death.

Not until 1987 did the final suits and claims reach their end. By then, only a pittance remained in Jay Panzirer's estate, initially valued at about $150,000. After Deco was satisfied and Leona got her money, and Mimi paid some, though not all, of her $50,000 legal fees, she ended up with $2,020, which was immediately garnished by Deco to pay for its court costs, and so she found herself still in debt to her lawyers. "I was one hundred percent wiped out," she says. "To this day I don't know why they did it."

As for Jay Panzirer's four children, Leona Helmsley's grandchildren, each got $432.91. A Helmsley spokesman would later say that even so, Leona "has made provisions for them. She set up significant trust funds for them fifteen years ago. She loves them and she is taking care of them." If so, to what degree remains a mystery.

Her son's family were not the only ones she assaulted. With those who worked for her, she had always been difficult. Now she was close to impossible. Her fury was barely controlled, and anyone might be a target, any offense, real or imagined, enough to set it loose. The mere sight of her would often create fear and trembling in her employees.

The mere mention of Jay's name would invariably set loose tears, though in moments they would be replaced by renewed wrath. "You sometimes had the feeling," says a witness to these episodes, "that she felt nobody had the right to mention his name, that nobody was worthy of mentioning it."

In her mourning, Leona was forced to inflict on others the pain she felt. No one could escape, not those who worked for her and who had long suffered at her hands anyway, and not even a daughter-in-law she had once lavished affection upon and who had fulfilled her son's last years, or her son's children, her grandchildren.

"The sad thing," says a woman who worked with her at the time, "is that she'll never understand what she did, and she'll never know what she lost."

20

IN THESE YEARS, another sort of demise was taking place. Though certainly not as traumatic as a son's death, its course was directed as surely by the inexorable hand of fate. Harry Helmsley was growing old, and his empire was aging and decaying with him.

Looking out often from the terrace of his Park Lane penthouse, or from the windows of his fifty-third-floor office in the Helmsley-controlled Lincoln Building—"Taking inventory," Leona once described it—he would exult, "I own this, I own this, I own this and that one and that one and that one." Indeed he did.

He continued to go to his offices every morning, the one in the Lincoln Building and the newer one in the Helmsley Palace, continued to take out folders containing all his projects, and study them. They were impressive. A vast television and motion picture complex on Manhattan's West Side. New office buildings around the country. New condominiums. New hotels. The folders and the plans piled up. And remained only folders and plans.

He built nothing. The Helmsley Palace and the New York Helmsley had been his last major endeavors. His plans for the television city, on land he had bought from *The New York Times* nearly a decade before? He abandoned them. A major condominium complex rising in Miami? He let it go into foreclosure. The chance to build a new skyscraper on Lexington Avenue over the Grand Central Post Office? He hesitated, and then let it fall to somebody else. A major office and apartment development across the Hudson in Fort Lee, New Jersey? It came to nothing. The opportunities to acquire property on Madison Avenue, on Third Avenue for new office skyscrapers? He let those pass on to Donald Trump, to the Zeckendorfs, to foreign consortiums. So it went with project after project, opportunity after opportunity. There were only the folders and the dreams they contained, yellowing with age and disuse.

He bought little, and what he bought was mainly for the pleasures and comfort of himself and his wife, spending millions to acquire the mansion and estate called Dunnellen Hall in Greenwich, Connecticut, looking at but not quite closing on other properties in Barbados, the Bahamas, other places where he and Leona vacationed.

He sold some, finding buyers for buildings that were not doing quite as well as he wanted, buildings that required an outlay of cash to renovate, buildings where the tenants were making trouble for him. And he sold the St. Moritz, the first hotel he and Lawrence Wien had bought so long before, the hotel that had revealed to him the possibilities in that business. They had bought it in 1958 for a little more than $3 million. In 1985, Donald Trump, reaching out in every direction to create his own empire, one that would surpass Helmsley's or anyone else's, made an offer that Helmsley thought irresistible. He was willing to pay $31 million for the hotel, ten times what it had cost Helmsley and Wien. They jumped at the offer, Helmsley certain that he had gotten the better of Donald Trump, telling associates that Trump's offer was far more than the hotel was worth. Trump didn't think so then, and, he says, he knows so now: Three years later, in 1988, he turned around and sold the St. Moritz to Alan Bond, the Australian yachtsman and entrepreneur, for $181 million, all in cash.

Harry Helmsley's fortune continued to grow, yes, but now it consisted of paper billions, money derived from the steadily escalating value of real estate, not from the addition of properties as in the past.

As the dynamism, ingenuity, and visions that had propelled Harry Helmsley to his preeminent position seemed to fade, so the companies he had used so effectively also began to languish. In essence, he had run a one-man show. No matter how large and complex his empire became, his hand was in every aspect. Nothing was done without his knowledge and without his approval. He knew, he was fond of saying, the details of every deal and every operation down to the cost of the nails and the brooms. The modern techniques using computer printouts, data analyses, and telex transmittal systems, among others, have found little place in the world of Helmsley Enterprises and its various offshoots. What worked in the past—the dog-eared address book, the Rolodex, and buttonholing the personal contact— was good enough for him. That they might not work now was the fault not of these old tried-and-true methods but of the people who plied them. And so, Harry Helmsley, the master of all the old ways, remained the indispensable man. He had trained no successors, and without the Harry Helmsley of old, his organization was leaderless.

"In the old days," says the head of a rival real estate firm, "when I was just beginning in the business, Helmsley was the best. Make no mistake about it. His people were aggressive, they knew the market from top to bottom, they could spot trends, they knew what was around even before it was around, and they could cut a deal like nobody you ever saw. You couldn't go anywhere without stumbling over the Helmsley people. But that was before the Queen came along and he got bitten by the hotel bug. New ways of doing things came along and the rest of us adapted to them, but not Helmsley. He just kept doing things the way he'd always done them. So, what happened? His bright young guys up and left. Today you'll find them high up in just about all the good firms and in their own companies. What's left are a bunch of *alte cockers* who've made their pile and don't really give a damn anymore, and some young guys who don't know what the hell they're doing. Everybody used to worry about Helmsley. Not anymore. Nobody even thinks about Helmsley today. He's not a factor, and his whole place is just marking time.''

The only possible successors, besides Leona, are Alvin Schwartz and Irving Schneider, his two closest associates, partners in many a deal and, as a result, multimillionaires. They may be experts in the art of making real estate deals, but neither Schwartz, past seventy, nor Schneider, approaching seventy, has the flair to run a vast enterprise. And below them in the Helmsley echelon? There is no one. Nor are there any modern management programs to develop those bright young men so necessary for the continued success of any business.

Worse still, those with the potential to lead have fled, some out of disenchantment, some summarily fired, often after conflict with Leona Helmsley. Joseph Grotto, for instance, went to work for Brown, Harris, Stevens in the mid-1950s and eventually Helmsley made him president of the residential brokerage arm of the empire. Some thought that when Helmsley himself departed, Grotto would be among the most likely candidates to take over. Enter Leona Helmsley. Power more and more accrued to her. Helmsley more and more deferred to her as she took an ever more active role in day-to-day operations. And then, though she had hired her own brother, Alvin Rosenthal, to work as a Helmsley executive, she decided that nepotism was bad business. Out went a notice. No more relatives were to be hired. It so happened that a few years before, Grotto had hired his son to work for Brown, Harris, Stevens. The young man, according to several former Helmsley executives, was good enough at his work so that even without paternal intervention he would have been a success. But he was Joe Grotto's son, and Leona said no relatives. Then, offering no particular reason, she ordered Grotto to fire another Brown, Harris, Stevens executive, this one a man who had been with the company for years. This time Grotto refused. So Leona fired Joe Grotto instead. Harry backed her action.

Another top candidate was James Boisi. In 1984 Harry wooed him away from Morgan Guaranty Trust Company, where he had been vice-chairman, to take the newly created title of vice-chairman of Helmsley Enterprises and, it was assumed, he was heir apparent. When Boisi took the job, though, he wasn't aware that he would be answerable to Leona. She didn't take to him. Picking an excuse, she started going over his expense vouchers and screamed when she saw how much he had been spending entertaining clients. It mattered not that he had been entertaining them at her Helmsley Palace. She summarily fired him. Harry did not demur.

He objected to little that she did, appearing rather to enjoy everything about her. There had been rumors that upon his departure, for whatever reason, his business would be offered to Schwartz and Schneider, but the indications were that neither had any special interest in buying and running it, that rather when Harry Helmsley went, both intended to retire. But Helmsley himself let it be known that on his passing, all would become Leona's, all the money, all the properties, all the power. And so as fear of Helmsley's penchant for retribution receded, it was replaced by an even greater fear of Leona.

In a sense, of course, the power and the wealth were hers already. And she had no compunctions about instilling terror in those who worked for her or for him. All those dreams that had filled her early days of privation and struggle had come true. She was Leona Helmsley. She was Queen of the Palace and she was heiress to a vast domain.

She had become, as well, though she did not realize it, increasingly an object of ridicule.

Her portraits that filled the pages of the newspapers and glossy magazines provided fodder for a growing round of bad jokes about tucks and face-lifts, about daily sessions in beauty salons, about hours at makeup tables. Her eternal smile, a comedian quipped, must have been surgically frozen on her face, and if her expression ever changed the whole face would shatter and look like fissured porcelain. Another entertained cabaret audiences by holding a photograph of Leona and asking, ''Will the real Leona Helmsley stand up?'' at which a woman wearing a Lena the Hyena mask rose. Available in souvenir shops around Times Square and in Greenwich Village were rubberized Leona Helmsley masks. On Halloween in the latter half of the 1980s, among those who rang the doorbells and shouted ''Trick or treat,'' there inevitably seemed to be at least one Leona Helmsley in company with the Wicked Witch of the West and Snow White's stepmother.

She had courted admiration and envy. There was still envy, though even that was fading as the stories about her cruelties, petty and large, and the malicious and sarcastic jibes took hold and became rife. The admiration had vanished. To the world beyond her domain, she bore only a resemblance to the Queen of Hearts screeching, ''Off with her head!''

In the late fall of 1988, a visitor wandering through the lobby of the New York Helmsley happened upon a stack of brochures for all the Helmsley and Harley hotels around the country, ranked neatly in a stand on the front desk. Their covers were illustrated with a photograph of Leona Helmsley standing on the grand staircase of the Helmsley Palace, adorned in a long gown with red skirt and low-cut black top with bouffant sleeves, tiara on her head, diamonds dangling from her ears, arms spread wide to welcome her guests. On the display brochure fronting the stack, though, someone had inked in a mustache and a Van Dyke on her face. It was impossible to miss. No one had bothered to remove the offending object.

They became, as time passed, ever more friendless and isolated, even irrelevant. With Harry Helmsley's advancing years came the afflictions of age—a heart ailment, a stroke, a debilitating eyelid condition that required multiple operations.

His longtime friend, Lawrence Wien, had grown old, too, and he had used his remarkable philanthropy to soften the resentment of his business ways. Helmsley, in these later years, would embark on his own philanthropic path, though in a much more limited and self-aggrandizing way.

Under the influence of his first wife, whose Quaker faith had instilled the virtue of charity, Helmsley had given to a variety of good causes. If he was not as generous as his wealth might have indicated, he had still been generous, and he had even served on several boards, though without leaving a mark. In the first years of his marriage to Leona, however, charity became celebrated more in its absence than in its presence.

Changes were slow in coming even as the Helmsleys became more publicly prominent, their wealth ever more publicly noted, and the tales about their misuse of power spread ever more widely. But at last, perhaps to counter the impression of mean-spiritedness and unbridled greed that was taking hold, they began to give, and make sure their gifts were widely known.

In Greenwich, they gave to religious organizations and other charities, though mainly in small amounts, a few thousand here and a few thousand there, and little notice was taken of them. But as the era of unbridled greed reached its height, some of the gifts became large enough that they could not escape attention. For instance, when the lights designed to illuminate the courtyard of St. Patrick's Cathedral crashed onto the Lady Chapel, the Helmsleys' donated a new system that bathed the chapel and the whole cathedral in a mantle of light. It made a spectacular view from the windows of the Helmsley Palace across Madison Avenue, which stood on the land Harry Helmsley had acquired for a song from the archdiocese.

There were other well-publicized gifts, too, but they all paled beside the one the Helmsleys made in 1986 to New York Hospital. Shortly before, Helmsley had suffered mild heart problems and had checked into the hospital's cardiovascular center for treatment. He had made a good recovery, and now he and Leona decided to repay the hospital. They donated $30 million to the hospital's modernization program and another $3 million to the cardiovascular research center, which would be renamed for Harry Helmsley. The $33 million was the largest gift to New York Hospital in nearly sixty years, topped only by $40 million given in 1927 by the philanthropist Payne Whitney that had been used to construct much of the hospital, and one of the largest gifts ever made by an individual to a single institution.

Helmsley was modest in acknowledging this huge contribution. Though he had made small donations in the past to a number of other institutions and charities, he said, "It is the size of this gift which is unusual for me. I have been having treatments at the hospital and they seem to handle things with the heart with great skill. So the whole idea of giving to them seemed to strike a chord." Besides, he added, "I'm trying to make myself one of the important people in New York and so I wanted to do something for New York."

However awkwardly he echoed Lawrence Wien, it was a noble gift all the same. And it was rightly hailed by the press and the public. That it put a little sheen on a tarnished reputation hardly mattered.

The one thing they stopped giving was the annual "I'm Just Wild About Harry" party. Those nights of waltzing cheek to cheek across ballroom floors became fewer. They might still go to their offices, though Harry was doing so with less frequency, but when night came, they tended to withdraw more and more into a private solitary world. Leona was still glimpsed at the Helmsley Palace bar, or in the lobby. But sightings of her husband became fewer.

In late winter and early spring of 1988, as Helmsley's seventy-ninth birthday approached, there were no plans for a big party. Instead the Helmsleys took themselves off to Arizona, and Leona gave a small affair at the Scottsdale

Princess resort outside Phoenix. It was, according to all reports, a decidedly low-key party with only a few guests. The two did some shopping and bought a birthday present for Harry. It was a ten-acre estate in the hills of Arizona's Paradise Valley, complete with a twenty-one-thousand-square-foot house, swimming pool, and tennis courts. It cost $6 million.

At the end of March they flew back to New York. Looking tanned and rested, they appeared at the offices of Helmsley Enterprises to let the staff belatedly commemorate the birthday. There was a cake decorated with an idealized New York skyline. Among the few speeches, Harry thanked everyone for their devotion, and those who worked for him praised him for all he had accomplished through all the years. It did not last long. And then the Helmsleys departed.

Awaiting them was a maelstrom of their own creation.

Part Four
Trial and Judgment

21

BETWEEN INDICTMENT AND trial lie months, even years of legal maneuvers that have made speedy trials for wealthy defendants something more celebrated in the absence than the presence. So it was with Harry and Leona Helmsley. Originally scheduled for September 1988, the trial was postponed time after time—to November, to January 1989, to April, and then finally to June 26, nearly fifteen months after the indictments had been handed down.

The reason? The Helmsleys did not want to face a jury of their peers. Their attorneys filed motion after motion, to higher and higher courts, seeking to have the indictments dismissed. They were faulty, the lawyers alleged, too broad, too far-reaching. If crimes had been committed, they had been committed by the Helmsley aides, Joseph Licari and Frank Turco, who had devised a scheme "to steal blindly from the Helmsleys" without their knowledge. The reasons piled one on another. And if the attorneys couldn't knock out the indictments, they wanted a change of venue because the publicity surrounding the Helmsleys would make fair trial impossible in New York. But time after time, on petition after petition, they lost.

Their one victory was a pyrrhic one. Though Harry Helmsley's friends and associates continued to maintain that they saw no outward changes in him, only the little slowing down natural in a man of his age, others began to differ. Employees at the Park Lane reported that he seemed stooped when they saw him. He had a vacant look in his eyes. He sometimes had to be helped. Sometimes he seemed not to recognize longtime employees.

And then his attorneys went before the court and said that Harry Helmsley, the man who had built an empire and ruled it as an absolute monarch, was no longer capable of assisting in his own defense, as required by law. His physical and mental condition had so deteriorated that he could not stand trial. After a panel of five medical experts from New York, selected by prosecution and defense, had offered conflicting views on his mental state, the court appointed Dr. Martin L. Albert, professor of neurology at Boston University School of Medicine, to examine him. Dr. Albert's diagnosis: Harry Helmsley had "memory difficulties and difficulties in reasoning . . . He would not be cognitively fit to respond to a hostile cross examination . . . He could not substantially assist in his defense." A series of small strokes and other ailments—cerebrovascular disease due to hypertension, reactive hypoglycemia, arrhythmia, and apnea (a temporary cessation of breathing during sleep), among others—had "caused substantial brain damage," the court and its experts agreed. Not only was his memory no longer reliable, but he had difficulty even holding conversations for any period of time. Nature knows not wealth and power, and the vicissitudes of time afflict the rich man as surely as they afflict the homeless beggar huddled in a doorway. Without objection from the government, Harry Helmsley was separated from the case. Though he would remain under indictment, he would not face the judgment of his peers, only the judgment of posterity.

That left Leona. Though her trial loomed, she acted as though little had changed. Those glossy, retouched ads celebrating the Queen guarding her palace continued to pour forth week after week. She continued to rule her empire, and Harry's, as before. She bought herself a new limousine that the maker described as "a beautiful, beautiful car," and then added, "I hope she's around long enough to use it."

And she earned the deeper enmity of the Helmsleys' long-time rival in the world of high-flying real estate, Donald Trump, who for years had attempted to play down any thought that a feud might exist. The Helmsleys owned some property in Atlantic City, where Trump was carving out a vast gambling and hotel empire. Trump wanted that property, as players of Monopoly, that Atlantic City-based board game, always want more. He offered a high price. Leona demanded lots more. Trump upped his ante, to $21 million. Leona countered, not a penny less than $24 million. Trump put on the pressure. Leona held out. The pressure mounted. Finally in early May, a deal was struck for Trump's final offer.

He was enraged by her intransigence, nevertheless, and he was anything but generous in accepting what he then called his victory. Leona, he said, "totally conceded defeat in her irrational attempt to deprive me of something to which I am entitled. . . . Her judgment should not be used to run Harry's empire. She's set businesswomen back twenty years."

And why had she exacerbated the long-rumored feud with Trump? "She always wanted to go to his parties," said Trump's attorney, Pat McGahn, with a grin, "and he wouldn't invite her." Trump himself added, "She invites me to her parties and I don't want to go to her parties."

Still, this was only a minor diversion as the trial approached. Though neither her attorneys nor the government would comment, efforts were apparently being made so that she could avoid the ignominy of a trial. From the beginning, the government, despite the popular view that she was the real culprit, had seemingly felt that nothing had been done without Harry Helmsley's knowledge and/or active participation. Thus it was prepared to let her plead to a lesser count and mete out only a fine if she would provide it with evidence. She adamantly refused, convinced, it was said, that she had nothing to fear.

From the moment of Harry Helmsley's separation from

the case, new whispers started about possible negotiations. By now, though, the government's stance had hardened. The crimes of which she was charged, not merely income tax evasion, but extortion and more, were too serious to be dismissed with only a slap on the wrist. A lesson had to be taught to Leona Helmsley and anyone else who would follow her route.

Thus, according to reports, to avoid trial she would have to plead guilty to some of the main counts, pay a very heavy fine, and trade her diamonds and penthouse for the severe garb of a convict in federal prison for six months.

She would have none of it, despite, it was whispered, some gentle urging by her attorneys. She countered, it was said, by offering to plead no contest, a legal nicety that would avoid the stigma of a felony conviction, which a guilty plea would entail. She would pay a fine. But she would not go to prison.

Through spring, the positions of government and Leona Helmsley remained frozen, neither side willing to give. And so there they stood as the moment for trial and judgment arrived.

22

DESPITE THE FORMALITY and outward civility of its codified rules and ancient rituals, a court of law is a pitiless place. Fear, rage, and hatred are never far from the surface, though held under tight rein. The defendant sits, silent and powerless, and listens to recitations, coated with venom, of events that happened years before. Perhaps worst of all, his or her fate rests in the hands of twelve strangers.

On June 26, 1989, the long-delayed case entitled the *United States of America* v. *Helmsley, et al* finally came to trial in a high-ceilinged, paneled courtroom with muddy, threadbare carpeting on the third floor of the Greek-columned federal courthouse in New York's Foley Square.

It was the last of the celebrated courtroom dramas that had titillated New Yorkers, and much of the nation, in the latter 1980s. Filling headlines and columns of newsprint day after day were the trials of defendants who were as famous as the television reporters who night after night stood out in front of the courthouses. There had been the Mafia trials, starring John Gotti; the ''preppie'' murder case, starring Robert Chambers and his victim, Jennifer Levin; the affair of battered and slain Lisa Steinberg, starring Joel Steinberg and his longtime lover, Hedda Nussbaum; the political corruption trials of Bronx boss Stanley Friedman and his cohorts; the trial of one-time Miss America and close friend of Mayor Koch Bess Myerson. Most had been produced and directed by Rudolph Giuliani, the United States Attorney for the Southern District of New York, headline-grabbing prosecutor often portrayed as the successor to Thomas E. Dewey as scourge of all wrongdoers high and low. Now the trial of the Queen of the Palace, Leona Helmsley, was to be the ultimate jewel in the Giuliani crown.

And so, at 10:23, seated beneath the seal of the United States and flanked by an American flag and the witness box, Federal District Judge John M. Walker, Jr., called his court to order. A first cousin of President George Bush, to whom he bears a distinct resemblance, he had been, until his appointment to the federal bench in 1985, assistant secretary of the treasury for enforcement and operations, and thus was an expert on tax matters. His reputation was that of a fair, no-nonsense jurist who kept tight control of his courtroom. As events in the months to follow would amply demonstrate, he had little patience with repetition, vagueness, or incompetence, and had little compunction in reframing a rambling and incoherent question so that witness and jurors would clearly understand what was being asked. And yet he had as well a mischievous glint in his eye. There was one instance late in the trial when one of the defense lawyers was having trouble framing a question for a witness. He looked toward Walker. Walker looked back, waiting. The lawyer finally said, "I was hoping you'd help me again, Your Honor." The judge shook his head and grinned. "This time you're on your own."

On the first day of the trial, he dismissed a defense motion for a change of venue to Philadelphia, on grounds that Leona Helmsley could never get a fair trial in New York because of the publicity. Gesturing toward the huge pile of newspaper clippings, magazine articles, and radio and television transcripts that the defense had submitted, he noted that the articles were from all over the country. There were venomous ones from Philadelphia as well as New York, which gave him pause to wonder just why the defense thought they'd get a better deal there. Further, he noted, among the items submitted was an article about heavyweight champion Mike Tyson and his troubles with his one-time wife, Robin Givens. "Let both sides be warned," he said, "this is one judge who reads all of the papers put before him."

From his bench high over the courtroom, Walker looked out over, first, a long table for the prosecution. At one end sat James DeVita, an assistant United States attorney for New York's southern district and leader of that team, and stretching down from him other assistant United States attorneys, IRS agents, and lawyers from the office of New York State Attorney General Robert Abrams, who had his own indictments against these defendants but who had decided that the federal government should carry the day, and bear the expense. DeVita, who would celebrate his forty-first birthday during the middle of the trial, was a veteran of eight years as a government trial lawyer; his previous major case had been the successful prosecution of the Reverend Sun Yung Moon. A soft-spoken, auburn-haired man who eschewed histrionics, he resembled, both physically and in manner, a bulldog. He had built his reputation on detailed preparation rather than oratory, but both would be in evidence throughout this long summer.

At the table behind the government sat the defense. At one end was Frank Turco, a deeply tanned man in his forties with a thin, sharp-featured face and tinted glasses. In twenty-one years as a Helmsley employee, he had risen through the ranks to become comptroller and chief financial officer of the Helmsley Hotels and a close aide of Leona Helmsley. He had done her bidding without question and had been well rewarded financially for stoically bearing her imperious demands, her two A.M. phone calls, and so much more, until, in early 1986, she had peremptorily fired him. He had, it was said, met with the government time after time, for more than eighty hours, and offered to plead guilty and become a witness for the government in exchange for leniency. But DeVita and the government were sure they had all the witnesses they needed. His offer was spurned, and now he sat at the same table, charged with the same crimes as his one-time employer, though he rarely looked in her direction and she rarely looked at him.

Separated by Turco's lawyer, William Brodsky, a bearded man given to sudden, sometimes fumbling objections that Judge Walker more often than not overruled, was Joseph Licari. A small, slightly rotund man in his fifties, he looked like the bookkeeper he was. He had become through twenty-one years in the Helmsley empire the chief financial officer of Helmsley Enterprises. A close associate of Harry Helmsley, he had sometimes been called Helmsley's alter ego, entrusted with investing more than $200 million of Helmsley money in ventures that would make more money. Everyone agreed that he was a nice guy who tried desperately to avoid making waves. His career had come to a sudden end in 1986 when Leona Helmsley, whom, said his attorney, "he avoided like the plague," and whom he had seen perhaps three times over the years, and who caused him to throw up whenever he heard her voice, fired him during that third and final meeting. His lawyer was Joseph R. Benfante, a pleasant if often overblown and excitable man who was never at a loss for a cliché or a joke and who sometimes seemed out of his depth in this kind of case. Both his fees and his expenses, and Brodsky's as well, were being paid by the Helmsleys.

Down the table, separated by more attorneys and aides, sat the chief defendant, the focus of all eyes, Leona Helmsley. On that late June day, she looked anything but the self-assured, glamorous queen her publicity made her out to be. Her clothes were expensive and stylish, of course—a chartreuse suit, pearls around the neck, white pumps.[1] But she

1. All through the trial her clothes would be expensive and invariably different. Indeed, one of her lawyers finally told her to stop wearing such expensive designer clothes; it didn't sit well with the jury. She did not always heed that advice, however, though as time passed she wore some of those dresses more than once and tried to stick with ones that were conservative.

seemed jittery, her hands frequently shaking, mouth frozen
in a turned-down expression, her face scarlet beneath carefully and artfully applied makeup, as though she had been
in the sun too long or had just come through another chem-
ical treatment (though it would later be said that the high
color might well be the result of dangerously high blood
pressure or a skin allergy), and the skin seemed stretched
so tight that it would crack if her countenance changed. The
only heavy makeup she wore was deep layers of black mascara that seemed to conceal eyes so sad they seemed forever
on the edge of spilling over.

If Licari and Turco had a single lawyer each, neither
skilled in the world of high finance and taxes, Leona Helmsley had at her side four experts, trained in threading through
the intricate tax jungle. Most important, the chief of this
team was Gerald A. Feffer, partner in the Washington law
firm of Williams and Connolly. A handsome, suave man in
his mid-forties, once himself an assistant U.S. attorney in
New York's southern district and later boss of the Justice
Department's tax division during the Carter administration,
he was a specialist in tax fraud cases. He might exude a
nice-guy air, but beneath it lay steel; Feffer was a heavyweight.

The job those first days was picking a jury, twelve men
and women, and six alternates. They would have to sit for
two to three months, Judge Walker warned them. Though
some observers thought it would be no easy job finding an
impartial jury for Leona Helmsley, given all her publicity,
the panel of more than a hundred potential jurors had been
carefully screened. All had completed lengthy question-
naires running to more than forty pages, covering everything from financial and family status to attitudes about
women striving to get ahead in business to whether the rich
get and/or deserve different treatment from the average cit-
izen.

Within three days more than fifty had been screened, and
on July 5, the day after Leona Helmsley's birthday, after the

defense and the government had exercised their peremptory challenges, a jury of seven women and five men, seven blacks and five whites, of the middle and lower-middle classes, was seated in two rows in the jury box, the six alternates behind them. (Over the next months, two jurors would be dismissed by Judge Walker, one because she arrived forty-five minutes late for a trial session because her train had broken down, and the other because his wife was about to undergo major surgery. As a result, the panel that ultimately deliberated was composed of six men and six women, six blacks, one Hispanic and five whites.) Outside, more than two inches of rain inundated the city as Jim DeVita rose, went to a rostrum set at the end of the jury box, and began to outline the government's case against Leona Helmsley, Joseph Licari, and Frank Turco.

If Harry Helmsley was physically absent, his name was never far from DeVita's lips, never far from the minds of those in the packed courtroom. Righteous indignation filling his voice, DeVita told the jury that although what they would hear might "seem like the script for a movie or a TV show, it is not fiction. . . . Harry and Leona Helmsley used their position, power, and privilege to avoid paying income tax. They acted as though they were above the law." By the use of phony invoices and other means, they illegally charged more than $4 million of personal expenses to their businesses and so "they cheated the government on their income tax of over $1 million in 1983, 1984, and 1985. The evidence will show that they were arrogant and greedy." As for Licari and Turco, they "served as henchmen in carrying out the scheme of fraudulent practices, of fabricating and falsifying documents, of coercing employees to help."

Most of this fraud, DeVita said, stemmed from the more than $8 million spent on renovations and redecoration of Dunnellen Hall, most of which was simply charged to seventeen of their businesses, which Leona Helmsley "considered her personal piggy bank." Because they had the value of the goods on which the money was spent and their businesses got tax deductions for business expenses, their actions constituted tax fraud.

Furthermore, there was the matter of extortion. According to DeVita, Leona Helmsley and Frank Turco extorted money, goods, and services from vendors either doing business with Helmsley companies or seeking their business. They extended this practice to employees by threatening to fire them unless they came across. And so those employees "who participated did so because their jobs depended on it."

The jurors, he said, will hear about all this and a lot more from nearly a hundred witnesses, many of them Helmsley employees, past and present. They would be shown documents from the Helmsley files, bills and invoices that had been altered and fabricated, checks and memos and notes asking that bills be falsified or "deep-sixed" or "garbaged," and notes from Turco to Leona saying he had done this, and notes from Leona saying she wanted nothing done without her approval. When the government's case was finished, the charges would be proven conclusively and the jury's only choice would be to return verdicts of guilty.

How would Gerald Feffer respond? Would he, as pretrial papers and rumors had indicated, attempt to blame it all on the co-defendants, Frank Turco and Joseph Licari, claim that Leona Helmsley knew nothing of what had been done in her name? Or would he find some other course to deflect the government's charges?

DeVita would later say that Feffer had "a silver tongue to go along with his silver hair," and he was not far from the mark. For just over an hour that afternoon, the Washington lawyer put on a stunning show, often acting like a reluctant advocate whose own opinion of his client was not much higher than her prosecutors'.

The government, he said, "will wheel into this court grocery carts full of documents, I guarantee it.''[2] The defense, he said, would not contest the authenticity of most of those documents; indeed, the defense agreed with much of what the government alleged, and the facts were not in dispute. What was in dispute was Leona Helmsley's intention to cheat the government of its just due. "Mrs. Helmsley made mistakes," he said, "and she exercised bad judgment. But there was no deliberate decision to commit crimes."

This case was not the United States versus Leona Helmsley, "but rather the Internal Revenue Service versus Leona Helmsley. The IRS is responsible for all of us being in court this summer. It's the IRS's case and the IRS wants to put a show on for all the world to see. For three years the IRS has tried to nail Mrs. Helmsley. This extravaganza was created by the IRS and they love it. We will demonstrate that in their haste to make big headlines they forgot that they were representing you, and the people of the United States."

What is not an issue in the case, Feffer asserted, is the Helmsleys' extravagant lifestyle. "I have confidence you'll be fair to Mrs. Helmsley despite the fact that she's a billionaire." The kind of person she is is not an issue, though the government will attempt to make "her personality a central pivot, they will bring in witnesses to paint Mrs. Helmsley in such a way that you will hate her. . . . There is no question that she overcompensates to make it in business. She is and was extremely tough and abrasive, and she is an absolute perfectionist. An employee makes a mistake, the employee pays. She has an explosive temper. She has no patience with those who fail to live up to her expectations. But I don't believe that Mrs. Helmsley is charged in this indictment with being a tough bitch."

All those documents that the government would show to

___

2. He was right. Before the week was out grocery carts heaped to the top with documents, nearly a score of tall filing cabinets bulging with papers, and as many cardboard shipping transfiles filled the well of the court and lined one of its walls.

the jury, he said, did not show intent to cheat the government, for "if they did, why weren't they destroyed if she wanted to commit a crime?" The reason was, he said, that there was no intent. Because the Helmsleys did a lot of work at home, at Dunnellen Hall, they were entitled to have the Helmsley companies pay a portion of their expenses, and if the way they did it "was an unusual and unconventional system, it was a practical one." Further, the incontrovertible proof that Harry and Leona Helmsley had no intention of cheating the government was there for everyone to see: In the three years covered by this indictment, 1983 to 1985, they had actually paid more than $57 million in income taxes. Why, then, would they try to get away with a measly $1 million?

As far as a conspiracy to defraud the government, it just didn't exist. Her co-defendant, Joe Licari, "was overworked and not well organized. He didn't want to deal with Mrs. Helmsley. Dunnellen Hall was a giant pain in the ass for Joe Licari and he didn't want to become involved with Mrs. Helmsley on any level." What's more, in the middle of this so-called conspiracy, Joe Licari, Frank Turco, and a lot of others involved in the scheme were fired. "What's going on here?" Feffer asked rhetorically. "It doesn't make sense."

As for the charges of extortion against her and Frank Turco? The people who were supposedly extorted "were tough, aggressive business people, people who were looking to make a buck. They were not victims. Ask yourselves how much did these victims make off the Helmsleys. They made out like bandits. They made tons of money."

Leona Helmsley, Feffer insisted, had no intention of committing a crime, and without intent there was no crime. Nobody was hurt. The IRS was defrauded of nothing. What this case comes down to is that "the IRS is out to kill these people. This case demonstrates how far the IRS is willing to go to get someone."

Neither Benfante nor Brodsky took long in outlining their

defense. Both Licari and Turco were longtime, loyal employees of the Helmsley organization. Both carried out the orders of Harry and Leona Helmsley. They had done nothing wrong and there was no conspiracy and there were no crimes. It was as simple as that.

In essence, then, the defense contended that a major part of the expenses for Dunnellen Hall, even for personal items, was legitimate business expenses and so the Helmsleys were entitled to deduct them on their income tax returns. The falsified invoices had been falsified not to defraud the Internal Revenue Service but rather in an effort by Turco and other Helmsley employees to circumvent Leona Helmsley in order to pay vendors and contractors that she, for one reason or another, was refusing to pay. Finally, the so-called extortion was merely a means to secure rebates for the Helmsley companies, especially the hotels, from the suppliers who would ultimately benefit greatly from vastly increased sales to the Helmsleys.

23

FEFFER WAS RIGHT on one count. Though Leona Helmsley had not been indicted for her personality, it nevertheless would be brought into such sharp focus that the jurors would be unable to avoid it, though they would later say it had not entered into their deliberations. Of the forty-four witnesses DeVita summoned to testify over the next seven weeks (Judge Walker told him to slash his list of a hundred to cut out redundant and cumulative ones, even to narrow the scope of the charges, so that everyone could go home by Labor Day), hardly a one did not add to the already huge stockpile of Leona Helmsley tales of outrage.

Those stories were merely a fillip, though, a kind of enlivening color added to the testimony, supported by thousands of documents, memoranda, invoices, ledgers, and checks, that related directly to the charges.

The Helmsley scheme, as the government and its witnesses unveiled it for the court, began almost immediately after Harry wrote his $11 million check for the castle in Connecticut in late June 1983. Dunnellen Hall lacked much they thought essential to their future happiness. Prime among them was an enclosed pool. An architect was hired to do renderings for the pool enclosure without delay. By the end of June, he had them ready. Leona and Harry looked them over and approved.

The next step was to hire a contractor. Chuck Olivieri, chief operating officer of a company called Riverview Interiors, got a call from Carl Morse, chairman of Morse Diesel, for whom he had worked during construction of the Helmsley Palace. Morse told him of the Helmsleys' new home and asked if he would be interested in doing the work on the pool enclosure. Within a few days Olivieri met with Harry Helmsley at Dunnellen Hall. When he departed, architect's plans in hand, he went back to his office and drew up a budget.

It came to $600,000, a figure that did not make Leona Helmsley happy. Olivieri met with the couple again in late summer at Dunnellen Hall, and Harry told him that although he liked the proposal, it seemed very expensive. Leona was more acerbic. "She said," Olivieri testified, "that she wasn't building the Taj Mahal, that she only wanted her pool enclosed, and it shouldn't cost more than $150,000 to $200,000." Olivieri explained that the job wasn't as simple as it looked. Not only did they want the pool enclosure to blend in with the existing masonry and old brick at Dunnellen Hall, they wanted him to use stainless steel and limestone and other materials that were very expensive. Then Leona decided that she also wanted the enclosure air conditioned, and she wanted that system also to be built with stainless steel and the ducts placed underground rather than exposed. "I told her I didn't think air conditioning was necessary. She said it was necessary." The additional cost came to $50,000.

When the Helmsleys finally approved, Olivieri began preliminary work. But he had no desire to lay out his own money and wait for payment, so he submitted two invoices up front to Harry Helmsley, one for $6,000 and one for $4,000, basically the cost of work already completed and for some essential supplies. Helmsley looked them over, offered no objections, and then told Olivieri to send them on to Joe Licari, Helmsley Enterprises' chief financial officer. Licari, Helmsley explained, was handling all the financial arrangements regarding Dunnellen Hall, just as Frank

Turco was handling all the technical matters, making, under
Leona's direction, all the day-to-day decisions.

So the invoices went to Licari. Olivieri waited but received no payment. In late October he finally reached Licari
and they met in the Lincoln Building. Licari said, well, yes,
Olivieri ought to be paid, but in order to be paid, he'd have
to combine the two invoices into a single one for $10,000.
Plus, the work described on the new invoice should not be
for work on a pool enclosure at Dunnellen Hall, but rather
for work done at the Helmsley-owned Graybar Building,
where Olivieri's company had never done anything. When
the "corrected" invoice had been drawn up, Licari said, it
should be submitted to Frank Turco, who would arrange
payment. If this was the only way to get paid, then Olivieri
was going to do what he had been told. Sure enough, he
was paid immediately.

A month later, he met with Licari again and told him he
was about to submit a request for an additional payment of
$24,000 to cover materials he had to buy and other costs.
Licari said that Olivieri wasn't the only one having trouble
getting paid. The architect who had drawn up the plans for
the enclosure back in June was still waiting for his money.
The architect's fee was $55,000, and if Leona ever found
that out, she'd hit the ceiling. The thing to do was up the
invoice to $79,000 and submit it as work done on the Gray-
bar Building. Olivieri did, received a check from the
Graybar Building, and sent the architect his fee.

Early in January, under orders, he sent in another invoice,
this one for $36,000, including $4,000 for refinishing wood
floors at Dunnellen Hall and the rest for the pool enclosure.
Under directives from both Licari and Turco, the invoice
declared that the work had been on the elevator shaft at the
Helmsley Building, 230 Park Avenue, and the check he got
was from 230 Park Avenue.

His work apparently satisfied Leona Helmsley enough so
that just before the end of the year, she approached him
with a proposal for another job. It seemed that she didn't

have enough closet and dressing-room space in the Helmsleys' nine-room duplex penthouse atop the Park Lane Hotel. So she was taking over another apartment adjacent to the penthouse with the intention of turning it into closets and a beauty salon.

Olivieri drew a proposal. The cost of breaking through walls and all the rest came to $111,000. "She told me this was outrageous, but I should proceed anyway." Then she threw in a zinger. Olivieri would do the work, but he wouldn't get a fee for it "because, she said, I was getting so much for the pool enclosure at Dunnellen Hall." Nevertheless, Olivieri proceeded, hiring two subcontractors to do the actual work. And he sent in a request for $30,000 to cover partial material costs and labor. What he got was a check for $10,000, not from Leona Helmsley but from the Park Lane, an amount that he handed over to the subcontractors as a deposit on the sink and cabinets.

Suddenly, in March 1984, Olivieri's involvement in both Dunnellen Hall and the Park Lane came to an abrupt end. He got a call from the head of security at Dunnellen Hall telling him there was a problem. The pool enclosure was not satisfactory to Mrs. Helmsley. In order to cut costs, Olivieri had substituted fiberglass for stainless steel on the air conditioning ducts. Leona was somehow under the impression that he had substituted asbestos, and she wanted him gone. He tried to explain to her husband, but Harry said he had been told by the people on the estate that Olivieri's work was not satisfactory and the job was going to be handed over to a company called LaStrada. There wasn't much Olivieri could do about that decision. Still, he was owed $17,000 for the work he had already done. Harry eventually arranged for the builder to get $12,000, not out of his own pocket but from the law firm that represented the Helmsleys at the Palace Hotel, supposedly for consulting work at $1,000 a day.

* * *

Jeremiah McCarthy was the chief engineer of Helmsley-Spear. Earning over $100,000 a year, he was a man for whom Harry Helmsley had special affection. When the Helmsleys bought Dunnellen Hall in 1983, they turned to Jerry McCarthy to supervise all the renovations they had in mind, under Frank Turco's overall command. That's when his troubles began.

Among the many additions Leona wanted was a barbecue pit. McCarthy had a friend in the construction business, Eugene Brennan, who was willing to take on what was, in essence, a small job as a favor. He went to work, finished the barbecue pit, and sent in a bill for $13,000. Leona took a look at the finished job and didn't like what she considered shoddy workmanship, for there was trouble with the drainage system and the area flooded. And so when McCarthy sent along Brennan's bill, "Mrs. Helmsley called me up," he told the court, "yelling and screaming, ranting and raving, saying I was an idiot and that she wasn't going to spend $13,000 for a barbecue." Nothing McCarthy said could get her to okay the payment. He pleaded with her that Brennan had done the job as a favor, that he had six kids and needed the money. Her response was a sarcastic "Why didn't he keep his pants on? Then he wouldn't need the money."

It was too much. So McCarthy went to his friend, Harry Helmsley. He sighed, told McCarthy to get Helmsley-Spear to write the check to Brennan, and so settle the matter. McCarthy did just that. Then Leona found out about it. Enraged, she screamed at him for going to her husband over her head. If he wanted to keep his job, he was going to pay for the barbecue pit with a personal check for $10,000 out of his own pocket. Once more he went to Harry Helmsley. Helmsley told him, "Give her the check and get her off your back." If he did, Helmsley would see that he was reimbursed. So McCarthy did just that, making the check out to Leona Helmsley and handing it over to Frank Turco. But that wasn't good enough. In this case, Leona didn't want the check herself, she wanted it made out to Helmsley-

Spear, and after a couple of months, McCarthy did as ordered.[1]

But even that did not soothe Leona Helmsley's growing displeasure with him. Nothing that McCarthy did, at Dunnellen Hall or anywhere else, satisfied her. For instance, there was an emergency at the St. Moritz Hotel when the water pressure drastically fell off. McCarthy rushed over, took a look, and grabbed two hundred dollars from petty cash for the materials necessary to make the repairs. Harry Helmsley told him he was a genius for the way he had handled the emergency. Not so Leona Helmsley. ''She told me I was a thief and an idiot and I was fired.'' But then, that was not the first time she had fired him. She had fired him, it sometimes seemed to him, every other day, only to rehire him an hour later.

But McCarthy's troubles mounted as the Helmsley scheme to funnel Dunnellen Hall expenses into their business entities accelerated. As the man in charge, there came a day in the summer of 1984 when he was told to sign some invoices prepared by Frank Turco falsely describing work actually done on the estate as work done on several Helmsley hotels and other properties. McCarthy refused. Turco told him Mrs. Helmsley was ''going to be furious. You're going to be gone.'' McCarthy went to Licari and told him he thought what Turco was requesting was wrong. Licari ''agreed it wasn't the right thing to do. But he said the situation was out of his hands.''

And then Leona herself called. ''She said, 'Fuck you, you're not my partner. You don't tell me how to spend my money. You sign what you're told to sign.' '' Even with

---

1. Whether he ever got repaid, as Harry Helmsley had promised, is unclear. McCarthy claims not, that this was the only promise to him Harry ever broke. Still, he did get a raise to $110,000 a year on a new five-year contract in the early summer of 1985, and then when Leona forced his firing a few months later, he got a $75,000 bonus, or severance pay, from Harry, who sighed and said, ''This settles it out,'' which McCarthy took to mean the firing and not the reimbursement.

that, McCarthy still refused. Why? Jerry Feffer demanded
on cross-examination. Explained McCarthy: "This lady has
spent years calling me a thief and telling everyone I'm a
thief. And now she wants me to be one, and I wasn't going
to do it."

For McCarthy, the end at Dunnellen Hall came when a
newly installed sprinkler system sprayed water on a drive-
way rather than on the flower beds. "She got upset and told
me never to come back on the property." This order did
not upset him at all, though a year later, when she had him
fired, that was something else.

The man who replaced McCarthy at Dunnellen Hall was
William Piacitelli. At thirty-two, Billy Piacitelli had worked
his way up in fourteen years with the Helmsleys from a
mail-room boy to comptroller of Hospitality Services Company, a Helmsley tax shelter initially used to handle aspects
of the Helmsley organization's advertising and then much of
the financial affairs of Dunnellen Hall before Leona fired
him in 1986. Unlike all the other former and even present
Helmsley employees who had been cited as unindicted co-
conspirators and given grants of immunity in exchange for
their testimony, Piacitelli had pleaded guilty to three criminal misdemeanors growing out of this conspiracy. Among
his jobs had been checking the books to see what was being
spent on Dunnellen Hall and which of the Helmsley companies was paying the bills. He had received a suspended
sentence in exchange for his agreement to testify.

He had his funny, or not-so-funny, revelatory anecdote,
of course. In the summer of 1984, when under Turco's direction he was supervising much of the work at the Connecticut estate, a telephone system was installed. One thing
Leona Helmsley could not abide was the ringing of a telephone, and so in her bedroom she substituted the familiar
ring with melodious chimes placed under her bed. At lunch
one day, however, she complained bitterly that the chimes
weren't working properly, going ding-dik instead of ding-

dong. After lunch Piacitelli went up to the bedroom crawled under the bed, and saw that the chimes were leaning against the wall. He moved them away from the wall, which got them working. He then proceeded downstairs and reported the miracle he had wrought to Leona. Instead of praise, he was the object of vituperation. She screamed at him for daring to go into her bedroom. Nobody was permitted in her bedroom. She then banished him from Dunnellen Hall and told him never to enter the grounds again.

It was a funny story. Judge Walker, the attorneys, the jurors, and even Leona Helmsley laughed when Billy Piacitelli told it. But he had more damaging stories about his nine-month tenure at Dunnellen Hall. When he left the Helmsleys in 1986, he took with him copies of all his files and all of Frank Turco's files, most relating to the affairs of Dunnellen Hall. Among these documents:

- A 1983 memo from Turco summarizing the expenses of the Greenwich estate, including the fact that Hospitality Services was paying the salary of the Dunnellen Hall caretaker (whose salary was later listed on the books of the St. Moritz Hotel until it was sold to Donald Trump)
- Another memo from Harry Helmsley to various executives discussing the allocation of the estate's expenses between Helmsley-Spear, Hospitality Services, Deco Purchasing, the Park Lane, and the hotels in the Harley chain
- Memos sent every month to Harry or Leona Helmsley and some to both from Turco, detailing all bills relating to Dunnellen Hall and which of the Helmsley entities was paying them
- A memo noting that Deco was purchasing, and paying for, outdoor furniture, outdoor pool sets, sheets,

towels, walkie-talkies, even two golf carts for the estate.

He talked about using correction fluid on invoices so that the bills would look to outside accountants as though they were directed to Helmsley entities and not the Helmsley estate. He testified that Leona had directed that Hospitality Services pay her sister, Sandra Schulman, several thousand dollars for costume jewelry, with checks made out to cash. He had created phony documents so that Harry and Leona Helmsley could come away with five thousand dollars in cash for a trip to Las Vegas. On an ongoing basis, he found a way to cover all the chits for a few hundred dollars here and there that Leona sent in for reimbursement by having "guys in the office bring back blank restaurant receipts from lunch."

One day he discovered that Ed Kleiner, the manager of the Park Lane, was actually listing on the hotel's books the payments made for Dunnellen Hall without any attempt at subterfuge. Piacitelli told him to stop doing it that way, to set up some kind of code. Kleiner refused. Piacitelli went to Turco, and from that point on, Dunnellen Hall expenses were on the books and check stubs as relating to "DH." When one of the outside accountants going through the books noticed the initials and asked what "DH" stood for, Piacitelli told him, "Don't Hask." The accountant apparently didn't.

The use of Helmsley companies—mainly those owned totally by Harry Helmsley, though on occasion even those in which there were partners—was not limited merely to paying the costs of the renovations of Dunnellen Hall, but went so far as even to include personal goods and living expenses. Though meat and other major items were delivered weekly from the Park Lane, accounts were set up at the local Greenwich grocery stores for eggs, bread, ginger ale, carrots, potatoes, milk, onions, and all the rest. When the bills

came in, they were sent on for reimbursement to the Park
Lane and Helmsley-Spear if they had been paid out of a
petty cash fund over which Leona had total control. (She
had such control that she even checked to make sure that
she was getting reimbursed for bottle deposits.) On the
books of the Park Lane and Helmsley-Spear, they were listed
as miscellaneous expenses. After a time, though, those local accounts were closed when Leona Helmsley declared
that she would no longer approve such expenses because
most of what they were buying locally was available from
the Park Lane on its regular run up to Greenwich.

Piacitelli also testified on count forty-seven in the government's forty-seven-count indictment, extortion. There was
a day, he said, when he and another aide of Frank Turco,
Vince Sclafani, went over to the Helmsley Palace. When
they arrived, Leona was standing in the lobby talking to
someone. Piacitelli walked on, then looked back and saw
Sclafani "take out [an] envelope and hand it to her. She
continued the conversation." On another day he saw Sclafani go through the double doors into Leona's executive offices at the Palace. He was carrying an envelope of cash that
had been dropped on his desk earlier by liquor salesmen
who were paying monthly kickbacks in order to obtain the
Helmsley business.

Asked DeVita, "Did you ever have any conversations
about what was happening to the monthly money?"

"It was going to Mrs. Helmsley."

"And that was told to you by who?"

"Frank Turco."

Piacitelli's career with the Helmsleys came to an end early
in 1986. His boss, Frank Turco, was also on his way out at
the time, and Turco's office was being disbanded. For Piacitelli, who had spent his entire working life with the organization, it was a bitter blow, and so he decided to make
a direct appeal to Leona. She was that day being fitted at
the shop of her dressmaker, Julia, and he went to her and

pleaded for his job. She listened and replied, "I don't want
to hurt you, but I don't need you any longer."

Under cross-examination, Piacitelli rarely wavered. Was
Mrs. Helmsley having a lot of trouble with contractors at
Dunnellen Hall? Yes, and she was constantly complaining
about them, writing on one invoice for paneling her living
room walls: "Why so much? This is getting out of hand."

Isn't it true, Feffer pressed, that she thought everybody
was cheating her?

"I don't know. That's for her to answer."

Isn't it true that people were afraid they wouldn't live up
to her expectations?

"Speaking for myself, yes."

And what about all the kickbacks from the liquor vendors, the extortion, if you will? Turco, Piacitelli explained,
was always asking for kickbacks, and when somebody said
yes, then Turco said, "We don't want a kickback, just lower
the price for the Helmsley organization." But, still, everybody in the office knew that the liquor salesmen were coming in and dropping envelopes with cash on Turco's desk.
But, "Turco never took anything for himself."

Near the end of Piacitelli's nearly two days on the stand,
Turco's lawyer, William Brodsky, made a last effort to im-
peach his credibility. Why did Piacitelli agree to plead guilty
and then to testify, Brodsky asked. Wasn't it because he
and his wife were in the middle of trying to adopt a son and
"did they threaten to take him away, prevent the adoption
if you didn't agree?" And wasn't it true that he and his wife
had decided to adopt a second child and they were afraid
that if he were indicted and convicted the adoption would
not go through?

Well, Piacitelli said, he was certainly concerned and he
hoped by cooperating to protect the adoptions. Whether that
had anything do with it or not, he didn't know, but he and
his wife were able to adopt both children.

Jim DeVita was enraged. He drew himself up stiffly and
demanded, "Did the United States government or anyone

in the United States attorney's office every threaten you or
indicate anything to you in regards to the adoption of your
children if you did not agree to plead and to testify?''
   ''No,'' Piacitelli replied.

   Then came John Struck, a bearded bull of a man who had
worked his way up through eleven years from handyman to
director of engineering on a number of Helmsley-owned and
-managed properties. As an added responsibility, he was
assigned the task of overseeing the Dunnellen Hall renovations during the eighteen months following the departure of
Billy Piacitelli. At the time he thought it another step up the
Helmsley ladder.
   Had he had even an inkling of what lay in store for him
in Connecticut, he might have had second thoughts. The
troubles that had afflicted McCarthy and Piacitelli multiplied. Among many instances, one day when the workmen
who had been doing some lawn work happened to leave a
forklift on the grass, Struck recalled, ''There was a voice
in the distance. It was Mrs. Helmsley, sticking her head out
of the window, yelling at us to get it off her grass.'' Another
day he was explaining a problem to her and she wasn't buying the explanation. ''She picked up a telephone and threw
it across the room at me. I escaped injury.''
   According to Struck, phony invoices for work done on
the estate—billing Helmsley business properties and finding
the right ones to bill and inventing a logical explanation
for the bill—were the rule rather than the exception. When
devising phony invoices first came Struck's way, he went to
Turco to find out if that was what he was supposed to do.
''This is the procedure that has been followed, and the procedure will continue,'' Turco told him.
   And so it did. It had to be inventive, of course. ''I didn't
submit a bill for landscaping or tree-trimming to the building at 420 Lexington Avenue,'' he explained. ''There are
no trees there.''
   Struck's testimony about such inventive manipulation of

invoices was backed by Robert Sullivan, the controller of
the Harley Hotel chain based in Cleveland. One day, he
said, Frank Turco called him and asked, "What's our hotel
in Enfield, Connecticut, like? How much grass does it
have?"

"It's got a front and back lawn," Sullivan told him.

"Okay," Turco said. "Now it's got ten thousand pachysandras to go along with the grass." The pachysandras,
costing $1,535, were shipped to Dunnellen Hall, and billed
to and paid for by the Harley at Enfield, as were a lot of
other gardening expenses, sometimes running as high as
$35,000.

Above all, Struck oversaw the work on the pool and its
enclosure. When LaStrada took over from Olivieri, its executives promptly told the Helmsleys, as contractors are
wont to do, what a terrible job Olivieri had done. Much of
it had to be ripped out, and an enormous amount of work
would have to be done to put it all to rights. And so the
costs mounted, not merely because LaStrada was redoing
what had already been done but also because the Helmsleys,
and especially Leona, kept changing their minds about what
they wanted. For instance, workers had spent hours putting
up a wall on one side of the enclosure. Then, Struck testified, "They wanted two thirteen-foot bay windows cut into
the wall so they'd have a better view." The wall had to be
torn down and rebuilt, and what was worse, "It was the
dead of winter and we were fighting the weather." The
Helmsleys decided that instead of a roof over the enclosure,
it would be nice to have a dance floor up there, since dancing was as much a passion with them as swimming. And so
a dance floor of red marble they had.

In came LaStrada's bills, staggering by mid-1985—$1.2
million for the pool and enclosure, another $800,000 for
the dance floor up above. Struck, following orders from
Turco and Licari, orders they told him had come from the
Helmsleys—and Struck was sure they had since he helped
prepare monthly reports for them detailing all the Dunnellen

Hall expenses, and since he regularly saw bills and invoices
on which their initials appeared approving payment—
phonied-up invoices so everything went down on the books
as work done at the Helmsleys' Garden Bay Manor apartments in Queens and on other Helmsley properties.

By late fall of 1985, LaStrada was still owed $588,000
and the builder was having a lot of trouble getting its money.
The old tried-and-true method of falsifying invoices and
sending them on to Helmsley corporate entities for payment
had ended some months earlier. Why? Dunnellen Hall was
no longer the personal property of Harry and Leona. Looking to the future and the prospect of huge Connecticut in-
heritance taxes, they had sought a way out and so had set
up the 521 Corporation in Delaware—521 Round Hill Road
being the address of the estate—with themselves as the sole
shareholders. They then turned title over to the corporation,
and a little later Harry gave his shares, and so total ownership of it, to Leona. With a corporation now owning the
estate, the Helmsleys gave orders that all requests for payment were to go directly to them for approval and payment.
So Struck prepared a memo on the LaStrada outstanding
bill and handed it to Harry Helmsley one morning in the
library at Dunnellen Hall. Harry scanned it, shook his head,
and said he wasn't about to authorize payment based on that
memo. He ordered Struck to go back and prepare a more
detailed one.

Struck did as ordered, and about two weeks later, he and
Frank Turco went out to Dunnellen Hall and again met with
both Helmsleys in the library. Harry went over the new
memo, sighed, looked over at his wife, and said, "Lee, if
only you didn't order so much, maybe the costs wouldn't
be so high."

As Struck remembered it, "Mrs. Helmsley began to yell
and scream at Mr. Helmsley, 'You're being sucked in, too.
Can't you see they're all trying to steal things from us?
They're all trying to rob us. We don't owe them anything.'
Mr. Helmsley got very quiet. Mr. Turco got very quiet. I

thought it was time for me to leave, so I did. Mr. Turco remained. I stood about two or three rooms away and I could hear her screaming and yelling. I waited around to see if Mr. Turco would come out alive.''

"Did he?" DeVita asked.

"Yes," Struck said, and motioned toward the end of the defense table where Turco sat. "He's here."

Leona got her way. LaStrada wasn't paid and eventually brought suit against the Helmsleys, as did so many other contractors.

For eighteen months, Struck followed his orders faithfully, and though he ran afoul of the mistress of the estate now and again, he always escaped without being sacked. But his luck was about to end.

Just before Thanksgiving in 1985, the Helmsleys were about to depart for a two-week vacation. On the eve of their departure, Struck met with Leona in the butler's pantry and received a list of jobs she wanted completed before her return on December 8. Among those jobs was refinishing the eight doors to her bedroom so they would match the walnut floors. It was not as simple as it seemed. When the doors were stripped, he discovered that some had been made of one kind of wood and some of another, and making them match each other and the floors as well was a painstaking chore. Still, Struck thought he had time. As soon as the Thanksgiving holiday ended, the painters went back to work, labored through Friday and Saturday, finishing about noon on Sunday, December 1. On Monday they were scheduled to rehang the doors.

About two o'clock Sunday afternoon, Struck was at home when the phone rang. It was the groundskeeper at Dunnellen Hall. "He told me Mr. and Mrs. Helmsley were on their way home. I said, 'Thanks for the information. It's been nice knowing you.' Usually we kept each other informed beforehand if they were due so we could get prepared. It didn't happen this time. I wasn't going to have time to rehang the doors, and I knew she wouldn't be happy having no doors on her bedroom.''

The next morning he reached Dunnellen Hall about eight-thirty and immediately called Turco to tell him what had happened. Turco said, "John, I'm sorry, but you're fired.''

Struck thought maybe he could still save his job if he went directly to Leona. When she saw him, she began to scream that she'd had to hang the doors herself. "You're fired."

He immediately called Turco, and Turco said, "Go see her again. She fires people all the time and then changes her mind. Maybe she'll change her mind with you.''

Back to the library he went. "You came home a week early," he tried to explain. "The doors were supposed to be hung today. If you'd come home when we thought, the job would have been done.''

"I'm not allowed to come to my own house?'' Leona said.

"Of course," Struck said, and continued to explain, pleading with her for his job.

She wouldn't listen. "I'm sorry," she said. "I don't want to hurt you, but I have to make an example of you.''

And so John Struck's eleven-year career with the Helmsleys came to an end.

Korean-born Steve Chang was a composed, articulate, and convincing witness. A forty-nine-year-old engineer with a master's degree, he had come to the United States in 1971 and gotten a job as a mechanic at the Park Lane. Six years later, he decided to go into business for himself. "Mr. Helmsley told me if things didn't work out, there would always be a place for me in the Helmsley organization.'' As it happened, Chang's venture didn't work out and in 1979, he called Helmsley and was offered a job which amounted to that of a troubleshooter. Soon thereafter he was in charge of the engineering department at the Helmsley Building on

Park Avenue, though he was often called upon to handle problems at the St. Moritz and other Helmsley hotels.

In the summer of 1984 he got a message that Harry Helmsley wanted to see him at Dunnellen. "Mr. and Mrs. Helmsley were in the swimming pool. Mr. Helmsley said, 'Hello, how are you? How's the family?' And then he swam away. Mrs. Helmsley remained. She said there were maintenance problems at Dunnellen Hall; it was always too hot or too cold. She asked me to look into it. It was close to the weekend and I said I'd be back on Monday to see what was the trouble. She said, 'Why not tomorrow?' I said, 'Okay.' "

From that point on, he was at Dunnellen Hall three or four times a week, sometimes on weekends, often bringing with him the chief engineer and mechanic from the Helmsley Building. He was introduced to Turco by Leona and told he should confirm with Turco whatever jobs had to be done.

About a month after his first visit, Leona asked him to check out her indoor stereo system because she was very unhappy with the sound. He told her he was not familiar with music systems, but he would get the specs and see what could be done. What he discovered was that the system had been poorly designed and installed. Worst of all, the speakers had been set in a particularly inappropriate place. "I got in touch with the president of the company and said this is not the right way to install the system and Mrs. Helmsley is very unhappy. They offered to come and correct it, but when I told her, she said, 'Never mind. I am suing them.' "

Still, Leona loved music and she wanted it not only indoors but outdoors as well. She told Chang that she wanted an outdoor system "that would provide calm and nice music and she wanted the speakers underground. She said she had seen such a system at Disney World in Florida, and would I contact contractors to see how it could be done at Dunnellen Hall?" Leona's desire was to have music in the front yard, the outdoor pool, the tennis courts, the gazebo area, and the barbecue area. Chang advised against having music

at the tennis courts, saying, "I don't think people playing
tennis have a chance to listen to music." When Harry and
Leona thought about that, they agreed, and the tennis courts
were dropped. Leona wanted the system to contain fifty-
eight speakers. "I tell her this is too many, you can't get
nice, calm music with so many." Leona agreed, and cut
back to twenty speakers.

Now Chang had to get somebody to do the job. He got
one recommendation from a salesman he knew in building
supplies, then contacted four companies selected at random
from the Yellow Pages, and asked for bids. Those bids
ranged from a high of $230,000 down to $57,304 from Audio Sound Productions, the company recommended by
Chang's salesman friend. That was the bid accepted. Contracts were drawn, with Audio Sound to receive 50 percent
up front, 20 percent on delivery, and the final 30 percent
on satisfactory completion of the job.

All seemed well—until Chang got an invoice from Audio
Sound for the down payment on an "outdoor music system," addressed to him at Dunnellen Hall. According to
Chang, he sent the invoice on to Turco. Turco called and
told him, "I cannot approve this as it is."

Chang said, "Why not?"

Turco said, "Because it says it's for the installation of a
music system at Dunnellen Hall. Can you make it for some
kind of security system at 230 Park Avenue?"

Chang said, "No. We already have a security system. I
feel very uncomfortable about approving this. I cannot approve of something we already have."

Turco said, "Can you contact the vendor and have him
make another invoice regarding a security system at 230
Park Avenue?"

Chang said, "I would feel very uncomfortable about
that."

Turco said, "Do you want me to tell Mrs. Helmsley that
you feel uncomfortable?"

The way it was put to him, Chang was sure that if he

didn't do what he was told, he would be out of a job the next day. He called David Rosen, the president of Audio Sound. "I tell him that the invoice wasn't any good, and he'd have to make another regarding an electronic security system at 230 Park Avenue and did he mind. Rosen said, 'I don't care as long as I get paid.' "

Chang was still very disturbed. He called John Trainor, a senior vice-president of Helmsley-Spear, which managed 230 Park Avenue, and asked his advice. Trainor said, "I cannot advise you. You have to do it to the best of your knowledge." Chang said, "Then you will get the invoices. It's in your lap." Trainor replied, "When I get them, I will do what I have to do."

The new invoice, for an electronic security system at the Helmsley Building, arrived on September 9, 1984, with a request for a deposit of 50 percent on the total cost of $57,450. Chang, following the normal routine, sent the invoice up for a work approval and purchase order. On October 2 the check for $27,000 was ready, Chang picked it up, and gave it to Rosen.

Three weeks later, the charade was replayed: An invoice for an electronic security system arrived with a request for $16,000 payment. This time the invoice was sent by Chang to Leona at her office in the Helmsley Palace, because she had to approve all payments. She approved, in writing, and Rosen got his check. On December 15 the final "security system" invoice arrived, was signed and approved by Leona, and the payment made.

Initially, Leona was happy enough with Audio Sound's outdoor system to tell Chang to contact them once more to install another system. This one would provide music to the indoor pool, the dance hall, and the breakfast room. Audio Sound surveyed the area and on January 4, 1985, sent a proposal for a music system, otherwise to be called a security sound system at 230 Park Avenue, that would cost $36,392. Leona looked at it and wrote, "Okay. Leona Helmsley."

And then, as so often happened, Leona decided that she wasn't really as happy as she had thought. The outdoor system, she complained to Chang, wasn't working, at least the remote control wasn't working. Chang and Audio Sound checked it out. The system was set up in four zones, and the remote control unit had to be aimed at the receiver in the right zone and the right button pushed. If, for instance, the unit was aimed at the barbecue and she pushed the gazebo button, obviously it wouldn't work. They tried to explain this to Leona. "She says it does not work," Chang remembered. "We explained that you had to aim the right control. She said, 'I don't care. It does not work.' We explained how it worked. She was very annoyed and did not listen."

Then early one morning, his phone rang and he was ordered to Dunnellen Hall immediately; the entire music system had suddenly gone on at four-thirty in the morning. "I was very shocked." He called Audio Sound, which dispatched an emergency crew, and he himself sped up to Connecticut. There he met Leona, who was very upset. The Audio Sound specialists and Chang checked the main installation panel, and everything was in perfect order. "I tell her it doesn't make sense. She said the emergency generator went on. That's what set it off. But the emergency generator was not related to the stereo system, so it couldn't be. I say to her, 'Who told you that?'

"She said, 'Charlie told me.' Charlie was the gardener and general yard cleanup man.

"I said, 'What does Charlie know about it?'

"She said, 'Charlie knows a lot.'

"I said, 'This is not something he knows about.'

"She said, 'If Charlie told me, then that's what it was.'

"I said, 'If you believe Charlie's word over mine, then maybe we ought to change jobs.'

"She said, 'You'll pay for that.'

"I said, 'I have nothing to pay.' "

(As Steve Chang related this tale, spectators, lawyers, the

judge, even Leona Helmsley herself broke into howls of
laughter.)

The sound systems were Chang's bane at Dunnellen Hall.
When the new system was being installed in the dance hall,
Leona said she didn't want the speakers to show. Chang and
the sound experts decided to conceal them under large flower
pots. Leona was furious. Chang said, "You have any other
idea, we'll follow it."

"You are in charge," Leona said. "You're supposed to
handle it. If you didn't know what you were doing, why
didn't you tell me?"

Chang said, "I'm the supervisor. I rely on experts."

Leona walked away, and then a servant appeared and told
him he was wanted in the library. Both Helmsleys were
there. Leona said, "You don't know what you're doing. The
whole thing is a mess. I'm not happy with the system."
Chang told her, "You're not saying why you're unhappy. I
take full responsibility and I will wait for your instructions."

As Chang recalls, "The instructions were 'You're not to
come to Dunnellen Hall anymore.' I say to myself, 'God is
on my side.' "

So Chang, too, departed the Connecticut estate. But before he did, another occurrence disturbed him greatly. The
building supply salesman who had recommended Audio
Sound had stopped by his office one day and said that the
company wanted to show its appreciation for getting the
Dunnellen Hall contract. An envelope was left on Chang's
desk. Inside was two thousand dollars. He broached Rosen
about it, and asked whether this hadn't, perhaps, increased
the price to the Helmsleys. "I asked if there is any funny
business and Dave Rosen said, no, I do a fair business and
don't play games." Still, Chang was not happy about the
situation and he mentioned it to Leona. She merely walked
away. For a time, he said, "I was afraid I had insulted her."

His conscience continued to bother him, he said. "I don't
believe the money belongs to me. I was very uncomfortable.

I worked seventeen years at Helmsley, and I always walk and talk straight. I feel I have to buy something to give it to her to get the money off my hands.'' He used a small part of the money to take the Dunnellen Hall crew out to lunch. And then he did more. At the end of 1984, while he was still at Dunnellen Hall, Leona asked him if he knew anything about Oriental art and where the Helmsley might get some classic antiques. What she wanted in particular were steel masks for the walls. Chang went to downtown Manhattan and found an unusual bronze statue. He described it to Leona and she said, ''Go get it.'' He bought it for eight hundred dollars and gave it to her, and she set it in the library beside the fireplace. He told her that there was a twin to that statue, and she told him to get that one, too, and give her the bills. He did as ordered and was reimbursed, with two checks for eight hundred dollars each, from Deco Purchasing. Now, with the money from the supply salesman, he went back down to the Oriental art store and used most of those funds to buy two wood masks, two baked-mud masks, a tea table, and a steel belt. These he had packed and delivered to Dunnellen Hall as a present to Leona.

Chang may have been fired from Dunnellen Hall, but, unlike so many others who worked there, not from the Helmsley organization. When he left the estate, he returned to his job as troubleshooter and head of the Helmsley Building engineering department. All the same, by November 1987 he thought it was time to strike out on his own once more. He quit and set up his own engineering and consulting firm.

What followed were the tales of a willing witness and an extremely reluctant one. In the four years before he was fired in 1986, Ed Kleiner had been comptroller of the Park Lane Hotel, where the Helmsleys made their permanent home in a duplex aerie. Geoffrey Lerigo, who had once been general manager of the Park Lane, had become executive vice-president of the Helmsley Hotels, a job he still held. Together, they gave the court intimate details of just how the Helmsleys had used their hotel empire for personal purposes, not only on a grandiose scale but on a petty one as well. Though no one seemed to realize it during the years of the scheme, the Park Lane was a potential source of trouble. Most of the Helmsley subsidiaries that were used to funnel money for Dunnellen Hall and other personal expenses of the couple were owned 100 percent by Harry Helmsley personally or through one of his corporations. Not so the Park Lane. Though he was the largest stockholder, he had as partners a group of banks who were investors in a company called Realesco Equities, which owned about 25 percent of the Park Lane and some other Helmsley-controlled properties.

Kleiner didn't go up to Connecticut, but he knew plenty about what went on there and elsewhere in the Helmsley empire. A slim, nervous man who kept rubbing his hands, he had dark hair, a mustache, and glasses; his forte was numbers, and though not a CPA, he considered himself an expert accountant. When he first went to work in the Park Lane office, the bookkeeping system, he said, was a disaster. There were books upon books, accounts upon accounts for any number of small items. So Kleiner suggested to Turco that the system be modernized and consolidated to make it all easier to calculate.

Turco shook his head. Forget it, he said. "The only system we have around here is the Helmsley-cheat-the-government system."

Kleiner was stunned. "I thought perhaps he was joking. I later learned that perhaps he was not."

The effect of that statement on the jury was palpable, and the defense did its best to counter it. During cross-examination Feffer forced Kleiner to admit that before the grand jury he had testified that what Turco said was, "The only system we have around here is the *Harry*-Helmsley-cheat-the-government system." Why, Feffer demanded, had

Kleiner changed his testimony? Obviously flustered, Kleiner stammered that he had said "the Helmsley" inadvertently. Wasn't it, Feffer pressed, because Leona Helmsley was on trial here and Harry Helmsley wasn't? Perhaps, Kleiner admitted. But even with that admission, the damage had been done.

What's more, Kleiner was able to back it up. He had no stories of Leona Helmsley's outrages; he had, in fact, never even had a conversation with her save at staff social affairs. But he had journals, account books, ledgers, invoices, dozens of memos he had written to Turco and others over the years, and a series of memos he had written to himself in the privacy of his office at the end of working days. He kept a careful record of all that went on at the Park Lane during his tenure, worried that trouble might one day descend and he would need such a record to protect himself. He was worried enough, in fact, that he began looking for another job within months after he was hired by the hotel, though it was not until after he was fired in 1986 that he found one.

At first, as Dunnellen Hall bills began to arrive for payment at the Park Lane, he entered them on the books as costs of the estate. He even had a rubber stamp made reading "Dunnellen Hall" for the accounting staff to use. Then, in August 1983, Billy Piacitelli ordered him to stop doing that because outside auditors would pick up the fact that the hotel was paying the Helmsleys' personal bills. "Make up some code word to use because of taxes," Piacitelli told him. Kleiner did, from that point on using either the initials "G.C.," for Greenwich, Connecticut, or "D.H." for "Don't Hask," when entering estate expenses.

Guided by DeVita during the next two days, Kleiner went through the Park Lane accounts and through his memos, and in so doing laid out a scheme that was blatant in design and execution. All the expenses for Dunnellen Hall were put into the operating accounts of the Park Lane, not as advances to Harry and Leona Helmsley. If they had been listed as advances, they would have been a debt to the hotel and so repayable by the Helmsleys. As operating expenses, they were part of the hotel's operating costs and so a tax deduction for the hotel. It was Joe Licari, Kleiner said, who had given the instructions to do that, and when he asked Licari to put those instructions in writing, Licari replied, "We prefer not to do that."

Kleiner proceeded to detail just what kind of Helmsley personal expenses the hotel paid. There was a $210,000 invoice from Ashkenazie and Co. supposedly for an inlaid mahogany end table, initialed for payment, "HBH," for Harry B. Helmsley. Acting under Turco's direction, a convoluted method was devised to hide the transaction. It was first charged as an advance to Harry Helmsley and then a credit for $210,000 was entered, canceling out the advance, and the $210,000 for the purchase was then entered into the "Fixed Assets-Fine Arts" account of the hotel itself, so that any auditor looking over the books would assume that the hotel had bought an inlaid mahogany end table worth $210,000. The only thing was, no end table fitting this description existed at the Park Lane. There wasn't even an end table. Ashkenazie had supplied a jade statue for Dunnellen Hall.

That Fixed Assets-Fine Arts account, in fact, accumulated a lot of costly things that never saw the inside of the hotel—an 1850 rosewood inlaid cabinet worth $13,800 and two Chinese figurine pots at $800, to name just two. The invoices were okayed for payment by "LMH," standing for Leona Mindy Helmsley, or "HBH," meaning Harry B. Helmsley, showing that the Helmsleys knew all about the purchases and approved the payments.

A Fixed Assets-Furniture account served the same purpose. It absorbed a $94,364 bill from Deco Purchasing for mirrors, glass art, chairs, ottomans, paintings, and even a personal check Harry Helmsley wrote for $9,498. Among those furniture assets of the hotel was a $45,000 silver-and-gold-plated clock in the shape of the Helmsley Building. "What," DeVita asked suave, British-born Geoffrey Lerigo, "was the clock for?" Before Lerigo could respond, Judge Walker drew a laugh from the courtroom with a question of his own: "Was it to keep time?" Not precisely, Lerigo finally explained. It was a birthday gift from Leona to Harry, though Leona didn't pay for it, the Park Lane did.

And where is the clock? DeVita asked.

On Harry Helmsley's desk in the Helmsley's duplex suite atop the Park Lane.

How much were the Helmsleys paying for that apartment? A thousand dollars a month.

And what were the room rates at the Park Lane?

The cheapest rooms went for between $150 and $160 a night.

"By paying the room rate, you don't get to visit the clock, do you?" DeVita asked.

Lerigo only shrugged.

The hotel, of course, had more than Fixed Assets-Fine Arts and Fixed Assets-Furniture accounts. A Rooms and Uniforms account was charged, with Leona's initialed approval, more than $20,000 for three-piece morning suits, dresses, aprons, jackets, and four-in-hand ties for the Dunnellen Hall major domo, butler, maids, cooks, and all the rest of the staff. But that account didn't only pay big bills, it paid little ones too, such as $40 to have Leona's stone marten coat cleaned and $45 to Columbia Stage and Screen in Hollywood for makeup.

The Food and Beverage account for the kitchen, Kleiner and Lerigo detailed, had bought Dunnellen silver, crystal, and china, and paid $16,750 for fifty silver plates, $5,528.40 for one hundred pieces of plain white china, $7,762.73 for china with an Indian Tree pattern, $1,185.19 for twelve cups and saucers in the Hong Kong pattern, $10,000 for a silver-plated gallery tray and Gorham silver centerpiece, $396 for twenty-four silver card holders, and $698 for seventy-two nine-inch silver-plated trivets—the list seemed nearly endless.

When Harry and Leona took a trip to the Far East in

December 1983, they stopped off in Hong Kong and Harry spent $40,000 for pearls, writing a check on the Park Lane. The purchase was initially classified as an advance to Harry, until Ed Kleiner received a memo from Joe Licari telling him to give Harry a credit for $40,000 and list that amount on the Maintenance and Decorating account. And that account also paid $2,976 for a pair of eighteen-karat-gold cuff links with the representation of the Helmsley Building that Leona gave Harry as a present.

The Park Lane, it became evident, was paying a staggering amount of the Helmsleys' personal expenses. Once a week, a van left the hotel carrying food and beverages destined for Dunnellen Hall. The Helmsleys, though, thought perhaps they ought to pay part of that cost, and so Harry reimbursed the hotel for 40 percent. Most of the Dunnellen Hall staff was paid by the Park Lane until 1985, when Turco sent a memo to the hotel saying those employees were to be placed on the payroll of the Harley in Enfield for insurance and other benefit reasons. In 1985 the hotel even paid $10,260 for Christmas presents for the people at Dunnellen Hall.

In that same year the Helmsleys decided to take a ten-day vacation on the Caribbean island of Mustique. They chose Exclusively Cruises in Palm Beach to make all the arrangements, including $7,000 for a house in Palm Beach, and $18,000 for a boat charter from the island of St. Lucia to Mustique (the landing strip on Mustique was not long enough to accommodate their private jet, hence the need to charter a yacht). As it happened, the Helmsleys cut short their stay because the mosquitoes were swarming, returning home a week early (an event that led to the firing of John Struck because he didn't have the bedroom doors rehung in time). The total cost of that vacation came to nearly $30,000. And who paid for it? The Park Lane, naturally. And what did the books show? An expense for Advertising and Promotion.

This fraud was extended to petty cash. According to Kleiner, Leona used to drop by the offices at least once a week and take $20 or $30 or $40 from the petty cash account, and she ordered that no petty cash was to be dispensed to anyone for any purpose until the vouchers had been sent to her office at the Helmsley Palace and approved by her personally.

"What, if anything, does Mrs. Helmsley have growing in her Park Lane apartment?" DeVita asked Lerigo, to another burst of laughter.

Well, Lerigo explained, there was a greenhouse with plants. Park Interior Landscape provided those plants and those on the terrace and sent people three times a week to take care of them.

Who paid for the plants and the maintenance?

The Park Lane.

"Is the greenhouse open to the hotel guests?"

"No."

The capstone of this monumental greed was still to come, though. In October 1985 Joe Licari sent a memo to Ed Kleiner saying that "effective immediately" Leona Helmsley was to be paid $83,333.34 on the first of every month as a consulting fee, or $1 million a year. And the check was to be delivered to her office at the Helmsley Palace no later than the morning of the first of the month. The Realesco investors, despite their interest in the hotel, were never told of this, as they were never told of all the other personal expenses of the Helmsleys that were being picked up by the Park Lane.

The Helmsleys had a particular passion for jade, and this was where the prosecutor probed next. On that trip to the Far East they stopped off in San Francisco for a visit with an old acquaintance named Sidney Ashkenazie, who ran a shop specializing in Oriental art in the Fairmont Hotel. While in the shop, they chanced on a jade water buffalo. Leona was entranced, and the $220,000 asking price didn't faze her. "Chances are," she told Ashkenazie, "we'll buy it when we get back from our trip."

By February the Helmsleys were back in Connecticut, and Ashkenazie got a call from Leona. She had decided she would, indeed, like to own the jade water buffalo. Only she'd like a better price. Ashkenazie, who usually did not negotiate prices, agreed this one time to come down $10,000 to $210,000. Envisioning a long-term relationship with the billionaire Helmsleys, he said, "Every art dealer dreams of having a client like the Helmsleys." Then Leona said that before she finally committed herself, she'd like to take another look at the piece. Ashkenazie agreed to personally carry it to Connecticut along with about fifteen other jade pieces that the Helmsleys might find of interest.

At Dunnellen Hall, the jade was spread out. Harry and Leona examined what Ashkenazie and his wife, Robin, had to offer, and ended up deciding on the water buffalo and four other items—a *koro,* or jade incense burner, an eighteenth-century jade mountain, and a pair of small lavender jade water buffalo with children perched on their backs. The total price: $500,000.

The Ashkenazies left the jade behind and headed back to San Francisco with the promise of payment of the $500,000 within two or three days. Once home, Robin Ashkenazie wrote a letter of thanks to Leona: "It was certainly thrilling to see such a fantastic house, though I'm not sure fantastic adequately describes such a house. . . . As you discussed with Sidney regarding payment," she was sending along invoices, one for $210,000 for the large jade buffalo, which was owned by Ashkenazie, and $50,000 for the pair of smaller buffalo, $80,000 for the koro, and $150,000 for the jade mountain. The check for $210,000 should be made out to Ashkenazie's company, Alcar, while the check for $290,000 for the other items should be made out to Dennison Investment, Ltd., of Hong Kong, which had given the pieces to Ashkenazie on consignment.

Then the Ashkenazies notified Dennison that its jade had

been sold to the Helmsleys for $290,000 and that payment was due in a day or two.

The day or two passed and no check arrived. Five weeks passed and still no check appeared in the mail. Ashkenazie was now under a lot of pressure. He owed money to Dennison and he was owed $210,000 himself, and for a small business, which his was, such large unpaid bills spelled disaster. He was well aware, he testified, "from rumors that Mrs. Helmsley could become disenchanted with something easily, and I was worried that this might be the case, and I knew that a sale is not a sale until the check is in the bank." So he called Leona and politely requested payment as soon as possible. She was most apologetic. She told him she thought Harry had taken care of the bill and, obviously, Harry had thought she had. But Ashkenazie was not to worry. She would personally see that it was taken care of immediately.

The next day, Ashkenazie got a call from a man who identified himself as Joseph Licari. Licari said he was speaking on behalf of Harry Helmsley and asked Ashkenazie to send a set of new invoices. "Send me different invoices," Licari said. "Send me invoices indicating that the things the Helmsleys bought are furniture."

"I can't do that," Ashkenazie said. "I don't deal in furniture."

But Licari pressed and Ashkenazie, knowing the money was essential to the survival of his firm, finally capitulated. Still, he told Licari, he was very concerned that if anyone decided to look into the matter, such invoices wouldn't hold up.

Licari replied, "Then send me some blank invoices and you can put on yours whatever you want and I'll put on mine what I want." That's what Ashkenazie did, sending a number of blank invoices to Licari with a note that it would be all right to enter furniture in the case of Dennison because that firm did deal in furniture.

Within days the art dealer received a series of checks for

full payment, along with photo copies of the blank invoices and a letter from Licari noting, "Enclosed are four checks." When the Ashkenazies looked at the checks and the invoices, they discovered:

1. The Helmsley Windham Hotel was paying for the pair of small jade buffalo, only they were now some antique tables.
2. The Helmsley Carlton House was paying for the koro, which had become chairs and tables.
3. The Park Lane was paying for the large buffalo, which had turned into an inlaid mahogany card table.
4. The St. Moritz Hotel was paying for the jade mountain, which had been transformed into a cherry-wood highboy and several other valuable pieces of furniture.

Over the eighteen months that followed, Ashkenazie offered several other jade pieces, but failed to elicit any interest. Then, in September 1985, he received a call from Leona. She had decided she wasn't completely happy with the $150,000 jade mountain. Could she return it? Ashkenazie assured her that of course she could. Then he and Robin set off for Greenwich to retrieve it, carrying with them several other jade pieces in hopes of making a swap. Leona examined them and chose two, worth $79,000, which left Ashkenazie owing her $71,000. He agreed to make the refund without delay, but when he got back to San Francisco, he had some trouble raising the money. Instead he sent her a check for $41,000, and a couple of months later, a second check for $30,000. Both checks were made payable to Leona M. Helmsley. Both checks were endorsed and cashed by Leona M. Helmsley. There was no record of Leona M. Helmsley reimbursing the St. Moritz, which had paid for the jade. (Indeed, when Donald Trump bought the St. Moritz, those valuable pieces of "furniture" for which the hotel had paid $150,000 were still on the books among the hotel's assets, only they were nowhere to be found on the premises. In order to forestall any action, legal or otherwise, that might grow out of such a disappearance, Harry Helmsley made out a personal check to Trump to cover the value of that "furniture.")

Elizabeth Baum was a middle-aged, German-born housekeeper living in Texas when a call came in the summer of 1983 that Leona Helmsley would like to hire her to supervise the growing staff of chefs, butlers, seamstresses, maids, and other household help at Dunnellen Hall. It would be a long move, but that was all right because Mrs. Helmsley was paying the $3,988 moving bill—if not Mrs. Helmsley, then the Park Lane, on whose books the move would appear not as one from Texas to Connecticut but from Texas to New York. And the salary was good—though she soon discovered that her salary and those of the others on the staff were being paid not by Leona or Harry Helmsley but by the Park Lane and the Harley hotel chain, based in Ohio. So Elizabeth Baum agreed and made the move.

She quickly learned that working for Leona Helmsley was not the most pleasant of experiences. The mistress of the household "screamed at everyone . . . everyone was scared of her . . . she was very nasty." When Baum, who placed the weekly order for groceries and household supplies for delivery from the Park Lane, happened to pay for a few things she ordered at the local grocery for the staff and asked for reimbursement, Leona Helmsley snapped, "You bought it, you pay for it."

She had been at the estate for about six weeks when she encountered Leona in a back hall. In a moment of idle conversation, as Baum surveyed the domain with awe, she remarked, "You must pay a lot of taxes." The Queen's facetious response turned out to be the most memorable one of the trial: "We don't pay taxes. Only the little people pay taxes."

Baum's reign over the Dunnellen Hall staff lasted a mere six months before she was called into the kitchen. Without any preliminaries, "She screamed and yelled at me. She cursed me and said I was fired." Baum went upstairs and began to pack. Leona summoned her again and told her, "Everything's okay. You can stay." The reprieve lasted less than a week and then Turco took her aside and said, "Mrs. Helmsley wants you off the property." And so, like so many others who passed briefly through Leona Helmsley's life, Elizabeth Baum was gone.

Were the Helmsleys ignorant of just what was being done in their name? That was the contention of the defense. It was all being done behind their backs simply to make sure that contractors and suppliers were paid. On cross-examination Feffer wrung from most of the government witnesses the admission that bitter experience with Leona Helmsley's volatile temper and imperious demands so cowed them that they would do almost anything rather than face her and suffer that wrath once more. He wrung from them, too, the admission that they took their orders from Frank Turco, and sometimes Joe Licari. Most shared the view that this was often the only way anyone would ever be paid, given Leona Helmsley's conviction that everyone was out to cheat her.

Ed Kleiner, though, had prepared the Park Lane monthly reports not just for Turco but for the Helmsleys as well. And Geoffrey Lerigo testified that no bills were ever paid without Leona Helmsley's express permission. He had once paid a voucher for flowers, on his own, only to discover that "Mrs. Helmsley was not happy with the flowers and said she would not pay the bill. I told her I had already approved the payment. She was very angry and she made me repay the company. After that, I never paid a bill without her approval."

Further, the Helmsleys kept complete records, in excruciating detail, of every item bought for Dunnellen Hall. This vital link was uncovered by Martin Goldstein, Leona's personal assistant from 1985 until he quit in early 1989 because "I couldn't stand all the yelling." The records were kept in what came to be known as the "Dunnellen Hall A-File." One copy existed, along with regular business records and files, on the bookcase behind Harry Helmsley's desk in the Lincoln Building, updated regularly by his secretary. And Leona Helmsley had a duplicate. Goldstein told how he and Leona had been going through her desk one day in April 1988 in search of some documents when he came upon the file. The government had known that it existed, had subpoenaed it, but it had somehow vanished. Now, Goldstein exclaimed to his employer, "That's the Dunnellen A-File that the government's looking for." By then wise enough in the ways of the law, Leona told him to send it on to her lawyer, who, as required, passed it on to the United States attorney's office.

The appalling and incriminating tale of Helmsley chicanery extended even to the smallest and cheapest items. These were laid out for the court by IRS agent John Dennehy, aided by seven- by ten-foot charts and graphs detailing the personal expenses Leona charged to the Park Lane and other Helmsley companies.

Based on an analysis of books, records, check stubs, charge slips, and more, Dennehy's charts show that the Park Lane had paid the bill not just for $35,000 worth of designer Bob Mackie dresses, but for such things as:

- $19.75 plus $1.25 in postage for a yearly subscription to The Crosswords Club, entitling the member, in this case Leona Helmsley, to four crossword puzzles a month.
- $32 for Super Bug Away insect repellent.

- $58 for an Itty Bitty Book Light.
- $214 for apples.
- $355 for tomatoes.
- The hotel paid even for her hair rollers and pins, paid $58.49 to have her legs waxed, and paid $12.99 for a girdle from Bloomingdale's, among other items of lingerie and swimsuits.

When the defense on cross-examination contended that many of these items were legitimate business expenses because Leona wore them when posing for her "Queen Stands Guard" advertisements, Jim DeVita countered, his voice edged with sarcasm, by asking Dennehy, "You never saw an advertisement in which Mrs. Helmsley appeared in her underwear, did you? . . . You never saw an ad in which Mrs. Helmsley appeared in girdles or swimwear, did you?"

Dennehy's charts were fascinating, but for the most part the testimony that accompanied them was a dry, seemingly endless explanation of the intricacies of tax law that had the court, jurors included, nodding off, and many spectators fled. Not so when it came to Mary Ann DiMicco Eboli, Leona's one-time secretary and personal assistant. She not only knew the details of all the major expenses but also of the petty ones.

An attractive blonde dressed in a white suit, with eyes and nose swollen and rimmed with red from hay fever, she never once in her hours on the witness stand looked at her former boss, though Leona glared at her relentlessly. She had worked for Leona from 1979 until 1985, years in which she had been intimately familiar with the life- and business-style of the hotel queen.

When she (neither prosecution nor defense could make up their minds whether to call her Ms. DiMicco or Mrs. Eboli during direct and cross-examination; DiMicco was her maiden name, Eboli the name of the man she had married and later divorced) first went to work, Leona had a personal checking account out of which she had paid her own expenses. Once Dunnellen Hall became a reality, that changed. According to Eboli, a new account was opened in New York on the Florida-based Deco Purchasing, and from that point on the personal account was used only to make investments and pay medical bills before they were reimbursed by insurance. The Deco New York account, on the other hand, became the font "for buying and redecorating 'the house,' as Mrs. Helmsley called Dunnellen Hall," and not only the house, but gowns from Leona's favorite dressmaker, Julia, and other personal expenses. When Leona wanted money deposited into that account, something she seemed to want often even though Harry Helmsley was giving her a check for $3,000 a month in walking-around-money—which she immediately cashed at the Helmsley Palace and turned into thirty one-hundred-dollar bills—she "would call Frank [Turco] and tell him the amount, and he would get checks from various companies and then she would deposit them." And the checks on the Deco New York account were signed by Leona herself or, when she directed, by Mary Ann Eboli and Frank Turco jointly. "Was the account ever used to pay business expenses for the hotels?" DeVita asked. "No," Eboli said.

The defense might claim that the Helmsleys worked long hours at Dunnellen Hall and so had the right to charge off at least half the expenses against their taxes, but Leona had told Eboli, that "Dunnellen Hall was purchased for the sole purpose of their having a weekend, vacation, and holiday home in which to relax."

What was being spent on that home, and who was paying, was no secret from Leona Helmsley. "Nothing could be paid without Mrs. Helmsley's approval," Mary Ann Eboli said. "I would go to her with a bill and she would instruct me, and then I would issue checks and send copies to Frank." But never to Joe Licari. "She told me she hated Joe Licari and she didn't want him to see anything and she didn't want him to having anything to do with Dunnellen

Hall.'' Still, Eboli kept accurate records of all the transac-
tions. Leona, she said, usually dictated the memos to her,
and she entered into the Dunnellen A-File, which she kept
in her desk, just what was being spent, for what, who was
doing the work, and who was doing the paying. Mary Ann
had, among other things, typed the fake Ashkenazie invoices under Leona's direction, she said, though she couldn't
remember exactly where she had gotten the descriptions of
the furniture that had been entered on those documents.

Leona was not only well aware of what was being spent
on Dunnellen, she was equally occupied with just how her
mansion was being run. The rules were explicit and detailed, according to a memo she dictated to Mary Ann Eboli.
It read, in part:

> When the Helmsleys are expected and in residence
> at Dunnellen Hall, their quarters are to be checked
> for cleanliness; if cold outside, a fire is to be made in
> the bedroom or den fireplace.
>
> It is imperative and mandatory that *everything* must
> have a place. Whether it be a towel, or a needle, or a
> hairpin, or a dish pattern—each must be in its place.
>
> Keys to the wine cellar are to be kept by Mrs.
> Helmsley, and any request must go through her. A
> complete inventory must be prepared of the liquor and
> wines stored in the cellar. A log book will be pre-
> pared and maintained in the wine cellar with a per-
> petual inventory indicating removals, name and date.
>
> Guest rooms—all guest rooms are to have toilet wa-
> ter and/or perfume, hair blower, two robes, tooth-
> brush, fresh toothpaste, comb, scale, hot curlers,
> soaps in sink and tub, basket, towels, bath mat,
> Q-tips, bath gel, shower cap, or any other items that
> can make our guests feel comfortable.
>
> Food—all food in the large freezer is specifically
> for Mr. and Mrs. Helmsley's use only. If there should
> be a need for anything within this freezer, it must be

requested. The help has a refrigerator, freezer and
oven in their dining room. These were installed for
the purpose of being utilized by them for their meals.
   All employees at Dunnellen Hall must cook and
clean for themselves. All telephone messages for the
Helmsleys must be written down. All long-distance
calls made by the help are to be paid for by that person
making the call.

   Until 1981 Leona worked out of an office in the Park
Lane. Then she moved to more luxurious quarters in the
Helmsley Palace. With that, Leona said to her assistant,
"Things change now. I can't wear these slacks anymore.
I'm going to have to walk through the lobby. I have to dress
properly, look properly. I can deduct a lot of these things
now that I'm president of the Helmsley Hotels. From now
on, forget the personal account and submit all bills to the
Park Lane, except for the American Express, which goes to
Brown, Harris, Stevens."
   Among those American Express charges was a curious
sidelight on spendaholic Leona Helmsley. She was, it seems,
a catalog freak. Everybody gets mail order catalogs; they
pile up in mail boxes and on doorsteps. Almost everybody
throws most of them away. Not Leona Helmsley. "I used
to try to hide the catalogs from her," Eboli sighed. "It
didn't always work." L. L. Bean, Lands' End, J. C. Pen-
ney, Sears, Saks Fifth Avenue, Bloomingdale's, Bergdorf,
it didn't matter. Leona pored over them intently and ordered
voluminously, often the same items in several different sizes,
colors, styles, and when they arrived, kept some and sent
others back, telling Mary Ann to send the bills over to
Brown, Harris, Stevens and "tell them which to pay." Those
bills ranged from as little as $24.90 to $1,694.
   What finally led to Eboli's break with Leona was the 1985
firing of her brother from his job at the Helmsley Palace.
"The firing was done underhanded, and I was very disturbed with Mrs. Helmsley because she had not let me know

about it until later. I went to her and we had a long conversation and she said maybe she could get him another job at Helmsley-Spear.'' That job never materialized, and Eboli, seething, went home, wrote out her resignation, and sent it off Federal Express. She never went back to the office.

Though she had quit, her involvement in the Helmsley affairs was far from over. As with many of the Helmsleys' trusted employees, Eboli had been well rewarded for her work. Her annual salary of nearly thirty thousand dollars a year had been lavishly supplemented by Christmas presents and bonuses. It was one of those Christmas presents that landed her in a lot of trouble and ended up turning her into a witness for the government. Shortly before the holidays in 1984, Leona came to her and said, ''Did you hear about your Christmas gift? I'm not giving you anything this year. Frank is taking care of it.''

Frank Turco was taking care of it, indeed. Her Christmas gift was to be twenty-five thousand dollars, and she got it in a most unusual way. Billy Piacitelli arrived at the office and handed her ten thousand dollars in cash. Frank Turco arrived and handed her a check for ten thousand dollars, with a note saying it was a return on a joint investment they had made on a thoroughbred horse—an investment that had never happened. And she got two checks for twenty-five hundred dollars from a Helmsley supplier. The trouble was, she didn't bother to declare this bonus on her income tax return. When the IRS came knocking on her door, she anted up the taxes, penalties, and interest, and, in exchange for the government's decision not to prosecute, she agreed to testify about all she knew of the activities of her employer.

She had more to talk about, though, than just the bills and the records. She was the witness, the government seemed convinced, whose testimony would draw Leona Helmsley into the web of extortion.

By early August, it was apparent to most of those who had sat through a month of trial that the government's tax case was nearly unassailable. Nobody needed or wanted to hear any more about it, and Judge Walker, showing considerable impatience, put an end to it. He didn't want the trial to drag on for months more. One of the jurors had a son who was being married early in September, and she wanted to go to the wedding. Walker assured her that the case would be over by Labor Day. He told Jim DeVita that he wanted to government to finish its case by August 11. And so the pressure was on the government to move rapidly.

But DeVita had offered almost nothing about the conspiracy to commit extortion. Because it carried the harshest punishment, up to twenty years in prison, it was considered the most serious.

So far there had been little testimony. The only witness, in fact, who had directly talked about extortion had been Billy Piacitelli. He said he had seen salesmen dropping cash-filled envelopes on Turco's desk and the desk of Turco's aide, Vince Sclafani. Moreover, he said he had watched Sclafani hand one of those envelopes to Leona Helmsley in the lobby of the Helmsley Palace and disappear into her private office with another. But no one so far had corroborated Piacitelli.

Now the government turned to count forty-seven. It began not with cash but with goods, calling to the stand Milton Meckler, who had been executive vice-president of the Florida-based Deco Purchasing. It was, he said, a thankless job. Deco was buying and paying for "every conceivable or inconceivable thing that would go in a mansion-type place," and as a result its profits were disappearing fast. Worried that his bosses, especially Harry Helmsley, would blame him for being an incompetent executive, he went directly to Harry to explain. But Harry soothed, "Don't worry about it. I know all about it." Still, he was worried, so he framed a proposal to change Deco's bookkeeping system so the books would be cleared of the nearly $1 million in Dunnellen Hall expenses, and then he would be able to show a profit. He put the proposal in writing for all to see, including the auditors. The result? Frank Turco told him, "You've just cost the Helmsleys $800,000 in taxes," and Leona ranted that he was "an idiot."

But Meckler and Deco were doing more than hiding Dunnellen Hall costs, Meckler said. He was ordered by Turco to put the pressure on suppliers for free merchandise, with the threat that if they didn't come across, they either would lose Helmsley business they already had or not get Helmsley business they were after. On the list of vendors supplying various Helmsley hotels and other businesses, an "x" appeared after some. Meckler said that Turco explained to him that the "x" meant the vendor "is to eat the cost if he wants to keep our business. This is what Mrs. Helmsley wants and this is what I want. Do it." Meckler did it, and the suppliers who agreed to eat their costs kept the business and those that resisted lost it.

And there were things that Leona Helmsley allegedly wanted free as adornments for her estate, among them new mattresses, because the first ones they ordered had given her husband a backache, and red kimonos for the pool. But Meckler's memory may have been faulty, at least as far as the mattresses were concerned. Feffer produced canceled checks showing that, actually, the original mattresses had been paid for and then credited against the replacement ones, and that the Helmsleys had paid the difference.

His testimony about television sets was less easily shaken. RCA had once supplied Helmsley-owned hotels, but for some reason it had earned Leona Helmsley's displeasure, and the business had been handed over to Zenith. Now RCA was trying to get back into the Queen's good graces. After much bargaining with Deco, it agreed to supply six hundred television sets to the Harley Hotels at $305 apiece, which was $1.50 below cost. Meckler took the proposal to Leona. She wanted to know how many TVs she could get for Dunnellen Hall—free. And she wanted them immediately, in time for her birthday, before any order was placed. Meckler went back to RCA. RCA was anxious enough to recapture a share of the Helmsley business to ship off three TVs. Leona's reaction? According to Meckler, she said, "How many more can I get?''

That Leona got the three TVs for free, nobody denied. But Meckler's credibility was called into question during cross-examination. It turned out that Meckler himself had gotten a free twenty-five-inch TV from RCA, supposedly by telling the salesman that he needed it for demonstration purposes, leading to possible future sales, in Florida. But the TV was installed in Meckler's home. Just before Meckler was called to testify before the grand jury, he happened to run into that salesman and suddenly remembered that twenty-five-inch TV and asked why he hadn't been billed for it. He got a bill and paid it promptly.

She didn't want just TVs and kimonos, according to Meckler. He remembered a day when he and Turco spotted a representative of the Dom Perignon champagne company. Turco told Meckler all he had to do was ask and he could have as many cases of champagne as he wanted. But, he said, "I have more champagne than I need and so does Mrs. Helmsley. I don't want cases and she doesn't want cases. What I want and what he's going to give me is cash. That's what Mrs. Helmsley wants.''

And so at last it had come down to the cash.

Lee West was an impressive witness. An immaculately groomed man in his mid-sixties, with white hair and a neatly trimmed white beard, he spoke eloquently in polished tones. A one-time professional musician, he had gone on to become a wholesale liquor salesman for Peerless Importers, exclusive distributors of such popular brands as Dewar's scotch and Gilbey's gin, among others. Among his clients had been the St. Moritz and the Park Lane hotels.

In September 1983 he got a call from Vince Sclafani, asking him to come to a meeting at the Graybar Building in New York. The man in command of that meeting was Frank Turco. "Have any of the Helmsley food and beverage people ever asked you for a kickback?" Turco asked.

"Absolutely not," West said.

"Is it done in the liquor business?"

"I've heard of it being done," West replied, but, he added, mainly in dealing with retailers and not with such large customers as restaurants and hotels.

"If you were to get a large portion of the Helmsley liquor business," Turco asked then, "what will you do for us?"

West's answer was, "I will give you very, very good service." It was, he testified, a response that did not seem to make Turco very happy, for Turco said that other salesmen were offering him Jaguars, trips to Europe for himself and his family, and a lot more.

West said he couldn't match those offers. All he could do was provide good service and show Turco a way the hotels could save lots of money. The state liquor laws, he explained, set the minimum prices for wine and liquor, but there was an out; under those laws, if a customer bought over five cases at a time, he was entitled to a 2 percent discount. "You're buying the wrong way now," West said. The St. Moritz and the Park Lane were each buying only what they needed, usually four cases or less at a time, and so neither was getting the discount on quantity. If all the Helmsley hotels consolidated their purchases, they would be entitled to that discount, and with the amount of wine and liquor they bought, those discounts would add up to a large savings. They might get additional savings as well because a good salesman would also let them know what brands were on special each month.

"Mr. Turco listened to me and he said he liked the idea and he asked me to write up a proposal." West did, presented the proposal to Turco, and they went over it. Turco seemed to take to it and said he would let West know if the Helmsley hotels wanted to follow through, though the final decision was, of course, up to Mrs. Helmsley.

Then, in mid-December, he was called to another meeting with Turco. He was told that Turco had met with several other liquor salesmen who had also submitted proposals for taking over the Helmsley business, but he and Mrs. Helmsley had decided that West's proposal made the most sense and so, beginning January 1, 1984, the new centralized wine- and liquor-buying program would begin, and the business would be West's.

As West was absorbing the good news, Turco added his zinger. Of course, the Helmsley aide-de-camp said, the Helmsleys wanted a kickback. West worked on commissions, earning 5 percent of whatever he sold. What Turco wanted was 2 percent, equal to 40 percent of West's commissions. "This had never come up before in our conversations," West said, "and I was really shocked. I said, 'Let me think about it.' " Turco told him to think hard, because either he paid the 2 percent or "we'll get somebody else." So West considered, and even talked to a lawyer (what the lawyer advised, he didn't say, and neither DeVita nor Feffer asked, for, of course, a lawyer's advice to his client is privileged). Finally he went back to Turco and said, "Much as I dislike this, I will do it."

And so, he became the primary supplier of wines and liquor to the Helmsley Hotels in New York, supplying not only Peerless's exclusive brands but also the so-called house brands. As for the brands that Peerless didn't carry, he was told to deal with Capital and Standard Foods, and told that both had agreed to the same kickback.

On February 10, 1984, he made his first payment, delivering nearly one thousand dollars in cash in a white envelope to Turco's office in the Graybar Building, handing it either to Turco or a Turco aide, he couldn't remember which. What he did remember was that he asked, "Out of curiosity, who's getting the money?"

Turco's reply: "Mrs. Helmsley."

And Sclafani added, "We don't touch a penny of it. It all goes to her." (Before the grand jury, however, as the defense was quick to bring out on cross-examination, West testified that Turco had disputed Sclafani's comment, saying, "No. It all goes back into sales.")

"Why?" West asked.

"It was her idea and that's the way she wants it."

For three months, he delivered 40 percent of his commissions to Turco, before he complained that this was really hurting him a great deal. West was told, okay, the kickback would be cut in half. It went on for a year, during which he handed over between eight thousand dollars and ten thousand dollars.

The up side of it was that during that year, Peerless's wine and liquor sales to the Helmsley Hotels skyrocketed. In 1983 the company's sales to the chain had been $265,845. A year later, with the kickbacks in force, sales were up to $582,646.

And then the arrangement came to a sudden end. The first complication arose during the fall, when Turco suggested to West that it might be nice if Peerless took out an ad in Turco's son's school journal. West carried the word back and assumed that Peerless had agreed, but then Turco called him in, showed him the journal, and angrily demanded, "Where's your ad?" It wasn't there. West apologized and was sure the apology had been accepted.

In December 1984, as the first year was running out, Turco called West into his office. "He told me they were very pleased with the way things had worked out and that I had saved them a lot of money through my idea. Then he said Peerless had made so much money on the sales to the Helmsley Hotels that he wanted Peerless to do something for them."

"What?" West asked.

"We want you to take a suite at the Carlton House for a year." The rent of that suite would be fifty-five thousand dollars.

It seemed outrageous to West. Nevertheless, he took the Turco demand to his employers. They rejected it. When he reported the rejection, Turco said, "If you don't do it, we'll get someone else."

Back he went to Peerless, telling them, "We'll lose the

business unless we agree to take the suite." Still, they wouldn't agree. "We have no need for a room and we will not be blackmailed into taking a room," they said.

He carried that message to Turco. "You're out" was Turco's response. "Finish off the month and after that we're not going to do business with your company again." As for West himself, "If you get another job, we'll do business with you." In fact, Turco would even arrange for West to get a job with Star Industries. West considered it, then decided against it, for Star Industries' product line was not the equal of Peerless's and so he stood to lose other customers if he made the switch. He explained all that to Turco. "Okay," Turco said, "then get the hell out of here."

As for Peerless, though it continued to supply the Helmsley hotels with Dewar's, Gilbey's, and other brands available nowhere else, its sales to the hotel chain dropped dramatically, by more than 75 percent.

James Pursley, a liquor salesman for Star Industries, moved into the slot vacated by West. On January 31, 1985, he and his employer met with Turco and Sclafani, and Dave Feinberg of Standard Foods, who would handle the lines Star didn't have access to, in Turco's office. He knew all about the kickback arrangement; his boss had explained it to him on the ride over: "If we don't pay the kickback, we won't have the business." To make sure he wasn't hurt, Star Industries was increasing his commission to $6\frac{1}{2}$ percent, which meant he would still be pocketing $4\frac{1}{2}$ percent commissions and those commissions would increase sharply with the Helmsley business in hand.

Every month from then until February 1986, he turned up at Turco's office with envelopes filled with cash and handed them to either Turco or Sclafani, paying out about seventy-two hundred dollars. Like West, he was curious as to the ultimate destination of that cash and asked Turco about it one day. "None of the money goes to me," Turco said. "It all goes to Mrs. Helmsley. I don't take any. If you don't believe me, pick up the phone and call her right now and ask her. She pays all her employees well and so she puts the money in a vault and takes from it.'' Pursley, however, didn't take up Turco's offer to call Leona.

The arrangement finally came to an end in February 1986. Pursley was summoned to the Helmsley Palace, where Sclafani now had his office. Turco's office had been disbanded, Sclafani told him. Sclafani was taking over, under Mrs. Helmsley's brother, Alvin Rosenthal, and there would be no more kickbacks until further notice.

The arrangement entered into by Herb Cohen of Capital Distributors was different, and strange. But then everything about Cohen's arrangements was odd. He, and Capital, were supplying the hotels with the brands they carried, yes, but he didn't actually do any work. Lee West of Peerless did. West would visit the hotels, take the orders, centralize them, then feed to Capital the orders for brands that company carried and Peerless didn't. Cohen never even visited the hotels once West arrived on the scene, merely sat home and collected his commissions, and then made his kickback. And he didn't even make the kickback in cash; he entered into an agreement with Turco to pay by check, made out to Realesco (and under cross-examination, Feffer suggested that perhaps Cohen, by paying by check, might have been able to write off those kickbacks as a business expense on his taxes, an ironic idea in the midst of this case, indeed).

And so the envelopes stuffed with bills had finally come to center stage. But the man who had received them had been Frank Turco, and the only evidence that Leona Helmsley was their ultimate destination was what Turco had said to the salesmen. This point was hardly conclusive, easily interpreted as self-serving. Indeed, it seemed at that point that if anyone was going to be convicted of extortion it was going to be Frank Turco.

But that's when Mary Ann DiMicco Eboli tied the sovereign of the hotel chain directly into the scheme. One day in 1984, ''Frank Turco called and said he was coming over. He came running into the office and he went into Mrs.

Helmsley's office and he told me to shut the door. He was
carrying a letter-sized manila envelope with him. After
about a minute he opened the door and told me to come in.
Mrs. Helmsley had her desk drawer open and she was lifting
out a white envelope and putting it into her purse. I could
see that the envelope had been opened and resealed, and
Frank was holding the manila envelope, which was empty.''

That evening, Eboli, who regularly packed Leona's purse
and papers before they left, saw the envelope again in the
purse. She lifted it to move it in order to put other things in
the purse. "It felt like something that was rectangular. It
felt like money. You could see there was money in it.''

About a month later, Turco called again and said he was
coming over, that he had to see Leona right away. Turco
came running into the office. (According to Eboli, Turco
was always running when he was on the way to see Leona.)
He held up a fat envelope and said, "I'm going to make the
old lady real happy today.'' Then he disappeared into the
office, closed the door, and reappeared almost immediately
without the envelope.

That evening, when she was packing Leona's purse, she
saw the envelope again. She moved it. "It appeared to contain money," she said.

Of course, Frank Turco was given to some exaggeration.
For instance, he once told Mary Ann that he needed a suit-
case to hold $250,000 from Seagram and that he was giving
it to Mrs. Helmsley. Eboli said she laughed when he told
her that. But she said she didn't laugh about those visits to
the office with the white envelopes that would make "the
old lady real happy.''

And what did Leona do with the money in those white
envelopes, if, indeed, they did contain money? According
to her assistant, Leona maintained a number of large safety
deposit boxes at the Chase Manhattan Bank on Fifty-seventh
Street. The two of them would make regular visits to the
vault, mainly to clip coupons from the bonds and other investments held there. In the boxes, too, Eboli testified, were

various documents, jewelry, and eight to ten white envelopes on any given day, envelopes she was sure contained
money.

Perhaps there was an innocent explanation for those white
envelopes with money in the safety deposit boxes. At least,
that's what the defense maintained. For wasn't it true that
Harry Helmsley gave Leona Helmsley a check for three
thousand dollars every month, and wasn't it true that she
cashed that check every month at the Helmsley Palace, turning it into hundred-dollar bills, and wasn't it true that she
usually put those bills in blank envelopes?

As the government case drew toward its close, a question
still hovered over the courtroom. What about those outside
accountants who were paid so much money to protect their
clients from themselves?

Their names were Gerald Marsden and Hirschel Levine,
partners in the firm of Eisner and Lubin, longtime outside
accountants and auditors for the Helmsley empire. For years
they had audited the books of most Helmsley-owned and
-controlled companies, had prepared tax returns for some
of those companies, and had prepared the personal tax returns for Harry and Leona Helmsley. And they had earned
a fee of $1 million a year for their work.

Most reluctant witnesses, Marsden and Levine were
called to testify by the government, but were battered about
the courtroom by both sides. Their memories proved faulty,
perhaps conveniently so, both prosecution and defense suggested.

They said, for instance, that they thought Harry Helmsley
was paying all the expenses of Dunnellen Hall from his personal bank account.

Marsden couldn't remember getting a copy of a newspaper clipping from Joe Licari concerning the indictment of
fashion designer Albert Nippon for charging personal expenses to his business, nor did he remember that one of his
accountants, to whom Licari had shown the clipping, had

discussed it with him and said that Licari had "asked if this looked or sounded familiar."

Marsden couldn't remember a 1986 meeting with a number of top Helmsley officials during which Leona's imminent firing of Frank Turco was discussed and the fear expressed at that meeting that, as a Helmsley financial executive had testified, Turco "should be put out to pasture instead because he knew too much."

Marsden claimed that the first time he knew charges for Dunnellen Hall were being paid by Helmsley companies was in June 1986, though his accountants working on the books of the Park Lane and other Helmsley entities had, years earlier, come across related entries that had been whited out. And he had "no recollection" of saying upon this "discovery" that the way to handle it was not to file amended returns showing that charges were actually personal income of the Helmsleys that had been "accidentally" charged as business expenses of their companies, but rather to merely add an additional $2 million to the taxes the Helmsleys owed on that year's personal tax return.

Nor did he remember having been told of a meeting between Joe Licari and another Helmsley financial executive during which there had been discussion of the fact that the detailed lists of expenses and payment relating to Dunnellen Hall were being kept, and Licari rolling his eyes toward the ceiling and saying that having the companies pay the bills was the way the Helmsleys wanted it, and "It's not a bad idea to keep the lists should we ever decide to correct the charges."

What he did remember was that in 1984 he discovered that Helmsley-Spear was paying Harry Helmsley six thousand dollars a month rent on Dunnellen Hall because Harry was using it for business. That six thousand dollars could be considered income for the Helmsleys and so was subject to personal taxes. Marsden advised Licari that the payments ought to stop for that reason, and they did.

And both Marsden and Hirsch Levine remembered that

as far back as 1983 they had offered the opinion that Harry
Helmsley was entitled to write off 50 percent of the expenses
of Dunnellen Hall because he took work there several days a
week and was such a workaholic.

And Marsden remembered discussing with Harry Helmsley the fact that both Helmsleys were using corporate credit
cards for personal expenses, and Harry explaining, well, it
was easier that way, and if Marsden found records of such
use, he should simply charge the payments back to Harry.

When first Marsden and then Levine finished their testimony, one could only wonder what they had actually done
to earn their $1 million a year. Wasn't one of the prime
functions of an accountant to protect a client from his own
unwise decisions?

Finally, at just after three on the afternoon of Tuesday,
August 15, one day shy of six weeks since testimony had
begun, after calling forty-four witnesses and entering into
the court record nearly ten thousand exhibits, containing
some fifty thousand documents, Jim DeVita rested the government's case. It had been an overwhelming and often
numbing display of governmental power to amass and shift
evidence, to round up witnesses and compel them to testify,
often against their will. It had been, too, veteran trial observers agreed, another example of the government's penchant for overkill, of going not one but a dozen steps beyond
the necessary. But it had been effective.

24

Now it was the defense's turn. What could the defense do to blunt the government's overpowering case? What witnesses would there be? Two figures would certainly not be called. Leona Helmsley would never take the stand to testify in her own defense and so open herself to DeVita's cross-examination. Nor would Joe Licari. Although evidence had been raised against him, it had been scattered over six weeks, and long stretches had passed during which his name was never mentioned. The portrait of him that emerged was that of a loyal lieutenant trapped in a dilemma not of his own making. For him to testify and so face cross-examination might hurt more than help.

Frank Turco was a different matter. As the trial progressed, his name was spoken at least as often as Leona Helmsley's. He was the man who witness after witness said had given them orders to falsify invoices, the man who had handled the kickbacks, the man more than one witness said "had no saving graces." The evidence against him had piled to such Himalayan proportions that even Turco himself seemed resigned to the idea that he would probably be convicted. His only hope, it seemed, would be to testify and explain that he had only been carrying out the orders of his former employer. At one time he had wanted to testify and had met with the government to work out a deal. It had come to nothing, Bill Brodsky said later. The government's terms had been so onerous that he and Turco felt they might just as well take their chances with a jury. And, perhaps, the government believed that after hearing the evidence against him, Turco might take the witness stand anyway. And, indeed, as the evidence mounted, Turco wavered daily. In the end, he and Brodsky decided to follow the strategy adopted by his co-defendants and remain silent.

Who, then, would the defense call to the stand? Benfante said Licari would call no witnesses. Brodsky echoed Licari. Feffer said that he would call three to testify on behalf of his client: Licari's secretary, Geraldine Moore; Leona's personal assistant, Martin Goldstein, who had already testified for the government; and Harry Helmsley's secretary, who would give her evidence not in person but through a deposition.

And suddenly, with no advance warning, the court was thrown into a turmoil.

James Bruton, one of Leona Helmsley's legal team, a member of the same Washington law firm as Feffer, had an idea. A tax specialist, he had been struck by peculiarities on the Helmsleys' tax returns. Much of the income was derived from real estate partnerships in which Harry Helmsley had a major interest. And many of the Helmsley's deductions came from those partnerships. Under the law, owners of real estate are entitled to deduct from their income depreciation on their property. There are two kinds of depreciation, one for real property—the building itself (though not the land, which does not depreciate) and anything that is considered a permanent part of the building, such as walls, doors, and the like—and one for personal property, such as desks, chairs, bookcases, carpeting, and all the rest. Real property depreciates over fifteen years; personal property depreciates over five years. What Bruton noticed in the Helmsley returns was that the accountants who had prepared them (not Eisner and Lubin, as it happened) had ignored the five-year depreciation deduction for personal property and had deducted instead everything under the fifteen-year depreciation allowance on real property. As a result, he figured, the Helmsleys had been denied large deductions, for instead of depreciating personal property rapidly, over five years, that depreciation had been spread out over fifteen years.

It was only theory, of course. He needed backing. And so at the end of July, he approached Touche Ross, one of the nation's most prestigious accounting firms, and asked them to do a quick study to see if his hypothesis was right. On July 29, Robert Schweih, an evaluation consultant for Touche Ross, led a staff of experts through an appraisal of some seventy-eight buildings in which Harry Helmsley owned a major interest, separating out real property from personal property. It took them three weeks to complete the reappraisals, which revealed that real property accounted for 92.2 percent of the value and personal property 7.8 percent.

They finished on Sunday, August 13, and turned their analysis over to Gerald W. Padwe, a Touche Ross senior partner. He in turn recalculated the Helmsley tax returns, taking into account the new depreciation for personal property. He finished his initial estimate within a matter of hours.

Late Monday afternoon, August 14, Feffer and Bruton sprang their surprise. They had two additional witnesses they wanted to call, they said, Schweih and Padwe. The testimony of those witnesses would show that, contrary to the government's contention in counts two through seven that the Helmsleys had fraudulently evaded income taxes in 1983, 1984, and 1985, aided by Licari and Turco, there had been no tax evasion. Rather, the government owed the Helmsleys a refund, for they had overpaid their taxes by $696,000.

If this were proved, the government case against Leona Helmsley, Turco, and Licari might collapse. Certainly the charges of tax evasion would vanish, and if they vanished, the jury might well be persuaded that even those other charges, count one, conspiracy to defraud the IRS, and counts eight through forty-six, conspiracy to file false tax returns and mail fraud, had little merit. That would leave only count forty-seven, the extortion charge, remaining.

DeVita was so enraged that the back of his neck turned bright red. And his rage was justified. Despite Perry Mason and the other popular myths of lawyers, surprise has no place in an American courtroom. Each side is required by the rules of the court to provide the other with a list of witnesses to be called, and to give the other side access to all documentary evidence that may be entered into the record, and to do so in a timely manner so that adequate preparation may be made to combat that testimony and evidence. The defense had not notified the government that it had commissioned a re-audit of the Helmsley tax returns until the last moment, and had not provided the government with the documentary evidence on which those re-audits had been based. As a result, DeVita stormed, the government had no opportunity to examine what Touche Ross had done and so prepare to cross-examine Schweih and Padwe. If Walker permitted this evidence, DeVita said, then the government wanted the court's permission to do a new audit on those returns itself.

The debate over the admissibility of this unexpected evidence went on into the next morning. As angry as DeVita was, Judge Walker was even angrier. "I am extremely disappointed in defense counsel," he said, "for not furnishing this [evidence] earlier. To me it is inexcusable and I can't understand why it didn't happen. It is clearly called for under the rule. . . . You knew what effect this would have in this case. You know the problems we're having in trying to move this case along, and now, all of a sudden, a trial that was expected to finish in less than two months now looks like it is going to run more than three, just to have to deal with this issue." He was left with two choices, he said. He would either preclude the defense from calling these witnesses and entering their evidence, or, after hearing the other defense witnesses, call a recess in the trial, perhaps until mid-September, in order to give the government time to prepare.

Thus, while government and defense waited to hear how Walker would rule (the jurors, of course, knew nothing about this, having been sent from the courtroom while the debate was going on), Feffer called his other witnesses.

Geraldine Moore, a small, grandmotherly lady, had worked at Helmsley-Spear for twenty-four years and had been Joe Licari's secretary for fourteen of those years. It was she, she declared, and not Mary Ann Eboli, who had typed the fake Ashkenazie invoices. Licari had given her Sotheby catalogs, had selected various items from those catalogs, and told her which to enter on the various invoices and what hotels they were to be charged against. "I felt very uncomfortable typing them," she said, "but Mr. Licari told me not to worry."

But under cross-examination she became confused. When shown copies of some of those invoices, those relating to the Park Lane and the Carlton House, she didn't remember having done those. The implication, then, was that perhaps more than one set of fake Ashkenazie invoices had been typed, that she had typed one set and Mary Ann Eboli another.

If the point of her testimony had been to call into question the veracity of Mary Ann Eboli, it did not seem to work. And for Joe Licari, it was damning.

Then Martin Goldstein, now a defense witness, was called, simply to tell the jury how long and hard both Leona and Harry Helmsley had worked at home at Dunnellen Hall, and so why they were entitled to deduct the expenses of their mansion from their income taxes. He said that they were there every week, from Thursday night or Friday morning until Monday night, that Leona always took two or three cases of work along with her, and so did Harry. He himself went out to Dunnellen Hall at least twice a week, often staying overnight, and brought work for them with him. Harry, especially, worked much of the day, answering the phone constantly, conferring with people who were steadily coming and going. Even dinner conversation dealt only with business matters.

Such a workaholic was Harry Helmsley, Goldstein said, that once when he handed over some financial reports, he said they would put him to sleep. Helmsley replied, "They're not going to put me to sleep. They're the most exciting things I can read."

Perhaps one reason Harry and Leona worked so long and so hard in the palace they had bought for rest and relaxation could be explained in Goldstein's response to the question: "Do the Helmsley's have any friends?"

"No."

The deposition from Harry Helmsley's secretary dealt only with the fact that he kept the Dunnellen A-File among the files for all the properties he controlled on the bookcase behind his desk, and its existence and contents were certainly no secret, for she updated it regularly.

Then Walker made his decision on the new audit. He would allow the defense to present its new evidence, and permit Schweih and Padwe to testify. But he would recess the court until Monday, August 21, to give the government time to prepare, and when the court came into session, he would instruct the jury that the testimony of the Touche Ross executives related only to the tax evasion counts, two to seven, and not to the other counts. On those the government was not required to prove that taxes were due, only that a conspiracy existed.

Robert Schweih's testimony was merely a prelude to Gerald Padwe's. He simply explained that he and his staff had done the reappraisals and the various steps they had taken in doing them.

Then it was Padwe's turn. An affable gray-haired man, he appeared self-assured as he sat in the witness box and, often in technical terms, answered the questions put to him by Bruton.

Harry Helmsley, he said, had been involved in more than a hundred properties, syndicates in which he had a 60 to 90 percent stake. These properties were grouped for tax and legal purposes into three different types of partnerships, called Formula Partners, Formula X Partners, and Formula Y Partners. Each owned one or more building, with the partners often differing from one building to another within any one, and the sole common link between type and building was Harry Helmsley. What Bruton had asked him to do was review the tax returns of these partnerships with emphasis on changes in the calculations for depreciation. He and two assistants in Washington had spent a weekend examining about seventy of the partnership returns and then zeroed in on eleven. Adjustments were made on those returns, changing straight-line real property depreciation to a combination of real property and personal property depreciation. This, he said, was a requirement under the law, and the previous accountants had erred in ignoring personal property depreciation. Once these changes had been made, he said, it was apparent that Harry Helmsley had not taken enough depreciation during these years. Thus, Padwe had reached the conclusion that the Helmsleys had overpaid their taxes by $53,000 in 1983, $61,000 in 1984, and $477,000 in 1985, or a total of $591,000. And thus the Helmsleys were actually entitled to a refund

Whether the jurors followed all the technical jargon, one could only wonder. Certainly Jim DeVita followed it. He had prepared thoroughly over the weekend, and one could sense in him a barely controlled ferocity as he rose to cross-examine. If he had been a diligent bulldog through much of the trial, he turned now into a tiger. In the hour that followed, the confident and smiling Padwe was turned into a sweating, uncomfortable, uncertain victim. It was perhaps DeVita's best moment in the trial.

If Padwe's calculations were correct and Harry Helmsley didn't take enough depreciation on his properties between 1983 and 1985, DeVita asked, wasn't it also true that Harry

Helmsley must, then, have taken too much depreciation in 1986, 1987, and 1988?

Perhaps, Padwe answered.

Returning to those 1983 to 1985 returns. Had Padwe been asked to file amended returns for the Helmsleys for those years?

No. He hadn't done enough analyses to do that.

"Now, your first calculation was that Mr. and Mrs. Helmsley overpaid their taxes by $696,000. Right?" DeVita said. "Then over the weekend, you recalculated and you came with an overpayment of $602,000. And then, Sunday, yesterday, you recalculated again and came up with an overpayment of $591,000. At least we're moving in the right direction."

"That's your conclusion," Padwe said.

"If we give you another week," DeVita retorted, "maybe it will be gone altogether."

DeVita turned to the government table and picked up a stack of documents, the Helmsleys' tax returns and the partnership tax returns. He handed the 1983 return to Padwe and told him to turn to Schedule D and its supplemental schedule of gains and losses. That schedule, DeVita pointed out, showed a $31 million capital gain for the partnership, including a $23 million capital gain on the sale for $28.5 million of a building at 225 Broadway. "Was this entire transaction treated as a capital gain?"

Padwe examined the return and said it seemed so, since on the line that said, "If straight-line depreciation is taken, enter 0," and zero was entered.

"They had taken no depreciation for real property?"

"I don't know."

"And what about the personal property depreciation? If this had been properly reported, wouldn't there have been a significant amount recaptured? If personal property amounted to 7.8 percent of the value, as Mr. Schweih said was usual, wouldn't that personal property depreciation amount to $364,353, and if Harry Helmsley owned sixty percent of that property, then wouldn't his ordinary income have been $218,612?"[1]

Padwe had no answer. DeVita shot at him, "You didn't look at that transaction and you weren't asked to look at that transaction, were you?"

If this line seemed to leave jurors, and most spectators, bewildered, Judge Walker quickly cleared it up. He turned to Padwe and said, to make this less confusing, let's put forward a hypothetical case. Say you buy a piece of property for $1,000 and you use a five-year depreciation on it, at twenty percent a year. At the end of one year, what would the property be worth?

"$800," Padwe answered. "The $1,000 less the twenty percent depreciation."

All right. Now, at the end of the year, you sell the property for $1,100. What would be the profit and what would be the tax due?

The profit would be $300, Padwe said, since depreciation had reduced the value of the property to $800. The capital gain would be $100, the amount above the original cost. And there would be ordinary income of $200, because on the sale of property the amount that has been deducted for depreciation is treated not as a capital gain but as ordinary income.

DeVita drove forward. "Do you know," he asked, "if any part of the $31 million capital gain of that partnership

---

1. Capital gains result from the sale of stocks and bonds, buildings, fixed assets, and other properties, all generally long-term investments, and are taxed at a substantially lower rate than ordinary income from such things as wages, salaries, and commissions. However, when a major property is sold, the amount that was deducted over the years for personal property depreciation is considered personal income and not a capital gain. DeVita's point, thus, was that if both real and personal property depreciation had been taken, Helmsley's income from this and other partnerships could not be considered entirely capital gains, that part of it was actually personal income and so subject to higher taxes. Yet nowhere on the returns could such recaptured income be found.

should have been treated as ordinary income, which would have increased the Helmsleys' tax liability?''

Padwe didn't know.

DeVita picked up the returns for the Formula, Formula X, and Formula Y Partnerships. "Did they have any income?" he asked.

"No," Padwe said. "There were net losses."

And DeVita went through them. On all these Formula Partnerships for the three years in question, the tax deductions had amounted to more than $27 million. "And your testimony is that this is incorrect, that this is not enough, that it should have been more if the correct methods of calculating depreciation had been used? But you haven't spoken to the people who actually prepared these returns, have you?''

"No," Padwe admitted.

DeVita had. And he was prepared to call them, if necessary, to testify that they had used the fifteen-year straight-line real property depreciation rather than separating real and personal property depreciation because the Helmsley organization had told them to do it that way, thus masking a huge amount of personal income.

More damning was DeVita's discovery of a piece of property in which Leona and Harry Helmsley had been partners. In 1984 Leona had not sold but "traded" her $650,000 interest in the partnership to her husband, though what she got in return was unclear. Nevertheless, because depreciation had been taken on that property, once she was no longer a holder of it, she was liable for taxes on her share of the amount of the depreciation, which DeVita figured at about $65,000. Had it been declared? Had it been paid?

Padwe didn't know.

DeVita proceeded to explore a rather seamy aspect of that "trade." According to documents, it occurred on January 1, 1984. Only DeVita had a copy of a memo written by Licari, dated September 14, 1984, or more than nine months later, saying, "Regarding the Formula properties, Mrs. Helmsley *would like to be bought out* [emphasis added], and Mr. Helmsley will do it in a way that would reduce her base and would not be a taxable event."

It was a transaction whose implications DeVita did not explore. He did not have to.

When Padwe was excused, he did not look happy. One was left speculating on whether the defense, which had paid him $360 an hour, Schweih $300 an hour, and lesser sums to their assistants—in all, tens of thousands of dollars for their three weeks of work—had invested its money wisely.

At 2:21 on the afternoon of Monday, August 21, the defense rested. All that remained were summations, Judge Walker's all-important charge, and the jury's deliberations and verdict.

25

EVEN MORE THAN the openings, final arguments are the occasion for eloquence and dramatics, for the attorneys to take total command of the courtroom and become the actors so many of them secretly imagine they are. There are rules, of course. The lawyers are limited to discussing only what has taken place during the course of the trial; they are barred from invoking extraneous matters or debating issues that were never raised. But within those bounds, they are free to say and do what they will to win a jury to their side. For the prosecution, the time has arrived to lay out for the jury a logical and easily followed road map, detailing the charges and the evidence the jury has heard that supports them. The defense, in turn, tries to convince the jury that the road map is faulty, that the case against the defendants has been nothing but empty bluster unsupported by substance.

In anticipation of a smash hit show, the biggest crowd of the summer turned out early, standing in line outside the courtroom doors in hopes of gaining a seat. They had to take what few leavings there might be, and there weren't many. Reporters from around the country filled the press rows. Down front, other rows were set aside for the families and friends of the leading players, lawyers, and defendants, including Frank Turco's wife, Joe Licari's wife and daughter, Leona Helmsley's niece, Fran Becker, and her grandson, Craig Panzirer, all of whom had been court regulars. And so, long before Judge Walker called the court to order, indeed as soon as the courtroom doors opened, the 150 seats in eleven rows of benches had been quickly filled, and throughout the day there were lines waiting outside in hopes that one would be vacated.

At nine-thirty, Judge Walker took his place on the bench. The jurors were marched into the courtroom and took their places. The anticipation mounted. What would Jim DeVita say? How would he say it? For everyone believed that it would be DeVita's voice that would resound for the next hours. After all, he had been the lead prosecutor; this had been his case from the beginning. Tradition was that the person who had guided the prosecution was the person who both summed up and had the final word in rebuttal after the defense had finished.

And then, to everyone's surprise, twenty-eight-year-old Cathy Seibel, a tall, dark-haired assistant United States attorney, second to DeVita on the case, rose and, thick loose-leaf binder in her hand, walked to the rostrum facing the jury box. A tactical decision, DeVita would say later. Whatever, hers was not an auspicious beginning. For the first hour and a half she was hesitant, rambling, sometimes even inaudible over the microphone, which was placed a little too far away. Watching the jury, one could sense that she was losing them. Though she went through the forty-seven counts of the indictment, the clearly defined road map to mark those counts was not there.

Only after a short recess, during which the microphone was moved and fixed, did Seibel begin to show that perhaps the tactical decision had not been a terrible mistake after all. If she was never eloquent, nevertheless she became sharper and there was some acid in her voice over the next two-and-a-half hours.

"If these people thought it proper for the Helmsley companies to pay all of this, why did they go to all these lengths to hide the fact? . . . They knew that Eisner and Lubin disapproved of what they were doing, and so designed this scheme with that in mind. And when each scheme didn't work and Harry Helmsley had to repay some of the charges, they set up another scheme. Every time they got caught, they knew it was wrong and then they set up a different and more ingenious and complicated scheme.''

As for those accountants: "Shouldn't Eisner and Lubin have dug a little deeper? You're not going to hear anyone from the government say they were great accountants. But then they're not the government's accountants. They were the Helmsleys' accountants. They should have saved the defendants from themselves, but maybe they were too afraid of losing this large account. They looked the other way and buried their heads in the sand.''

As for the defense contention that because the Helmsleys worked at home they were entitled to deduct 50 percent, or maybe even 60 percent of the cost of Dunnellen Hall as business expenses: "Just because you bring work home doesn't make the home a business expense. Because swimming and dancing were the only relaxations in Harry Helmsley's life, you're supposed to think he thought a pool and dance floor are legitimate business expenses? Just what kind of business expense is a pool, a patio, a barbecue, gardens, indoor and outdoor stereo systems designed for the sole and exclusive use of Harry and Leona Helmsley?''

When it came to making phony invoices and hiding the costs of Dunnellen Hall in their business, "The criteria is where it's least likely to be caught.''

The defense had contended that no conspiracy existed because there were so many witnesses, and the essence of a conspiracy is secrecy. "There were so many witnesses to the crime, yes, but they were employees and vendors and those who depended on Leona Helmsley and were scared to death of her. She was a lady who was not worried about her employees turning on her. It all shows how inflated and arrogant these defendants were. The testimony of their employees shows this. They were arrogant and they thought they were above the law.''

"It was a huge project to get the Helmsley business to pay all those Dunnellen bills. It was a full-time job for Frank

Turco. That's what he said. But ask yourself, why did they
do it if it wasn't to evade taxes? Taxes were what was concerning these defendants. In fact, about the only option that
didn't occur to them was paying the bills themselves.''

The Helmsleys were rich, yes, but they were also
"cheap." Instead of paying for things themselves, they made
the Helmsley empire pay, and so they "got twice the bang
for the buck. Nobody wants to think about Mrs. Helmsley's
underwear. The government is not trying to embarrass anyone, but it's just the facts of the case. Just because you're
rich doesn't mean you're not cheap. It's not that a million
dollars means less to Leona Helmsley than to you and me.
It's that five dollars and ten dollars mean more to her.''

"Joe Licari and Frank Turco were good employees. But
when you're asked to commit a crime, you should refuse.
They knew what they were doing was illegal and yet they
did it. Fear of losing your job is no excuse. Following orders
is no excuse. Frank Turco worked hard and was devoted to
his job—which was to help the Helmsleys commit a
crime. . . . Joe Licari may be a nice guy. Everyone agrees
that he is. But that doesn't excuse his crimes. He wouldn't
have been so concerned with being caught if he didn't know
it was illegal.''

On extortion: "This charge is conspiracy to commit extortion; it has nothing to do with whether that extortion was
successful or not. All the government has to do is prove that
an agreement existed to commit extortion. Threats to break
legs or do physical harm are not the only examples of extortion. It is a crime of extortion to hold out the promise of
business against the threat of economic loss.'' And then
Cathy Seibel recited the list of those the government contended had been the victims of the extortion conspiracy:
Jerry McCarthy; the vendors who had an "x" placed after
their names, meaning, according to Milton Meckler, that
they would have to "eat" the cost or lose the business;
RCA, which was forced to hand over three free TV sets to
Leona Helmsley if the electronics giant wanted Helmsley

business; and most especially the liquor salesmen who brought cash-filled envelopes every month to Frank Turco. "We know that Frank Turco was not keeping the money. It was going to Mrs. Helmsley."

And finally, "What we have here is a disdain for the obligation of citizenship, which is to pay your taxes. Leona Helmsley believed that she was above the law, that she could exempt herself from the rules that apply to everyone else. Cheating the government out of a million dollars by putting herself above all those little people paying their taxes is certainly something she would have done."

It had not been a ringing summary of the government's case, but, toward the end, at least, it had been clear and forceful. It remained to be seen how effective. In any case, the government would have one more chance to seal its victory, if victory there would be. Because the burden of proof is on the prosecution, it is granted both the first word and the last in rebuttal to the defense. That rebuttal would be Jim DeVita's chance to soar.

But before that, the defense would have its say.

Jerry Feffer was not feeling well. He had been away from home for more than two months and had not slept well in hotel beds. He had lost more than fifteen pounds and now had trouble keeping his trousers around his waist. And the sallowness of his complexion seemed to indicate that he was coming down with something. His condition was not helped by the heat in the courtroom—the air conditioning worked only fitfully—and Judge Walker gave him permission to take off his jacket, loosen his tie, and address the jury in shirt sleeves. On the defense table before him he had stocked Cokes, raisins, and other snacks to boost his energy, and he turned to those refreshers often during the eight hours spread over two days that he spoke to the jury.

"I would like to sit down with each of you," he began quietly, "and ask you what questions you might have and what is troubling you."

Then, as though he knew, he began to try to tear apart the fabric of the government's case, using sarcasm, wit, eloquence, and obfuscation.

"Mr. DeVita in his opening remarks promised you the stars, the moon, and the sun. He promised and he must deliver, and I don't think he has. I promised you that this was a very simple case that the government would complicate beyond belief, and that's what has happened. What is in dispute here are not the facts, but the intent. What is in dispute is Leona Helmsley's intent to commit tax fraud. We agree that they charged all these things to their business. But it's the intent behind all this that counts. . . .

"If they were trying to cheat the government, why were they keeping all those records in desks and on a bookcase? We do not dispute that the invoices were false, and we never have. But were they to cheat the IRS? Were they made with the intent to deceive the IRS or the accountants? No. There was a different intent, and there were two reasons for it."

The first reason, Feffer said, was to see that the vendors who were doing the work at Dunnellen Hall got paid. "Mrs. Helmsley was not always paying them. She believed she was being cheated and ripped off. She was absolutely paranoid about this. Crazy as it may seem, maybe she had reason to believe she was being ripped off at Dunnellen Hall." It seemed, Feffer went on, that everybody complained about everybody else's work, that contractors said about those they succeeded that they had "never encountered such a poorly executed project. There was a first-class disaster going on at Dunnellen Hall, and Mrs. Helmsley with her first-class temper was right in the middle. She believed that everyone was a thief, that they were ripping her off even on the petty cash. But the issue is not that she's a tough bitch, or even that she was right in many instances. . . .

"There's no doubt about it, Mrs. Helmsley was a very tough person to do business with, and people went to any lengths to avoid dealing with her. Many of the government's witnesses said that if at all possible, they would not deal with her, that they would avoid her if they could, that they would do anything to avoid getting Mrs. Helmsley angry at them. . . .

"And so these people were trying to find a way to get people paid without letting Mrs. Helmsley know they were being paid. False invoices sound terrible. Gosh. But the purpose, the simple fact, and even the government witnesses testified to it, was that it was done to pay vendors Mrs. Helmsley was having trouble with. That was the reason for the creation of the false invoices, to get people paid, not to cheat the government. Out of all the false invoices in this case, her actual initials appear on very few. Frank Turco was responsible for Dunnellen Hall. All he had to do was go to her and have her sign false invoices. Yet he didn't . . . John Struck talked about false invoices with twenty-one different people, but never with Mrs. Helmsley. . . . There is nothing to show that Mrs. Helmsley knew about the false documentation and the false invoices. They were doing it behind her back. . . . There was a lot going on here and I submit to you that Mrs. Helmsley was not part of it."

"More is less. That's a key here. In a criminal conspiracy, you don't let so many people in and you don't create records like this and keep them in your bookcase. Everyone in the world knew that the corporations were paying for Dunnellen Hall. It was no secret. More is less."

"Joe Licari needed to be involved with Dunnellen Hall like he needed a hole in the head. Imagine Joe Licari's reaction when he got a memo from Harry Helmsley that he's to get involved with Dunnellen Hall. Imagine Mr. Licari sitting with Mrs. Helmsley to set up the record keeping on the business use of Dunnellen Hall to satisfy the IRS. It's laughable."

"Look at this as a scheme not to cheat the IRS but actually to benefit the IRS. Because they didn't keep records, they weren't able to charge off the expenses. If they had come up with the documentation, they could have written off 50 percent. Everyone believed a fifty-fifty split was not just fair but conservative, and that's the issue. We're talking about intent. These people at that time believed they were doing things right and properly.''

Feffer's second reason for the creation of the false invoices was to ''to get the bills paid through the bookkeeping department at Helmsley-Spear. The bookkeepers were fooled into issuing checks for hundreds of thousands of dollars. We agree with that. But fooling bookkeepers is not a crime. It was a way to get the invoices through the system and get the vendors paid.'' It was a statement Feffer repeated over and over.

And then he turned to the man he portrayed as the real villain. ''Someone failed to do their job with the records, and that someone was Gerald Marsden. Gerald Marsden screwed up. . . .'' Everything was available to Marsden from the very start, Feffer alleged, and so he had complete knowledge of everything that was being done, despite his denials or his forgetful memory.

''There was that meeting around Valentine's Day in 1986 regarding the fact that the companies were paying the expenses at Dunnellen Hall. They said they had just discovered a memo about that. And everybody says Marsden was there. But Marsden has to deny he was at that meeting or knew about it. Because the Helmsleys' tax returns hadn't been filed yet and he knew he would be guilty of filing false returns. So he has to deny knowing anything. He says he didn't get the schedules showing the companies were paying for Dunnellen Hall until June 1986. And he says the next time he addressed the situation was in October or November—five months later. Come on! . . .''

Feffer turned to the question of conspiracy to commit extortion. The prosecution charged that liquor vendors were being extorted and the money was going to Mrs. Helmsley. But, he said, when Turco took over the handling of the liquor business in 1983 and 1984, after Mrs. Helmsley had heard some of her people were taking kickbacks, she set up a system, with Turco in charge, to put a stop to it. Turco's

job was to get the best possible price for the hotels, and one
way to do it was to ask for a rebate. The kickback was no
kickback, then, but a simple 2 percent rebate on purchases.
"These liquor salesmen had exclusivity and they made a
bundle, they made a fortune. These extortion victims were
cleaning up. . . . And do you think that Turco and the rest
would have let one of these extortion victims pay by check?
I've never heard of an extortion victim paying by
check. . . ."

"The prosecution desperately wants you to believe that
Mrs. Helmsley got all this money for herself. But there has
been testimony that all she had to do was make a call and
she could get any amount of money she wanted."

And the story that Billy Piacitelli told of seeing Vince
Sclafani handing Mrs. Helmsley a cash-filled envelope in
the lobby of the Helmsley Palace: "Come on! Besides,
there was other money going over to her regularly. We've
had testimony to that effect. Why does this have to be liquor money? Because the government wants it to be liquor
money."

Feffer, fatigue etching lines in his face after nearly eight
hours, was finally coming to a close. He returned once more
to the theme "more is less": the more people that knew
about the scheme and were part of it, the less likely it was
to be a conspiracy. "Those who knew what was going on,
the list is endless, and many of them were fired or not paid.
And in the middle of this conspiracy, she fires her chief
henchmen, Frank Turco and Joe Licari. It doesn't make
sense."

During the years covered by the indictment, the Helmsleys paid $57.8 million in taxes. "And yet Mrs. Baum says
that Mrs. Helmsley said they don't pay taxes, only the little
people pay taxes. That doesn't make sense."

And then, finally, emotionally, "Mrs. Helmsley has a lot
of enemies and these people came here to pay her back, no
question about that. These people had an agenda and that
agenda was to get her. If, in fact, she has abused or mis-

treated people, I beg you, ladies and gentlemen, to leave
that decision for a higher authority. You have the future of
Mrs. Helmsley in your hands. I ask you, ladies and gentlemen, end the suffering, the long terrible suffering of Mrs.
Helmsley. Let her walk out of this courtroom a free
woman.''

It had been, in many ways, a brilliant performance. Feffer
had managed to obfuscate the issues and the evidence to
such a degree that Frank Turco said during a break, ''I
listen to him and I'm so confused I don't know what I'm
charged with anymore.''

Joe Benfante, summing up for Joe Licari, played the
clown. ''Poor Joe Licari,'' he said. ''He's on trial for his
life. Not for his own tax returns, not for his own money,
not for Dunnellen Hall that he never even got to go to. His
whole life is on trial because of a lousy mansion he never
even saw. He doesn't even get to hear the music from Disney World. Give me a break. Give me a break. This is ri-
diculous.''

What happened to Licari, he said, was he was just a good
guy trying to do his job and getting caught in the middle,
particularly because of Leona Helmsley's dislike. ''Why did
she hate Joe Licari?'' he asked. ''Because Joe Licari was
Harry Helmsley's Jiminy Cricket, his conscience. He would
tell Harry Helmsley, 'Mrs. Helmsley is spending your
money again' and she went nuts. The queen did not want
to go to the king and ask for an allowance. Money was no
object. Leona wanted to get it done her way.''

And all those fake invoices. Harry dreamed them up because he didn't want anyone to know how much Leona was
spending, or what she was spending for. ''He didn't want
everyone to know his wife was a little strange, his wife was
beating up on him. Nobody, but nobody, knew what Mrs.
Helmsley was going to spend or what she was going to spend
it on. Perhaps Mr. Helmsley was embarrassed that she spent

$500,000 on an ugly gray and brown buffalo. It was the ugliest buffalo I ever saw.''

It was all very funny, especially after eight hours of Feffer's so-deliberate confusion. But there were a few times when Benfante went just a little too far. He pointed to a couple of government witnesses and said, ''They lied through their teeth.''

''That opinion,'' Judge Walker interrupted, ''is not relevant.''

''Maybe not, but after eight weeks, they are beginning to know that,'' Benfante said, gesturing to the jury.

And Judge Walker wouldn't let him open a huge gold paper-wrapped box he brought into court intending to present it to the IRS. There was a card attached to the outside. It read: ''This is how I bought the bras.'' Inside was a huge stack of expense vouchers for Leona Helmsley's personal purchases.

Benfante was a hard act to follow. Fortunately, he finished late Thursday afternoon, so Bill Brodsky didn't have to compete right away. He had a night to think over what he would say in Frank Turco's defense.

''It's important to remember,'' Brodsky said, ''that Frank Turco was an employee. He is not a billionaire. He is not a millionaire. He was a working stiff. He is a blunt, abrupt, hardworking guy, a Damon Runyon character. . . .

''He was a conduit. Go see Turco. Turco do this, Turco do that, and all this on top of all his other jobs. He never went on cruises. He never wore gold cuff links. He never went to Dunnellen Hall on social occasions. He was working so hard on weekends that he didn't have time for his weekly card game, which was his relaxation. He had no ownership participation in any Helmsley entity, and so no benefit accrued to Frank Turco from the Helmsleys' personal or corporate tax returns.

''The only thing Frank Turco got out of this was a headache and losing his job. Despite all his efforts to get people paid and to please his employers, and you know how hard that was, all he got was fired. He's fired, thrown out after twenty years. And what's his reward? He gets indicted. He's told, because he paid the bills through the corporations, 'You're a crook, you're a cheat, you're a felon.' "

"Look, the government says, he's an extortionist. After the death of Jay Panzirer in March 1982, Frank got the job of negotiating with the vendors, and Milton Meckler thought he was in line for the job and he was very bitter because he didn't get it and Frank did. Frank had an unorthodox way of negotiating, but it was effective. He wanted to put a stop to the payoffs, and when he was offered one, he said, give it to the Helmsley organization. His job was to get the lowest price, and he did, by these means. We know Frank Turco took money from the vendors. We don't deny that. But the rebate went to the Helmsley organization, and it was worth it. Look at the business these people got for liquor from the Helmsley hotels. There's nothing wrong with saying we don't want to get ripped off and have an employee taking kickbacks, which is taking from the hotels, and so now the rebates went to the hotels."

"Jerry McCarthy, Milton Meckler, Mary Ann DiMicco, and a lot of others, they all lied on the stand, they all shaded the truth. They wanted to get at Mrs. Helmsley, but they also wanted to get at Frank. Meckler, because Frank got the job that Meckler wanted and so Frank stepped on Meckler's toes, and so this was a way to get at Mrs. Helmsley and Frank. Mary Ann DiMicco's motive was against Mrs. Helmsley. . . ." And so it went.

"Frank Turco never intended to commit a crime. There was no extortion. Frank Turco asks from you what you would want for yourselves. Review the evidence fairly and without bias, and you will acquit him."

And then DeVita had the last word. Watching him during Brodsky's two-hour summation, it was obvious that he could hardly wait. He strode purposefully to the lectern, looked over the jury, and began, in a deceivingly low key.

"After twelve or thirteen hours of summations for the defense, I promise not to filibuster or make your ears ring. . . . Mr. Feffer said that the government wants you to hate Mrs. Helmsley. I don't want you to hate Mrs. Helmsley. I don't want you to hate anyone. I want you to decide on your common sense and the evidence. . . . Mr. Feffer said I tried to humiliate Mrs. Helmsley by some of my questions. If so, I want to apologize. I was merely poking fun at some of Mr. Bruton's questions."

The low key didn't last. "We didn't rest our case on just a few witnesses. There were many, and all the witnesses and all the documents meld, like strands of cable, not like links in a chain. They are entwined together, like the cables on the Brooklyn Bridge, which has stood near here for more than a hundred years. If I may say so, the defendants are trying to sell you the Brooklyn Bridge with their theories."

The defense, he said, had offered two theories, and the two were contradictory "and they don't fit." The defense claimed that Turco and Licari had dreamed up the phony invoice scheme "to get the bills paid behind Mrs. Helmsley's back. That makes no sense. They didn't only pay bills that had not been paid, they faked all kinds of bills, even bills she wanted paid. And she sent a memo saying, 'I must okay all bills before they are paid.' So it's obvious they didn't go behind her back. . . . It's nonsense to think that they bypassed Mrs. Helmsley. They sent her a monthly memo telling her what they had done. It was a monthly confession—'Here I am, Mrs. Helmsley, chop off my head.' "

And he began to detail. The phony invoices went all the way back to the beginning. "The first bill paid was for the moving expenses for Elizabeth Baum. And Mrs. Helmsley knew. She wants Elizabeth Baum to come from Texas to Connecticut. She's already given authorization for the payment by the Park Lane. They're not trying to get around Leona Helmsley.

"And who gets the bill? Joe Licari, and he's sending it

to Frank Turco to alter. And she doesn't want anything to do with Joe Licari?

"It's a triangle. Leona Helmsley to Joe Licari to Frank Turco. The Bermuda Triangle where the real bills vanish."

As for Feffer's theory that the fake invoices were a way to fool the bookkeepers: "The bookkeepers are going to do what they are told to do. They're not trying to fool the bookkeepers. Do you think a bookkeeper is going to tell Harry Helmsley or Leona Helmsley, 'I'm not going to do that'?"

"The real reason for the phony invoices was to avoid taxes on the amount paid."

Frank Turco and Joe Licari? "The defense objects to my description of them as henchmen. I won't call them henchmen anymore. They were the two Helmsley lieutenants, his and hers, matching sets."

"The defense says that Harry Helmsley was a workaholic. Why does that create a business expense for a swimming pool and a garden? His only business expense was for all those little pens he used, and I don't see them on the list of expenses. There's got to be a connection between the business use and the expense. So how do you explain deductions for the gardener and the maid and the chef? Maybe the chef made a sandwich for lunch, so you can write off half a sandwich, but . . ."

"Actions speak louder than words. Between July 1, 1983, and June 30, 1984, 90.3 percent of the $2,289,900 expenses of Dunnellen Hall were paid by the companies and 9.97 percent by Harry Helmsley. Then Eisner and Lubin found out they were using Deco to pay those expenses, and so the ratio was changed. But it wasn't changed to fifty-fifty, as the defense claims they had a right to do, but to 70 percent by the companies and 30 percent by Harry Helmsley. And if Eisner and Lubin hadn't forced him to pay back $800,000 to Deco, the ratio would actually have been 80.4 percent by the companies and 19.6 percent by Harry Helmsley. And if they really thought he was entitled to write off 50 percent, then why didn't they merely make him pay back half of that $800,000 instead of all of it?''

As for Leona Helmsley: ''Do you believe she honestly believed it was legal and legitimate to charge all her clothes and makeup and other personal items to the Park Lane?''

As for the accountants, Feffer's villains: ''Eisner and Lubin is not a paragon. If Eisner and Lubin had John Dennehy [the IRS agent who analyzed the Helmsleys' expenses] instead of Marsden and Levine, we wouldn't be here today. If you learn anything from this case it's that the accounting profession has some real problems.''

On extortion: ''It's not a requirement that you have sympathy for the victim. It's the wrongful intent of the perpetrators. The evidence is clear that the vendors were told they have to kick back. There's no rebate. The price is established by law. There was no strongarm and no physical violence. Of course not. There doesn't have to be. What there was was the misuse of economic power.''

The defense contended that the proof that there was no conspiracy was the firing of Joe Licari and Frank Turco in the middle. ''Why fire Turco and Licari? Who are they going to tell? They're in up to their necks. They can't tell. Do you think Leona Helmsley thought that someday she'd be sitting in this courtroom? Do you think she considered herself subject to the same laws as everyone else in this country?

''The defense says that they did it out in the open, and so there was no conspiracy. Brazenness is not a defense.''

''There was a time in our history, in English history,'' Jim DeVita said as he neared the end, ''when we had something called sovereign immunity, where the king and the queen could not be prosecuted. It's no longer the law. Your belief that you are above the law is no defense.

''Mr. Feffer says that the money involved in this case is peanuts. Peanuts? The defense contends that they are too rich to be guilty. That's not a defense.

''The fundamental principle of this country is that every-

body is equal before the law, rich or poor, famous or not.
All are equal before the law. The government has carried
its burden and we ask you to return verdicts of guilty.''

Over nearly four hours DeVita had proved himself Feffer's
match, perhaps even more than a match.

All that was left was Judge Walker's charge to the jury.
It was already nearly four on Friday afternoon, and the
charge ran to ninety-four pages, which would take about
three hours to read. But Walker wanted no more delays. He
wanted the case in the jury's hands by the end of the day.
And so he ordered the courtroom doors locked, the courtroom sealed, and then he began to explain the law about tax
fraud, conspiracy, and extortion to the jurors.

His job was merely to instruct, but by the time he had
finished, there was little reason for the defense to feel san-
guine. His reading of the law filled the defendants and their
lawyers with foreboding. He had instructed the jury, for
instance, that:

- ''To establish a conspiracy, the government is not
  required to show that two or more persons sat around
  a table and entered into a solemn compact . . . to
  violate the law.''
- ''A conspiracy may exist between persons who are
  not socially close or who even dislike one another.''
- ''There is no requirement that to be a member a person have a financial interest in the outcome of a conspiracy. . . . An interest could be a direct financial
  one, or an indirect one, such as pleasing a superior
  or holding one's job.''
- ''If a conspiracy exists, even if it should fail of its
  purpose, it is still punishable as a crime. Conse-
  quently, in a conspiracy charge there is no need to
  prove an actual violation of another law.''

- "It is not necessary for the government to prove that any defendant on trial committed an overt act, so long as at least one overt act was in fact performed by at least one conspirator."
- "It is no defense that your ultimate purpose was an innocent one, such as keeping your job or getting bills paid. . . ."

About the only balm the defense could find in the charge was when Walker came to extortion. He told the jurors: "If the alleged victims stood only to improve their position by making the alleged payments or deliveries in question, and did not act out of fear that an economic benefit would be cut off or that they would be economically worsened if they did not pay or deliver, then the acts in question do not constitute extortion. . . . For there to be extortion, the alleged victim must have made the payments or furnished the goods not to gain an advantage, but out of fear that if the payments were not made he would be harmed economically."

Lawyers and defendants left the courtroom with gloomy faces. Frank Turco, for one, practically stormed out, saying, "It's all over."

The final chapter in the Helmsleys' tale of monumental greed was about to close.

26

So the wait began, that interminable period in any trial when there is nothing to do but wander the corridors and talk inconsequentials while the jury deliberates.

For no one did those endless days while the jury was out seem more agonizing than for Leona Helmsley. In the summer of 1989 she had become the nation's, and especially New York's, woman you most love to hate. It was nearly impossible to find anyone with a good word to say about her. And those who leaped aboard the "Hate Leona" bandwagon were not just the people in the street, who were glad to vent their opinions to anyone who would listen. The rich and the powerful joined the chorus.

Naturally enough, Mayor Ed Koch was lead singer. There had been a time when he had eagerly sought invitations to Leona's "I Love Harry" birthday parties, had just as avidly sought Harry Helmsley's support, financial and political. But those days were past. At the end of July, trailing badly in a political campaign for reelection, Koch apparently decided it couldn't hurt to echo the popular sentiment about the hotel queen. At one of his impromptu press conferences on the steps of City Hall, just up the street from the trial at the federal courthouse, the mayor offered his opinion that Leona Helmsley was "the Wicked Witch of the West. For a billionairess to be so chintzy distresses people. It's just the chintziness. The things that clearly she did, irrespective of criminality—and I'm not getting into that, that's for a jury to decide—just her general relationship with other people.'' (Such remarks didn't help. Koch lost the primary, and his hold of City Hall, anyway.)

Donald Trump, whose acid sentiments about Leona had become ever more public over the previous months, added his voice. After the testimony about the jade and the phony invoices listing it as antique furniture bought by the St. Moritz, he was asked about the personal check Joe Licari had urged Harry Helmsley to send him.

''She totally tried to screw me, and I loved making her pay,'' he declared, apparently ignoring the fact that it was Harry Helmsley who had done the paying. ''I guess I'm one of the few people that caught her, me and the government. And I was happy about it. I know her very well. Nobody knows her as well as me. I feel so badly for Harry. He's a great man, a wonderful guy. He was really embarrassed. But she's a sick woman. As bad as he's been portrayed, she's worse. I can feel sorry for my worst enemy, but I can't feel sorry for Leona Helmsley. She deserves whatever she gets.''

The same day that Trump let fly his sling, Taylor-Gordon, Aarons, the advertising agency that had brought to the world the ''Queen Stands Guard'' campaign, shot off some arrows of its own. They were dumping the $5-million-a-year Helmsley account, President Elaine Taylor-Gordon announced, ''and we say good riddance and we're relieved.'' It seems that when the agency sent out its bill for May and June, the payment that came in was 60 percent less than the bill. ''When we asked why, she said she needed the money, and besides, she said, 'I write the ads anyway. Take it or leave it.' We decided to leave it. We told her it was unacceptable. I've been reading the papers and I know this is part of the pattern. She squeezed other contractors. It was inevitable we would be, too. Eventually, no one escapes.''

Besides, Ms. Taylor-Gordon added, handling the Helmsley Hotel account had been anything but a pleasant experience. ''She let us know we were the servants and she was the Queen. One time she summoned me to her apartment and then kept me waiting forty-five minutes. Then she sat me on an uncomfortable bar stool while she drank martinis and I drank Brioschi. She said, 'Don't get comfortable. You're not here for a social visit.' "

Whoever takes on the Helmsley account, she added, "We'll be glad to send them our supply of Maalox and Advil and our armor."

Manfred Barg, once the manager of the Park Lane and then of the Helmsley Palace, had been fired while on a cruise to Alaska with his wife in August 1986. He and his wife had been evicted from their forty-third-floor apartment in the hotel. Though Barg was not summoned as a witness in the trial, he said the reason he was fired was because he refused to cash phony checks for the Helmsleys. And so, in August 1989 he filed a $2.95 million damage suit against Leona Helmsley, charging that he had been wrongfully evicted from his apartment and that he had been subject to "ruthless termination" of his job.

One day in mid-July, Dominick Turco, Frank's son, who had come up from Florida to give what comfort he could to his father, didn't show up in court. Another young man, about the same age, tall, slim, nice-looking, well-dressed in a light-colored suit, was, and he would be there for much of the rest of the summer. His name was Craig Panzirer. He was Leona Hemsley's grandson. He had once been a very close friend of Dominick Turco. But no longer, and when Dominick showed up in court, Craig did not, or if he did, he quickly departed.

Craig Panzirer's life had not been easy since the death of his father, since the day his grandmother, in her grief and search for answers, had accused him of killing his father. He had lived with his stepmother, Mimi, had returned to his mother, Myrna, had trouble at school, had trouble holding a job. But now he had apparently come to some kind of terms with his grandmother. She had given him a job with the Helmsley empire, though during this summer what that job entailed seemed to be coming to court and being at her side.

And he was, his arm often around her, her arm around him, her hand ruffling his hair as they walked together up the center aisle during breaks or at the end of the day. On the surface they seemed fond of each other.

Aside from her grandson, Leona Helmsley had only a niece, Fran Becker, a large blonde woman who appeared most days and who sat with Craig, and disappeared with her aunt at lunch, at recesses, and at day's end.

There was one other. His name was Sam Orenstein. He had known Leona Rosenthal back in the old days in Brooklyn, had courted her and lost her to her first husband, Leo Panzirer, who had been his friend. "I tell you this," said the seventy-eight-year-old Orenstein, a short, plump, balding retired restaurateur when he appeared on the first day of the trial—he would appear a few times more, and was there the day the jury returned with its verdict—"if Leona had married me, she never would have divorced," and, by implication, been in this kind of trouble. He had a brown bag lunch with her one noon, always approached her whenever he was present, though she never seemed particularly pleased to see him.

Leona Helmsley herself, with her expertly coiffured hair, her careful makeup, her expensive and understated clothes, her regal posture and manner, seemed the most alone person in the courtroom.

The one person she cared deeply about, her husband, Harry, was absent. Isolated during these difficult days in their Park Lane penthouse, he was a man whose health was deteriorating. And she did care. On the day of Judge Walker's charge to the jury, when the court was sealed until after seven, someone heard her say as she hurried out that she was very concerned that Harry might be worried because she was so late getting home; he knew when she usually arrived and if she were late it would upset him greatly.

* * *

Through the eight weeks, like almost everyone else, though I watched her closely, I did not talk with her. She made exceptions and talked sometimes, inconsequentially, with women reporters. But never with men.

Something was happening, though. It is not easy to sit in a public glare day after day for two months, become the object of so many curious and often hostile eyes, hear endless recitations of the evils one has inflicted on others and come away unaffected. Not even Leona Helmsley.

She had begun to bend a little, now and then, especially when there were children around. On August 8, Jim DeVita's forty-first birthday, DeVita's wife and six daughters, including his new baby, appeared in court. The girls were blondes and redheads. During a recess, Leona Helmsley, instead of heading quickly for the privacy of a closed room off the main hall, paused, bent and stroked the hair of one of the DeVita children, complimented her on it, chatted with her and the other children for several minutes. It was something that had not happened before.

A few weeks later, I brought my ten-year-old daughter with me to court. At a break in the middle of the morning, we drifted outside. As we stood to one side of the door, Leona appeared with Fran Becker, paused, looked toward us, and approached.

She bent toward Emily. "Good morning, dear," she said. "Did you come down here to see me?"

Emily nodded, and said yes.

"I'm flattered," Leona Helmsley said. "I'm Leona Helmsley."

Emily introduced herself. Leona took a package of Velamints from her purse, took one for herself and offered Emily one. They shared this little treat. And then they began to talk, about a pen filled with glitter that Fran Becker had noticed Emily using to take notes. Where had she bought it? Actually, she said, she had bought the shell of the pen empty, had filled it with water and glitter and then sealed it. Where could one buy one like it? They talked about bubbles, blowing them, big ones and small ones. They talked about school. Leona patted Emily's cheek, she held Emily's face between her fingers. She seemed interested, even fascinated with the talk.

And then, while Emily and Fran Becker talked on, she turned to me. She knew who I was and what I was doing. She had asked someone and been told. "She's a very bright child," she said. "I've never heard a vocabulary like that on someone that age. It must be frightening to live with her."

I said it was, but it was fun, too, a constant adventure. But as much fun as it was, I didn't think I'd want to be that age and have to live through it all again.

"I would," she said.

A young man approached. He was a Helmsley employee in Florida and he had flown up to be with her at the end of the trial. I said to him lightly that he must be the first Helmsley employee to turn up on her side.

Leona looked at me and said, "I have lots of people who work for me who like me. They tell me so and they write to me. I'm not a complete monster, you know."

Several times that day, Emily had conversations with Leona Helmsley, private ones, off in a corner. What they talked about she would not say, would say only that she liked Mrs. Helmsley and they had become sort of friends, but she felt that what Mrs. Helmsley had done was wrong and she ought to be convicted. When we left at the end of the day, Emily thought she would not return, that she had had enough of court. Leona Helmsley went to her, bent, kissed her cheek, and said good-bye.

27

THE JURY HAD been out five days. It had sent in one or two requests for the rereading of testimony, but mainly there had been only silence. Late on Tuesday afternoon, the jurors sent in a message. They wanted additional explanation and instructions on the charge of conspiracy to commit extortion, count forty-seven. Judge Walker gave those instructions. The jurors returned to their deliberations.

On Wednesday morning, August 30, they were back at work. They ordered lunch, expecting to continue at least until the afternoon.

And then, suddenly, it was over. At 10:35 Judge Walker appeared. A message was brought to him. It read: "Judge Walker, good morning! We have reached a verdict. Thank you. Alvin Taylor."

Taylor, a black twenty-six-year-old postal worker, was the jury foreman. The jury had deliberated for thirty-five hours over five days.

Judge Walker said the courtroom would be sealed in fifteen minutes for the reading of the verdict. That would give anyone who wanted to use the bathrooms or have a smoke or walk around a little time.

At 10:47 the courtroom doors were locked and the jury brought in.

"Have you reached a verdict?" the court clerk asked.

"We have," Taylor said. He handed the verdict form to the clerk. The clerk handed it to Judge Walker. Walker

324

leafed through the ten pages. He handed it back to the clerk, who took it to Taylor.

Taylor rose. The three defendants and their attorneys stared at the jury foreman. The spectators in the overflowing courtroom, like spectators at a tennis match, kept flicking eyes from the jury to the backs of the defendants.

The clerk said: "As to count one of the indictment, conspiracy to commit offenses against the United States and to defraud the Internal Revenue Service. How do you find as to defendant Leona M. Helmsley?"

"Guilty."

"How do you find as to defendant Joseph V. Licari?"

"Guilty."

"How do you find as to defendant Frank J. Turco?"

"Guilty."

For the next eight minutes that question was repeated again and again, for all the counts of the indictment. And thirty-three times the words "guilty" as to defendant Leona M. Helmsley and defendant Joseph V. Licari and defendant Frank J. Turco came from Taylor's lips.

Only when the clerk asked, "How do you find on count forty of the indictment, mail fraud against the minority shareholders of Realesco?" were the words "not guilty" heard for the first time. They were repeated for all the mail fraud counts relating to Realesco, and for count forty-seven, conspiracy to commit extortion.

The Realesco mail fraud charge had been an iffy one. The victims were New York banks, and there was no evidence that the fraudulent statements had been mailed to them rather than delivered by messenger.

The extortion count had been the weakest. Even while the jury was out, experts, lawyers, and reporters in the courtroom had debated that count. Had extortion been legally committed, since the supposed victims had actually gained financially by paying the money and giving the goods? If court experts couldn't agree, how could one expect a jury to agree beyond a reasonable doubt?

As the verdicts were read, Frank Turco sat rigidly, his face expressionless. Joe Licari shook his head from side to side, saying no, no, his hands rising and falling. His daughter had gone to the ladies' room and when she returned, the doors had already been locked and so she could not get inside to hear the verdict against her father. When the doors were finally opened, she raced in. Someone stopped her. "Your father's going to prison," that someone said. She began to cry.

And Leona Helmsley. At first, she sat stiff, her head up, then it fell briefly, the back of her neck reddening, then it rose again. Most of the spectators could not see her face. But one who did said she had tears on her cheeks.

The court cleared quickly, but the defendants remained frozen in the seats at the defense table for nearly an hour.

Outside the courthouse, a huge crowd gathered. Television and still cameras were waiting everywhere. Reporters had been told the evening before that when the verdict came, Mrs. Helmsley would be spirited away by some side door. Nevertheless, everyone waited.

Joe Licari appeared and came down the long flight of steps, his wife, daughter, and Joe Benfante with him. He said nothing, and hurried to a waiting limousine.

Someone looked down the narrow street and spotted the Helmsleys' limousine. And then she appeared at the top of the steps. Someone must have advised her to do it, to face it this time and get it over with. She walked quickly down the steps, surrounded by bodyguards, Jerry Feffer a step behind. The crowd surged in around her. Microphones were thrust at her. Television and still cameras zoomed in on her. She said nothing. One of the cameramen, trying to climb onto the limousine, nearly got into a fight with a bodyguard, who thrust the camera lens away. Reporters and spectators screamed questions and imprecations at her. It was not one of the news media's better days. Sometimes privacy is a right to be jealously protected. Perhaps this was one of them.

At that moment, it was impossible not to feel pity for this very lonely and very proud woman. Though one could not like her or admire her, one could pity her. All through the trial she had seemed not to comprehend what it was she had done and what it was she had become. She was the Queen of the Palace, the woman who had obtained everything she had once desired with such an awful thirst, and it had come to this, it had come to nothing, and she did not know it. She had become a felon.

28

THOUGH SHE HAD escaped the worst, conviction for extortion conspiracy, carrying a prison term of up to twenty years, the crimes for which she had been convicted did not carry light penalties. Of the thirty-three counts on which the jury had found her guilty, count one, conspiracy to defraud the United States and the Internal Revenue Service, carried a maximum penalty of five years and a $250,000 fine; counts two to four, tax evasion, carried maximums of five years and $250,000 in fines on each count, plus court costs; counts eight to ten, making and subscribing false tax returns, carried maximums of three years and $250,000 in fines on each count, plus court costs, as did counts fourteen through twenty-nine, aiding and assisting the filing of false returns for Helmsley Enterprises and various subsidiaries and partnerships; and counts thirty to thirty-nine, mail fraud by mailing false returns to the New York State Department of Taxation and Finance, each carried maximum sentences of five years and $250,000 in fines. (Turco and Licari were liable for about the same sentences.)

If Judge Walker decided to sentence her to the maximum prescribed by the law and set those sentences to run consecutively rather than concurrently, she could theoretically receive 128 years in federal prison and fines and costs of more than $8.5 million.

Just about everyone agreed in the weeks following the trial's end that heavy fines were a necessity. If Leona Helmsley could easily afford whatever those fines might be, still she had never parted with money easily, and so the fines would hurt, if not her pocketbook then her pride.

The issue of prison raised more of a debate. Some thought a prison term would serve no useful purpose, that instead Mrs. Helmsley ought to be sentenced to perhaps a thousand hours of community service in a welfare hotel or an AIDS ward, and so be forced to make some useful contribution to society. It was an argument that had considerable support.

But others, especially among the prosecution, vigorously opposed such an idea. They said such noble-sounding sentences, especially for the rich and powerful, sounded a lot better than they actually were. Too often the rich just sent their maids to do that community service, and even if they did it themselves, still at the end of the day they returned to the luxury of their mansions and penthouses. Prison time, they argued, was an absolute necessity. It would show, as the trial was meant to, that the rich and powerful and the poor and powerless were treated equally before the law. It especially would serve as a warning for the rich who thought they, too, could get away with cheating this way on their income taxes and who could easily afford fines and monetary penalties if caught. The distinct probability of a time behind bars would serve as a meaningful deterrent.

Even as they waited to learn their fate on the federal conviction, Turco, Licari, and Leona Helmsley were told that the state of New York had no intention of dropping its own case against them. Though many thought that trying them again would be double jeopardy, the state was determined to press ahead. In addition, it was just as anxious to bring Harry Helmsley before the bar of justice this time. It scheduled mental and physical examinations by its own experts to see if the federal decision was wrong and the aging billionaire was really fit to stand trial on the state indictment.

For Turco and Licari, this was just too much. They had no desire to go through the agony once more. And so both agreed to plead guilty to the state charges, with the guarantee that the prison sentence and fines the state meted out would be no harsher than the ones they received from their federal convictions and would run concurrently with them. For his part, Turco essentially did what he had wanted to do for the federal authorities, becoming a witness against his former employers. He acknowledged that he had been part of the tax fraud conspiracy, had signed false invoices to conceal it, had done so under orders from Leona and Harry Helmsley, and that they had initialed and approved those fake invoices.

The key decision, then, remained Judge Walker's. It would be one of the last he would hand down in this court. Soon after the end of the trial, President Bush nominated him to a seat on the United States Court of Appeals for the Second Circuit, the nation's second highest judicial body. Throughout the fall he studied reports and recommendations from the government and defense. The day of decision originally had been set for November 14, but because of problems completing the probation reports, a necessary step prior to sentencing, it was rescheduled for December 12, not in the third-floor courtroom where the trial had taken place but in a larger one two floors above.

The trial had begun on a summer morning during a torrential rainstorm. Now it was ending on a snowy winter afternoon. By ten in the morning, a crowd began to gather, and by one-thirty, when the courtroom doors were opened, more than three hundred spectators—ordinary people, celebrities, and an army of the press—were shoving their way through to find seats. When the doors finally were closed, every seat was taken and onlookers stood three deep along the walls.

There was a holiday air about the vast room, and one was struck by a vagrant image of the crowds at the Place de la Concorde ringing the guillotine, waiting to witness the fate of Marie-Antoinette. They had come to witness the fate of another queen who instead of saying, "Let them eat cake," had said, "We don't pay taxes. Only the little people pay taxes."

The leading players drifted to their places. There was Joe Licari, slimmer than he had been a few months before, alongside his attorney, Joe Benfante. Frank Turco, who had grown a beard touched with gray, appeared with his attorney, Bill Brodsky. Jerry Feffer, no longer gaunt but trim and rested, took his seat at the end of the defense table. Then, seemingly out of nowhere, Leona Helmsley appeared, her hair neatly coiffured as always, but now flecked with gray, wearing a black silk dress and a gold chain around her neck from which hung a locket that contained a watch belonging to her dead son, Jay.

Out in the crowd, the other leading player, absent through the long summer, had an aisle seat in the third row. At long last Harry Helmsley had appeared in court, to offer comfort to his wife in her ordeal. He was tanned, for they had only just returned from a stay at their new mansion-estate in Arizona, but there was a vacant look on his face, and as the hours passed, his head frequently slumped to his chest, his eyes closing, and then suddenly would jerk straight up again. But the expression remained unreadable, vacant.

At the table between the defense and the judicial bench were the prosecutors, though Jim DeVita was there on a kind of sufferance. After nearly a decade of being, as he said, "on the side of the angels," he had left the government right after the trial to take a high-paying job with a prestigious Wall Street law firm. He was back as a special assistant to witness the final act.

Precisely at two, Judge Walker entered from the rear and took his place on the high bench. The crowd fell silent. Walker looked out over the spectators, looked down at the defendants, and then stated that he was aware of the great public interest in this case, of how much notoriety it had received in the press, and how one of these defendants had been pilloried. However offensive that might be, it was no substitute for the punishment that must be handed down by this court, and would not affect it. But before he meted out that punishment, he would hear from the defendants, their lawyers, and the government.

Feffer was eloquent as always. With Leona Helmsley at his side, her head bowed, he spoke of her advancing age, and said, "She understands and accepts that she must be punished for her crimes." But she has already been punished far beyond measure. "Mrs. Helmsley has been ridiculed, abused, and vilifed in an unprecedented way having nothing to do with her wrongdoing." She had received in the months following her conviction a barrage of hate mail, letters filled with anti-Semitic venom, the vilest of profanities, even death threats. Her photograph had appeared in a newspaper in company with murderers Charles Manson, Richard Speck, Lee Harvey Oswald, and Sirhan-Sirhan. "The emotional impact of all this has been catastrophic. She is a frightened, terrified woman who has become a prisoner in her own home."

That she should be punished was undeniable. "But the court should take into acocunt the way she has already been punished." And it should also remember that while she had evaded $1.2 million in federal taxes, she had also paid $34 million in federal taxes during that same period.

Further balancing the ledger was the fact that the portrait of Leona Helmsley painted during the trial had been a one-sided one. On the other side was a woman who had given millions to charity, who had provided medical care and financial help to needy employees and even strangers, and Feffer read excerpts from a sheaf of letters from the recipients demonstrating their gratitude.

Rather than prison—"It is not difficult to speculate what is waiting for Mrs. Helmsley if she is sent to prison"— Feffer asked Walker to impose an alternate sentence requiring her to work at the Homeward Bound shelter in Harlem

run by Mother Hale of Hale House for mothers and infants
born with drug dependence and AIDS. "You can ever order
her to live in Harlem with these mothers and infants," he
said.

In response, Jim DeVita stated that prison was a necessity
if a message was to be sent that everyone, regardless of
wealth and status, was treated the same. He had listened to
Feffer's tales of the outrages inflicted on Leona Helmsley,
but "this case was never about whether Mrs. Helmsley was
a good person or an evil person. It was not about whether
Mrs. Helmsley was unfairly treated in the press. And the
sentence should not be reduced because of that fact."

DeVita added a few scornful words about Harry Helmsley, whose head rose from his chest at the mention of his
name. Harry Helmsley had not been tried because the court
had ruled him incompetent, DeVita noted, but he had been
a major participant in all the crimes for which his wife and
Licari and Turco had been tried and convicted, and "Harry
Helmsley could have put a stop to the crimes and he was
unwilling to do so."

On behalf of their clients, Benfante and Brodsky admitted
they had made "mistakes," though those had been not for
personal gain but under orders of their superiors. Both were
pillars of their communities, active in social betterment;
they regretted what they had done, and now they stood convicted, their lives and their careers in ruins. Surely both
had paid a heavy enough price that rather than prison Judge
Walker should place them on probation or assign them to
some alternate service where they could help society.

DeVita scoffed. Licari, he said, had been invited into the
prosecutor's office, had been shown the evidence against
him, had been asked to plead guilty and help the government. He had refused and now he is sorry. He is a nice
man, DeVita said, but he was an active participant in the
scheme. "Next to Harry Helmsley, he had the best opportunity to stop this. Failing that, he could have left and gotten
another job. He had the credentials. But he did neither."

As for Turco, he "relished the game of fraud. His incli-
nation was in that direction, and Mrs. Helmsley's inclina-
tion was in that direction, and they fed on each other."

Then Walker looked toward the defendants. Did they have
anything they wished to say to the court?

There was dead silence as Leona Helmsley rose from
her seat and walked slowly, hesitantly to the microphone
set on a podium. In one hand she held two small sheets
of paper covered with handwriting. For the first time she
would speak in public after the months of silence. She
took a deep breath. She started and then paused, having
difficulty keeping her composure. Her voice broke, her
face crumbled.

"I'm guilty of a serious crime," she said in a voice so
low that one had to strain to make out the words. "I'm more
humiliated and ashamed than anybody could imagine. I feel
as though I have been living through a nightmare for three
years. For three years we have not gone out of our home,
we have not been able to walk on the sidewalk or go for a
meal in a restaurant or even go to a movie. A few years ago
I lost my only son—" Her voice broke, the tears started
streaming from her eyes, her body shook, she clutched the
sides of the podium as if on the edge of collapse. ". . . and
they have dug up his grave and ripped me apart in the newspapers with pictures of his grave. I beg of you, don't let me
lose Harry, too. Please don't. Our whole life has been work
and each other. We have nothing else. I'm sorry. I'm so
sorry . . ."

She could not continue. All the regal trappings and imperious demeanor had vanished at last. In that moment she
was a broken, defeated, vulnerable woman. Among the
spectators who had come to celebrate her moment of shame,
many looked away, unable to watch her as she turned and
stumbled back to her seat.

Judge John Walker's moment had arrived. He took Joe
Licari first. The man who had been Harry Helmsley's alter

ego had committed crimes not in a moment but over a three-year period and still showed scant remorse. And so he would spend thirty months in prison, three years on probation, and pay a $76,350 fine. Licari would begin serving that sentence soon after the Christmas holidays. He would be eligible for parole in ten months.

Next was Frank Turco. He had risen high in the Helmsley organization, and from his position he had been a willing participant in these crimes and yet showed little remorse for what he had done. And so Frank Turco would go to prison for twenty-four months, spend the following three years on probation, and pay a $51,350 fine. He, too, would begin his sentence after Christmas, and would be eligible for parole in eight months.

Finally, the moment this crowd had come for. The anticipation was patent, spectators straightening, leaning forward intently, straining. Leona Helmsley rose to face her judge. Walker looked down at her sternly. "You," he said, "bear full responsibility for this scheme. It was carried out under your direct orders for your benefit. Unlike many defendants who come before the court, you were not driven to this crime by financial need. Rather, your conduct was the product of naked greed. Throughout its course you persisted in the arrogant belief that you were above the law. Moreover, since the indictment and the trial, you have displayed no remorse or contrition. I trust that the sentence today will make it very clear that no person, no matter how wealthy or prominent, stands above the law."

Then he pronounced judgment:

Leona Helmsley had been convicted on thirty-three felony counts, divided into four groups of offenses: conspiracy, tax evasion, filing false tax returns, and mail fraud. Judge Walker sentenced her to four years in prison on each group of offenses. This was a total of sixteen years, but the sentences would run concurrently and thus amount to four years in federal prison. She could be paroled in sixteen months.

When she was released, she would be on probation for another three years, during which she would be required to perform two hundred fifty hours of community service each year at the Hale House shelter for drug-dependent and AIDS-afflicted infants and mothers.

On top of this were the staggering fines. Repayment of the taxes she had evaded—$1,240,000 to the federal government and $469,000 to New York state—plus interest and penalties amounting to $7,152,350. Moreover, payment of the costs to the government of its investigation and prosecution, an undetermined amount, could add up to more millions.

Leona Helmsley slumped a little, then straightened. Feffer announced that he would file an appeal, one that might take six months to a year before it was decided, and so delay for a time Leona Helmsley's journey from the Park Lane penthouse and Dunnellen Hall and Arizona estate to the women's prison camp in Danbury, Connecticut, ironically forty miles from Dunnellen Hall. There she would do menial labor seven hours a day, would wear a single, drab, ill-fitting prison uniform, would dine on tasteless institutional food, would share a cell with one or more inmates, and have only a small locker that would hold only the barest of essential personal possessions. Feffer would appeal, but few doubted that those appeals would fail and that, in the end, Leona Helmsley would make that journey.

So it was over. Some in the courtroom jeered in satisfaction, but outside, she had to face the growing mob gathering in the snow and cold to witness her last exit down the long flight of courthouse steps to her waiting Lincoln limousine. Harry Helmsley walked slowly down the aisle and passed through the barrier into the well of the court toward his wife. She put her arms around him and kissed him on the cheek. He held her, drew her close. She put her head on his shoulder and cried just a little. It seemed as though they were comforting each other.

Then she turned to a friend who had watched it all from a front-row seat. "See what they've done to me," she said bitterly. Not what she had done to herself and to so many others. Still oblivious. Still, in her mind, the queen.